The Rational Imagination

The Rational Imagination

How People Create Alternatives to Reality

Ruth M. J. Byrne

A Bradford Book
The MIT Press
Cambridge, Massachusetts
London, England

MIT Press books may be purchased at special quantity discounts for business or sales promotional use. For information, please e-mail special_sales@mitpress.mit.edu or write to Special Sales Department, The MIT Press, 55 Hayward Street, Cambridge, MA 02142.

This book was set in Stone Serif and Stone Sans on 3B2 by Asco Typesetters, Hong Kong. Printed and bound in the United States of America.

Library of Congress Cataloging-in-Publication Data

Byrne, Ruth M. J.
  The rational imagination : how people create alternatives to reality / Ruth M. J. Byrne.
    p.   cm.
  "A Bradford book."
  Includes bibliographical references and index.
  ISBN 0-262-02584-1 (alk. paper)
  1. Imagination (Philosophy). 2. Reasoning. I. Title.
  B105.I49B97   2005
  128'.3—dc22   2004063262

10 9 8 7 6 5 4 3 2 1

For Mark Keane and Alicia Byrne Keane with all my love

Contents

Preface

The human imagination remains one of the last uncharted terrains of the mind. This book explores one area of it, the creation of counterfactual alternatives to reality. The main claim in the book is that imaginative thoughts are guided by the same principles that underlie rational thoughts. Rationality and imagination have been viewed as complete opposites. At best, logic and creativity have been thought to have little in common. At worst, they have been considered to be each other's nemesis. But they may share more than has been suspected. Rational thought has turned out to be more imaginative than cognitive scientists previously supposed. This book argues that imaginative thought is more rational than scientists imagined.

The imagination of alternatives to reality has been of central interest to philosophers, artificial intelligence workers, linguists, and especially to psychologists—most notably social psychologists and cognitive psychologists. The application of a theory of rational thought to explain imaginative thought may interest anyone who wants to consider a new perspective on the exploration of imaginative thought, as well as anyone who wants to examine the potential impact of reasoning on other sorts of thinking.

The idea that the human imagination is rational has developed over many years in discussions and collaborations with many people. In 1983 when I began to study how people reason at Mark Keane's suggestion, I was struck by how they rely on background knowledge when they try to think logically, and I carried out experiments on this phenomenon when we were both undergraduates at University College Dublin and later as a PhD student at Trinity College, Dublin University. The idea that reasoning is an imaginative skill had just been proposed at that time by Phil Johnson-Laird in his book *Mental Models* and I owe a huge debt of gratitude to him for many enjoyable discussions about human reasoning. We developed the view of reasoning as an imaginative process for each of the main domains of deduction when we worked together at the MRC Applied Psychology Unit in Cambridge, and we summarized it in our book *Deduction* (1991). The idea that reasoning requires imagination captured the interest of many researchers (see the mental models website at http://www.tcd.ie/Psychology/Ruth_Byrne/mental_models/).

In 1993 I began to study how people imagine alternatives to reality. I had become interested in how discoveries about human reasoning might help to explain other kinds of thinking when I moved to Trinity College, Dublin University, after working first at the University of Wales in Cardiff and then in the computer science department at University College Dublin. Alessandra Tasso from Padua University visited for six months that year to carry out experiments on reasoning about imagined alternatives to reality, Susana Segura from Malaga University visited the next year to carry out experiments on counterfactual thoughts about what might have been different, and Sergio Moreno-Ríos visited from Granada University the following year to carry out experiments on semifactual thoughts about what might have been the same. Every year since, colleagues have visited for extended periods to collaborate on experiments about reasoning and imagination and I am grateful to all of them, not least for allowing me to describe our joint work in this book. Simon Handley from Plymouth University visited often when we carried out experiments on complex deductions, and Orlando Espino from Tenerife's La Laguna University has also been a frequent visitor to study conditional reasoning, in conjunction with Carlos Santamaría. Walter Schroyens from Leuven University and Yevgeniya Goldvarg from Princeton University came to work on conditional inference, too. At this time three PhD students at Trinity—Rachel McCloy, Alice McEleney, and Clare Walsh—studied the imagination of alternatives to controllable actions and the role of reasons and causes in thoughts about "if only ..." and "even if ...". Valerie Thompson visited from Saskatchewan University to study causal and counterfactual reasoning and Juan García-Madruga visited from UNED in Madrid to study "only if" reasoning, in conjunction with Cristina Quelhas and Csongor Juhos from ISPA in Lisbon. I learned a lot from discussions with all of these friends and colleagues, and I am very glad to have been part of so many interesting and enjoyable collaborations.

The ideas sketched here have benefited from discussions with many other colleagues at too many meetings to mention, and especially during visits to Phil Johnson-Laird at Princeton University, to Vittorio Girotto at Trieste University, and to the cognition laboratory at Freiburg University. I am grateful for regular criticism from the members of the cognitive science group, run jointly by the computer science department at University College Dublin and the psychology department at Trinity College, Dublin University, especially from Mark Keane and Fintan Costello and their PhD students, and my current PhD students, Michelle Cowley, Suzanne Egan, Caren Frosch, Julie Meehan, and Aisling Murray. Thanks also to earlier research students Nuala Gannon, Paul Larkin, Liz McLoughlin, Sinead Mulhern, and Vicki Panoutsakopoulou for discussions on related topics, including counterfactual thoughts in anxiety and depression as well as in young offenders, and to students who helped as laboratory assistants, including Ronan Culhane, Christina Curry, Michelle Flood, Peter Hegarty, Peter Keating, Joan Mallon, Patrick McAlinney, Maeve O'Brien, Emma Riggs, and Gry Wester. Thanks also to my colleagues in the psychology department at Trinity College for providing an environment that values cognitive science research.

I started to write this book when I was on a sabbatical funded by a Berkeley Fellowship from Trinity College, Dublin University. I am grateful to Tom Stone of MIT Press for his encouragement and patience in the years since and to the staff at The MIT Press who have helped produce the book —especially Jessica Lawrence-Hunt, Margy Avery, Susan Clark, Chryseis O. Fox, Elizabeth Judd, and Sandra Minkkinen. The studies described in the book were funded in part by the Irish Research Council for the Humanities and Social Sciences; the Irish Research Council for Science, Engineering and Technology; Enterprise Ireland; the Department of Education, Northern Ireland; and Trinity College's Arts and Social Sciences Benefactions fund.

Thanks to four people who generously read the whole manuscript and provided thought-provoking comments and counterexamples throughout: Mike Doherty, Phil Johnson-Laird, Mark Keane, and Bob Sternberg. Thanks also to colleagues who made helpful comments on individual chapters: Jean-François Bonnefon, Nyla Branscombe, Aidan Feeney, Juan García-Madruga, Vittorio Girotto, David Green, Peter Hegarty, Cristoph Klauer, Ned Lebow, David Mandel, Alice McEleney, Julie Meehan, Sergio Moreno-Ríos, Neal Roese, Susana Segura, and Cristina Quelhas. They helped me remedy many mistakes, and the book is far better for all their suggestions. The remaining mistakes are new ones I added or ones that are so deep-seated I cannot be shaken from them.

Thanks to my big family for their support: Mary Byrne; Cathy and Tony Fitzgerald; Linda and Noel Deighan; Lisa, Steven, and Jenny Fitzgerald; Paul and Laura Deighan; and Paul Byrne and Mary Alicia "Molly" Tracey. My biggest thanks is to my husband, Mark Keane, and my daughter, Alicia Byrne Keane, who are with me in every alternative reality I would ever want to imagine.

Dublin, April 9, 2004

1 The Counterfactual Imagination

Martin Luther King Jr. almost died when he was stabbed in 1958. A decade later he made the following remarks during a speech:

The tip of the blade was on the edge of my aorta.... It came out in the *New York Times* the next morning that if I had merely sneezed I would have died.... And I want to say tonight, I want to say tonight that I too am happy that I didn't sneeze. Because if I had sneezed, I wouldn't have been around here in 1960 when students all over the South started sitting in at lunch counters.... If I had sneezed, I wouldn't have been here in 1963 when the black people of Birmingham, Alabama aroused the conscience of this nation and brought into being the Civil Rights bill.... If I had sneezed I wouldn't have had the chance later that year in August to try to tell America about a dream that I had had.... I'm so happy that I didn't sneeze. (King 1968)

His reflections highlight the impact that something as insignificant and ordinary as a sneeze could have had on the course of civil rights in American history. King's remarks are particularly poignant given that he was assassinated the next day. He was thirty-nine years old when he died. Who can say what would have happened if he had lived longer?

This book is about how people imagine alternatives to reality. My interest is in how people think about what might have been. In daily life, people imagine how events might have turned out differently, "if only ...". Often, thoughts about what might have been can seem irresistible. They emerge at a very young age. They seem to exist in most cultures. Their existence demonstrates that thoughts are not tied to facts. Thoughts can go beyond facts to encompass other possibilities. People can think about facts—for example, that Martin Luther King was murdered. They can also think about *counterfactual* possibilities that may once have been possible but are no longer possible—for instance they can imagine that Martin Luther King had been killed when he was stabbed in 1958. They can even think about impossibilities that could never happen—for example, they can imagine that Martin Luther King was a European civil rights leader. This book focuses on counterfactual possibilities. It offers an explanation of how the mind creates alternatives to reality. The explanation relies on the idea that imaginative thought and rational thought have a lot in common.

Imagination

There are different kinds of imaginative thoughts. Thoughts about things that did not happen are one important kind (Thomas 1999). Counterfactual thoughts occur often in daily life—for instance, when someone thinks about how an event in the past might have turned out differently, or when someone creates a daydream or a fantasy. They also occur when a child engages in pretend play or chats with an imaginary friend or soft toy (Harris 2000; Riggs and Peterson 2000). Counterfactual suppositions can be close to the facts ("if Molly had joined the running team, she would have become slim"), or they can be remote ("if Molly had joined the running team, she would have become an Olympic gold medal winner").

This sort of imaginative thought may appear to be very different from creative thoughts. Creative thought occurs when someone writes a poem or a play or a piece of music or produces a work of art. It occurs when someone designs a crucial experiment or makes a discovery in science or invents a new product (Dunbar 1997; Sternberg and Davidson 1995). The term *imagination* has also been used to refer to other sorts of cognitive processes (Thomas 1999). In the history of the study of the mind, it has often been used by philosophers to refer to thinking. It has also been used to refer to imagery—for example, to the idea that the mind can form pictures akin to visual perceptions. But often when people refer to the imagination, they mean either counterfactual or creative thoughts.

Everyday imaginative thoughts may seem mundane in comparison to more exotic creative thoughts (Finke, Ward, and Smith 1992). Counterfactual thoughts differ in some ways from other sorts of creative thoughts. For example, the counterfactual imagination can seem effortless and at times involuntary, although it can be brought under voluntary control (Roese, Sanna, and Galinsky 2005). Other kinds of creative imagination can seem more deliberate and goal oriented. Even though the distance from counterfactual thought to creative thought may seem large, it is bridgeable. The cognitive processes that underlie the counterfactual imagination and other sorts of creative thoughts operate in an unconscious manner, and counterfactual and creative thoughts may rely on some of the same sorts of processes. Counterfactual thought can help people make discoveries and deal with novelty (Sternberg and Gastel 1989). In fact, creative works sometimes depend on the evocation of counterfactual alternatives. For example, Beckett conveys a view of the human condition in the play *Waiting for Godot* through the two main characters who anticipate something that never happens. An explanation of the counterfactual imagination may even contribute to an explanation of other sorts of creative thoughts. The penultimate chapter returns to this possibility.

Counterfactual Imagination
Speculations about what might have been are important in social discourse ("if the last government had invested more money in the health services …") and they can have a rhetorical force in debates about current affairs ("if Saddam Hussein had been killed in the first Gulf war …"). They can be helpful in historical analyses, say, in imagining whether the cold war could have escalated to a nuclear level (Lebow 2000; Tetlock and Parker 2005; Cowley 2001). One of the more surprising aspects of the counterfactual imagination is that there are remarkable similarities in what everyone imagines.

People create a counterfactual alternative to reality by mentally altering or "undoing" some aspects of the facts in their mental representation of reality (Kahneman and Tversky 1982). For example, the facts are that Molly did not join the running team, but you can imagine a counterfactual alternative by thinking, "if only she had joined the running team …". Some aspects of reality seem more "mutable"—that is, more readily changed in a mental simulation of the event—than others (Kahneman and Miller 1986). Different people tend to change the same sorts of things when they think about how things might have been different. These regularities indicate that there are "joints" in reality, junctures that attract everyone's attention (Kahneman and Tversky 1982). There are points at which reality is "slippable" (Hofstadter 1985).

To illustrate one of these "fault lines" of reality, consider the following story (adapted from Kahneman and Tversky 1982, 204):

Paul was 47 years old, the father of three and a successful banker. His wife has been ill at home for several months. On the day of the accident, Paul left his office at the regular time. He sometimes left early to take care of home chores at his wife's request, but this was not necessary on that day. Paul did not drive home by his regular route. The day was exceptionally clear and Paul told his friends at the office that he would drive along the shore to enjoy the view. The accident occurred at a major intersection. The light turned amber as Paul approached. Witnesses noted that he braked hard to stop at the crossing, although he could easily have gone through. His family recognised this as a common occurrence in Paul's driving. As he began to cross after the light changed, a truck charged through the intersection at top speed, and rammed Paul's car from the left. Paul was killed instantly. It was later ascertained that the truck was driven by a teenage boy, who was under the influence of drugs.

Suppose you are told that, as commonly happens in such situations, Paul's family and their friends often thought and often said "if only ..." during the days that followed the accident. How do you think they continued this sentence? There are many aspects of the facts that could be changed— for example, "if only Paul had not gone to work that day," or "if only the truck had not come through the intersection at just that time." But most people tend to think Paul's family will complete the sentence by saying "if only Paul had driven home by his regular route" (Kahneman and Tversky 1982).

A second group of participants were given a version of the scenario that contained a different set of sentences at the beginning:

On the day of the accident, Paul left the office earlier than usual, to attend to some household chores at his wife's request. He drove home along his regular route. Paul occasionally chose to drive along the shore, to enjoy the view on exceptionally clear days, but that day was just average. (p. 204)

They tended to complete the sentence by saying "if only Paul had left at his regular time." The experiment shows that most people imagine alternatives to exceptional events rather than to routine ones, regardless of whether the exceptional event was the route or the time (see also Gavanski and Wells 1989; Bouts, Spears, and van der Pligt 1992).

Once people have identified a fault line of reality, they often mentally change it in similar ways. They can imagine an event did not happen and they can imagine what might have happened instead. For example, they mentally delete a known aspect of reality from their mental representation of it ("if only Molly was not so lazy ...") or they add a new aspect ("if only Molly lived closer to a running track ..."). In the story about Paul, very few participants imagined an alternative to the least likely event in the scenario: two cars crossing an intersection at the exact same moment. The results indicate that most counterfactual thoughts do not focus on the least probable event (Kahneman and Tversky 1982). Instead people tend to change unusual events to make them more normal (Kahneman and Miller 1986). Exceptions to normality may be an important fault line of reality (Miller and McFarland 1986). There is a range of perceived fault lines in reality and they may correspond to core categories of mental life, such as space, time, cause, and intention (Byrne 1997; Miller and Johnson-Laird 1976).

What determines a perceived fault line in reality? In other words, why do people imagine alternatives to some aspects of reality more readily than others? This question is the key to understanding how the counterfactual imagination works. My aim in this book is to answer it. The book is organized around the fault lines of reality. Each chapter examines one of them, and sketches an explanation for it. To give a flavor of the sorts of phenomena to be examined in subsequent chapters, the next section briefly outlines each in turn.

What People Imagine

People mentally change various aspects of their mental representation of reality when they imagine how the facts could have turned out differently. A few of the more readily changed aspects will be outlined here. It is by no means an exhaustive list.

Actions   Take a moment to cast your mind back over the past week or so, and think about something you regret. Was it something you did or something you failed to do? One debated characteristic of counterfactual thoughts is the tendency for people to regret their actions—that is, things they did—more than their failures to act (Kahneman and Tversky 1982). As an example, consider two individuals, Mary and Laura, who invest their money in companies A and B. Mary invests in company A. She considers switching to company B but she decides not to. She finds out that she would have been better off by $1,000 if she had switched. Laura invests in company B. She considers switching to company A and she decides to do so. She finds out that she would have been better off by $1,000 if she had stayed in company B. Who do you think feels more regret? Most people judge that Laura will regret her action more than Mary will regret her inaction. People tend to imagine alternatives to actions more than they do to inactions. Chapter 3 examines this *action* effect. It also considers the important exceptions to it when people regret their failures to act instead.

Obligations   Now consider the last time you were late for an appointment with a friend. What sort of excuse did you offer? If it was based on something you were obliged to do, such as "I had to visit my parents," then your friend probably forgave you. But if your excuse was based on something socially unacceptable, such as "I had to have a stiff drink," then your friend may have been less understanding. Chapter 4 discusses the way the counterfactual imagination deals with forbidden actions. As another example consider an individual, Steven, who is delayed on his way home by several events. For example, he gets stuck in a traffic jam, he has to take a detour because of a fallen log on the road, and he decides to have a beer in a bar. He arrives home to find that his wife has had a heart attack and he is too late to save her. In the months that follow he is haunted by thoughts of what might have been, and he often says "if only ...". How do you think he completes this assertion? Most people believe that Steven says "if only I had not stopped for that beer" (Girotto, Legrenzi, and Rizzo 1991). The result shows that people imagine alternatives to events that are within their control more than to those outside their control (Markman et al. 1993). More than that, they tend to imagine alternatives to particular sorts of controllable actions: socially unacceptable ones.

Causes   Chapter 5 addresses a central question about counterfactual thoughts: their relation to causal thoughts. When you create an imaginary alternative—for example, "if only I hadn't left the bathroom window open, the burglar would never have gotten into the house"—you identify an important factor in the causal sequence of events, the burglar got in *because* I left the bathroom window open (Roese 1997). Philosophers have long noted that to think counterfactually is to think causally (Hume [1739] 2000; Mill [1872] 1956). The link to causal thoughts may underpin the role of counterfactual thoughts in helping people to learn and to prepare for the future—for instance, "I will not leave the bathroom window open in the future" (Roese 1994). But counterfactual and causal thoughts sometimes diverge in their focus. Suppose a taxi driver refused to give a couple a lift. The couple had to take their own car. As they were driving over a bridge it collapsed and they were killed. The taxi driver drove across the bridge safely a short while before them. How highly would you rate the taxi driver's role in causing the people's deaths? Most people judge the taxi driver to have had a causal role when they are told that he crossed the bridge safely, and they think that if only he had given them a lift they would still be alive (Wells and Gavanski 1989). But they judge the *cause* of the crash to be the collapsing bridge (N'gbala and Branscombe 1995; Mandel and Lehman 1996). Why do people wish that an event had not happened even when they know that the event did not cause the outcome? The explanation in chapter 5 emphasizes the identification of different sorts of causal relations, such as strong causal and enabling relations.

Chapter 6 examines the other side of the causal coin. Thoughts about how an event might have turned out differently "if only ..." can emphasize a causal relation; similarly, thoughts about how an event might have turned out the same "even if ..." can deny a causal relation—for example, "even if the driver had given them a lift, they still would have died." Consider the following scenario in which you are an Olympic runner faced with a critical dilemma (adapted from Boninger, Gleicher, and Strathman 1994, 301):

On the day before the 400 meter race, in a freak accident during training, you sprain your left ankle.... Your trainer recommends that you choose between two drugs, both legal according to Olympic guidelines. One is a well-known painkiller that has been proven effective but also has some serious side effects, including temporary nausea and drowsiness. The other painkiller is a newer and less well-known drug.... The newer drug might be a more effective painkiller but its side effects are not yet known.... After considerable thought, you elect to go with the better-known drug. On the day of the race, although there is no pain in your ankle, you already begin to feel the nausea and find yourself fighting off fatigue. You finish in fourth place.

Suppose you know that the runner had heard of other athletes who took the other legal painkiller but suffered the same side effects. She says "even if ...". How do you think she completed the assertion? Most people believe she would say, "even if I had taken the other painkiller I would have suffered the same side effects" (McCloy and Byrne 2002). This "even if ..." alternative affects people's judgment about the causal relations between the events. When they can create an "even if ..." alternative about the drug, they judge its role to be less causally important. Chapter 6 considers the impact of such "even if ..." alternatives.

Time   People imagine some of the most tantalizing counterfactuals about sports. Near wins, close calls, the drama of the final runner in a relay race, or the goal scorer in a penalty shoot-out—the perceived proximity of an alternative world can be heightened in key moments in sports, magnifying the disappointment or elation of the actual outcome (Markman and Tetlock 2000a). Chapter 7 deals with one last intriguing feature of counterfactual thoughts: people tend to imagine alternatives to the most recent event in a temporal sequence, rather than to earlier events. To illustrate the phenomenon, consider two individuals, Lisa and Jenny, who are offered the following attractive proposition. They both are to toss a coin and if both tosses come up the same—that is, both heads or both tails—they will each win $1,000. Lisa goes first and tosses a head, Jenny goes second and tosses a tail, and so neither wins. How do you think the events could have turned out differently? Who do you think will feel more guilt? And who do you think will blame the other more? Most people say "if only Jenny had tossed a head . . ."—that is, they imagine an alternative to the second event, rather than to the first event. They judge that Jenny will feel more guilt than Lisa, and they judge that Jenny will be blamed more by Lisa than Lisa will by Jenny (Miller and Gunasegaram 1990).

All these tendencies, to imagine counterfactual alternatives to actions, controllable events, socially unacceptable actions, causal relations, and actions that come last in a sequence, provide clues about the key fault lines of reality. Each of the following chapters explains the cognitive processes on which the counterfactual imagination depends. The explanation rests on the idea that the counterfactual imagination is guided by rational principles. The rest of this chapter sketches the counterfactual imagination, and the next chapter examines its relation to rational thought.

Imaginative Thoughts and Emotions

Glimpses of the counterfactual imagination are gained in various ways. In laboratory studies, people may be directed to think about what might have been—for example, they may read a vignette and complete an "if only . . ." sentence stem. Or their thoughts about what might have been may be spontaneous—for instance, they may be asked to complete a diary entry that reflects on a given set of events (Sanna and Turley 1996). Measures include not only the sorts of "if only . . ." alternatives that people create, but also the length of time it takes them to comprehend different parts of a story or to answer questions about it, and the sorts of inferences they make. In naturalistic studies, people are often asked to reflect on their own past lives, and sometimes on traumatic events that have happened to them (Davis et al. 1995). Most people tend to imagine the same sorts of alternatives regardless of how researchers elicit thoughts about what might have been.

Clues about counterfactual thoughts have also been garnered from judgments of various emotions such as regret and guilt, and from various social ascriptions such as blame and responsibility. The influence of counterfactual alternatives on subsequent judgments of causality and culpability has also been measured. These converging measures help build a picture of counterfactual thoughts not only when they occur in the laboratory, but also when they occur in field studies. For example, the fault line of action and inaction remains vital when people are asked to reflect on their own past lives (Gilovich and Medvec 1994; Landman and Manis 1992).

One intriguing manifestation of the counterfactual imagination is in the emotions that people experience, or that they judge other people to experience. Thoughts about what might have been seem to amplify certain emotions (Kahneman and Miller 1986; Roese 1997). Emotions such as regret, guilt, shame, relief, hope, and anticipation are counterfactual emotions (Landman 1993; Niedenthal, Tangney, and Gavanski 1994). The emotion is elicited by thinking about counterfactual possibilities, although the emotion itself is real. The emotion seems to depend on a comparison between how the event actually turned out and how it could have or should have turned out differently. The same is true for social attributions of culpability such as blame, responsibility, and fault, such as, "if you had not left the gate open, the dog would not have gotten lost" (Branscombe et al. 1996; Mandel 2003a). Emotions and social judgments can provide a window onto the underlying counterfactual thoughts, but sometimes there is a dissociation between them (Branscombe et al. 1997). Emotions and social judgments may be best viewed as imperfectly related to counterfactual thoughts.

What People Do *Not* Imagine

The things that most people focus on when they imagine what might have been provide a glimpse of the counterfactual imagination. So too do the things they do not think about. It is informative to consider what people do *not* focus on when they imagine how an event may have turned out differently. What aspects of their mental representation of reality do people leave alone, mentally unchanged? Most people do not tend to create "miracle-world" counterfactuals—for example, "if the Romans had had machine guns ..." (Tetlock and Parker 2005; McMullen and Markman 2002). They do not mentally alter natural laws—for instance, "she would not have fallen if there had not been gravity" (Seeleu et al. 1995). Everyday counterfactual thoughts tend to focus on counterfactual possibilities—that is, things that once were true possibilities. They do not tend to focus on impossibilities—that is, things that could never have been, given the way the world is, for example, "if Kangaroos had no tails they would topple over" (Lewis 1973). Part of the allure of great science fiction lies not only in what is changed but also in what is left unchanged. For example, Ridley Scott's film *Blade Runner* (based on Philip K. Dick's *Do Androids Dream of Electric Sheep?*) preserves familiar features of the real world, such as a Raymond Chandler–type main character, caught in constant rainfall and battling against larger forces. It combines these attributes with novel ones such as artificial intelligence beings so sophisticated in their memory and thinking that they do not know they are not human.

What people do not change when they create a counterfactual alternative depends on their beliefs. In general, people create plausible alternatives to reality. They judge a counterfactual to be plausible when it is consistent with their beliefs. How plausible do you think the following conjecture is: "If Kennedy had listened to his Hawk advisers he would have engaged in a nuclear strike during the Cuban missile crisis"? Political and military experts who believe that nuclear weapons could be deployed, judge it to be more plausible than experts who believe they would never be used (Tetlock and Lebow 2001). Are the perceived fault lines of reality, such as the tendency to imagine alternatives to actions, universal or specific to cultures? The tendency for people to say "if only ..." about their actions is present even in cultures that value collectivism rather than individualism (Gilovich et al. 2003). However, chapter 3 shows it may be more prevalent in reflections on particular times of the lifespan.

The plausibility of a counterfactual may also depend on its closeness to the current facts (Tetlock and Parker 2005). "Close counterfactuals" seem very near to the facts—for example, a runner who just misses first place in a race can imagine coming first instead of second. In fact, a runner who comes second feels worse than one who comes third (Boninger, Gleicher, and Strathman 1994). A small change can produce an imaginary alternative that is better than the actual reality, first place (Markman and Tetlock 2000a). Ironically, an objectively better position such as second place compared to third place is often not subjectively better.

Most people do not imagine remote or distant counterfactual alternatives. The phenomena sketched earlier, of the effects of normality, intentionality, social acceptability, causality, and temporal order, provide an important clue about how people imagine counterfactual alternatives. Counterfactual thoughts may be constrained by the need to create minimal changes (Byrne 1996). Larger changes to reality may be more creative (Roese and Olson 1993b). But counterfactual thoughts may be limited by the constraint that reality must be recoverable from the imagined alternative (Byrne 1997). This point will be illustrated in subsequent chapters, and the last chapter returns to it.

Most people do not imagine how the world might be different after every event. People engage in counterfactual musings most often after something bad happens (Roese 1997). They think about what might have been after dramatic life events, but also in their autobiographical reminiscences about lost opportunities or good luck (Kahneman and Tversky 1982). How often do people think about counterfactual alternatives in their daily thoughts? The answer is not yet known. But people spontaneously produce counterfactual thoughts frequently when they are asked to "think aloud"—for example, as they play a game of blackjack. They tend to generate one or two counterfactual thoughts on average when they discover the outcome of their game (Markman et al. 1993). Likewise, people spontaneously produce counterfactual thoughts frequently when they are asked to write a diary entry from the point of view of the main character in a story about moving to a new town and making friends (McEleney and Byrne 2000). In their diary entries, people generated on average two thoughts about what caused the actual outcome, and one thought about how it might have been different. When people were asked whether they would do something differently in their lives if they could do it over again, almost half of them said they would (Landman and Manis 1992; see also Davis et al. 1995).

Why do people think about what might have been? When they think about how the past could have turned out differently, they can think about how it might have been *better*—for example, they can think about an argument with a friend and say "if I had not said such harsh things, we would still be friends." These "upward" or "better-world" counterfactuals might help people to learn from their mistakes—for instance, not to say harsh things in the heat of an argument (Mandel and Lehman 1996; Roese 1994). They may prepare people for the future, and help them to plan how to prevent bad things from happening (Markman et al. 1993; Sherman and McConnell 1995). One vivid example of the usefulness of counterfactual thoughts is their role in helping aviation pilots who have experienced a "near-miss" accident. Their counterfactual thoughts help them to work out how to avoid a recurrence (Morris and Moore 2000).

Even young children rely on counterfactual thoughts to figure out how an outcome could have been prevented. For example, pretend a little doll walks across the floor with dirty shoes. What if the doll had taken her shoes off? Would the floor have become dirty? (Harris, German, and Mills 1996). By the age of 3 to 4 years, children can think about what the doll did, she wore her dirty shoes, and what she should have done, she should have taken her shoes off. Chapter 5 returns to the development of counterfactual thoughts and their relation to causal thoughts.

Better-world counterfactuals can help people to prepare for the future, but they can also make them feel bad. To feel good, people can think instead about how things might have turned out *worse*—for instance, "if I had told her how I felt, she would never have forgiven me," or "at least I did not say anything cruel ...". These "downward" or "worse-world" counterfactuals can help people feel better (McMullen and Markman 2000). However, they can encourage complacency.

Aside from thinking about better worlds and worse worlds, people can also think about how things might have turned out exactly the same—for example, "even if I had apologized to her, she would not have forgiven me." People can exercise some control over whether they imagine better worlds or worse worlds depending on their motivation—for instance, to console a victim (Seeleu et al. 1995). Whether a person creates an "even if ..." or an "if only ..." alternative may also depend on their current goals (Byrne 1997). For example, when you lose a game and you have the goal to improve on your next one, you may not say, "I would have lost even if ..." but instead you may say, "I could have won if only ..." (Roese et al. 2005).

Of course, people differ in their tendency to create "if only ..." alternatives about aspects of the past (Roese and Olson 1995). Some people may think about what might have been more than other people. Counterfactual thoughts can differ in their intensity as well as their frequency (Sanna and Turley-Ames 2000). Some people tend to think about how things might have turned out better, whereas other people think about how things might have turned out worse (Kasimatis and Wells 1995). Differences between individuals in thoughts about what might have been may be related to personality characteristics such as self-esteem and optimism (Feeney, Gardiner, and McEvoy 2001; Sanna, Turley-Ames, and Meier 1999; Sanna and Meier 2000). For example, people with high self-esteem imagine counterfactual alternatives to their own actions when the outcome is successful (in a scenario in which they imagine themselves as the protoganist). They praise themselves that if they had not acted the outcome would have been worse. But participants with low self-esteem imagine counterfactual alternatives to their own actions when the outcome is a failure. They blame themselves that if they had not acted the outcome would have been better (Roese and Olson 1993a). Differences between people in their counterfactual thoughts may also arise because of differences in motivation and mood (McMullen and Markman 2000; Kasimatis and Wells 1995). The next to last chapter examines some differences between people in the counterfactual alternatives they imagine that depend on cognitive differences. Individuals can differ in their preferred style of thinking (Sternberg 1997). For example, some people prefer to dwell on the facts, whereas others focus on the imagined alternative (Byrne and Tasso 1999). The phenomena to be considered in the intervening chapters are characteristic of *most* people, and chapter 8 returns to differences between individuals and preferred strategies.

This brief sketch of the counterfactual imagination provides a flavor of its broad characteristics, which will be refined in subsequent chapters. How does the mind give rise to counterfactual thoughts? The idea explored here is that the counterfactual imagination is rational. The next chapter outlines the idea that counterfactual thoughts are organized along the same principles as rational thought. In the past, rationality and imagination have been viewed as opposites, having little in common. Logical thought and creativity have even been considered mutually exclusive.

Contrary to this viewpoint, the argument made here is that rationality and imagination share a lot.

Summary

Imaginative thought about what might have been shows remarkable regularities. Most people mentally alter the same aspects of reality when they imagine alternatives. For example, most people imagine alternatives to actions, controllable events, unacceptable actions, causal relations, and recent events. This book explores the idea that rational thought and imaginative thought may have a lot in common.

Counterfactual thoughts are central to everyday mental life. Sometimes they can become too central. Some people continue to be plagued by thoughts about what might have been long after an event, even when these thoughts do not help them to learn from any mistake. For example, individuals who have experienced a traumatic life event, such as a severe paralyzing injury following an accident, are sometimes dogged by thoughts of how the accident might have been avoided if only they had done something differently. Individuals who have experienced the grief of the death of a spouse or child are sometimes haunted by thoughts of how they could have prevented the death—for example "if only I had checked on him more often during the night ..." or "if only I had not let her out to play that afternoon ...". The knowledge that their behavior was not the cause of the accident may do little to alleviate their suffering (Davis et al. 1995). Victims of traumatic attacks often recognize that the assailant caused the attack, but they still blame themselves for not doing enough to avoid it (Branscombe et al. 2003). After a traumatic life event, everyone thinks about what might have been to some extent, but people who continue to think about what might have been experience greater distress (Davis et al. 1995). Counterfactual thoughts may play a role in clinical disorders such as depression and anxiety (Roese and Olson 1995). A greater understanding of how people imagine alternatives to reality may contribute to the development of ways to help people for whom the counterfactual imagination has become dysfunctional.

2 Imagination and Rational Thought

This book provides an explanation for why people imagine the things they do when they create counterfactual alternatives to reality. The starting point is the idea that imaginative thoughts and rational thoughts have a lot in common. People try to think rationally in many situations. For example, you try to reach a rational conclusion when you estimate the likelihood that the next flight you take will be hijacked, or when you work out the risk that you may have contracted variant Creutzfeldt-Jakob disease (CJD) from your exposures to BSE-infected meat. You try to think rationally when you decide which treatment options to pursue for an illness you have, or when you make choices between different houses to buy or jobs to apply for. Rational thought takes many forms (Baron 2000; Galotti 2002). This chapter first examines rational thought and then considers the relation between rational thought and imaginative thought.

Often people are on their "best behavior" with regard to rational thought when they try to make deductions. Deductive reasoning requires people to reach a conclusion that is not just plausible or possible. The conclusion *must* be true, if the factors it is based on—the assumptions, beliefs, and knowledge that make up the premises—are true. A valid deductive inference has no counterexample—that is, the conclusion cannot be false and the premises true. Deductive reasoning is important for many aspects of thinking (Johnson-Laird and Byrne 1991, 3): "You need to make deductions in order to formulate plans and to evaluate actions; to determine the consequences of assumptions and hypotheses; to interpret and to formulate instructions, rules and general principles; to pursue arguments and negotiations; to weigh evidence and to assess data; to decide between competing theories; and to solve problems. A world without deduction would be a world without science, technology, laws, social conventions, and

culture." This chapter provides a sketch of rational thought, and it outlines
the idea that counterfactual thoughts are organized along the same principles as rational thoughts.

Rational Thought

Are people capable of rational thought? Do they have reliable strategies for
reasoning, a basic competence to be logical? The issue has been debated
(Evans and Over 1996; Gigerenzer and Selten 2001; Manktelow and Over
1993; Stanovich 1999). Clearly people can engage in hypothetical thought.
It is one of the remarkable achievements of human cognition. People rely
on hypothetical thought to conjecture and speculate, to plan and predict,
and to explore alternative trains of thought, as the cartoon in figure 2.1
illustrates. Most people can make inferences and solve everyday problems;

Figure 2.1
Reprinted by permission of www.CartoonStock.com

the very existence of a world with science, laws, and technology indicates that at least some individuals pursue rational conclusions. But most people make mistakes. They fail to make inferences that are valid—that is, they fail to reach conclusions that must be true, for which there are no counter-examples. They endorse inferences that are invalid; in other words, they reach conclusions that may not be true, for which there are counter-examples. And sometimes their emotions, beliefs, and opinions lead them to make inferences they would otherwise resist.

How compromised is the idea of human rationality by the existence of error? People's mistakes have led some researchers to suggest that people do not have any general capacity for rational thought, and instead their reasoning is based on a collection of biases and rules of thumb or "heuristics," which work well in some circumstances but not in others (Evans 1989; Kahneman and Tversky 1982). Others have suggested that people's seeming ability to think rationally in some circumstances may reflect nothing more than familiarity with a set of rules that govern a specific domain; once outside that domain, their reasoning is vulnerable to extraneous influences (Fiddick, Cosmides, and Tooby 2000; Holyoak and Cheng 1995). Chapter 4 shows that this view cannot be the full story about human reasoning.

Other researchers have suggested that people *do* have the capacity for rational thought. Some of these researchers have argued that people are rational because they have access to a "mental logic" of inference rules (Braine and O'Brien 1998; Rips 1994). The next chapter shows that the idea of rule-based rationality is too rigid to embrace the extraordinary flexibility of human reasoning. An alternative view is that people are rational because they can appreciate a simple semantic principle: an inference is valid if there are no counterexamples to it (Johnson-Laird and Byrne 1991). It is this last view of rationality that illuminates imaginative thought.

Hypothetical thought has been studied in many guises, and one good illustration is conditional reasoning. Within the domain of deductive inference, center stage has been occupied by reasoning about conditional relations, often expressed using "if"—for example, "if Alicia went to the stables then she rode Starlight." Conditionals have been considered the key to how people make suppositions and conjecture relationships between events (Johnson-Laird and Byrne 1991; Cheng and Holyoak 1985; Rips 1983; Braine and O'Brien 1991). For example, during the first round of the

World Cup Finals in 2002, an article in the *Irish Times* (June 11) described Ireland's chances in the upcoming competition. It began by providing the following background:

Group E: The permutations. The Republic of Ireland must beat Saudi Arabia to have any chance of reaching the second round. A victory by a two-goal margin (2–0, 3–1, etc) over the Saudis would be enough for Ireland to advance to the second round, regardless of the result between Germany and Cameroon.

The description depended on a sequence of conditionals:

If Ireland beat Saudi Arabia they would go through to the second round, regardless of the margin of their victory, if there is a winner in the Germany v Cameroon game (i.e. if the game doesn't end in a draw).

And it considered various options:

If Germany and Cameroon draw and Ireland beat Saudi Arabia the three teams would finish level on five points—in such an event Germany would definitely be through (their goal difference would be greater than Cameroon's) but the margin of Ireland's win would determine whether they beat Cameroon to second place. If Cameroon and Germany draw 1–1 on Tuesday and Ireland beat Saudi Arabia 1–0, Cameroon and Ireland would finish with identical records—lots would then have to be drawn to determine which of them would join Germany in the second round.

The description was not unusual. At every bus stop and in every pub similar descriptions could be overheard, as World Cup fever took hold. Conditionals can be put to many uses, and the example illustrates that ordinary people in their daily lives will come to grips with complex sequences of conditional relations, provided the topic is one they are interested in. (Aficionados may like to know that later that day Ireland beat Saudi Arabia, and Germany beat Cameroon, with the result that Ireland and Germany went through to the second round.)

People make inferences from conditionals. Consider the conditional: "if Alicia went to the stables then she rode Starlight." Suppose you discover that Alicia did not ride Starlight. What do you think follows? Some people say nothing follows. Other people say "Alicia did not go to the stables." What cognitive processes underlie their answers? One explanation is that people keep in mind possibilities of various sorts (Johnson-Laird and Byrne 2002). The next section outlines some of the key principles that guide the possibilities that people think about when they engage in conditional reasoning. The principles underlie deductive rationality. These same principles also help explain counterfactual thought.

The Interpretation of "If"

What did you think about when you understood the conditional, "if Alicia went to the stables she rode Starlight"? Take a moment to list what is possible (and what is impossible) given the truth of the conditional. To work out how people make inferences it is essential to work out how they understand what they are reasoning about. The conditional asserts a relation between two components, the antecedent ("Alicia went to the stables") and the consequent ("she rode Starlight"). Consider for a moment all of the combinations of these two components that could occur in the world:

(1)   Alicia went to the stables and she rode Starlight.

(2)   Alicia went to the stables and she did not ride Starlight.

(3)   Alicia did not go to the stables and she did not ride Starlight.

(4)   Alicia did not go to the stables and she rode Starlight.

Which of these situations did you think about when you understood the conditional?

The conditional is consistent with some of these situations, and it rules out others. Consider first the situations in which Alicia went to the stables (1 and 2). Do you think the conditional is consistent with either of these situations? Most people appreciate that its meaning is consistent with the first situation, Alicia went to the stables and she rode Starlight (Evans, Newstead, and Byrne 1993). Most people list this situation as possible (Johnson-Laird and Byrne 2002). The conditional can be true and situation 1 can be true at the same time. Do you think the conditional rules out any of the situations? Most people judge that it rules out the second situation, Alicia went to the stables and she did not ride Starlight.

Now consider the situations in which Alicia did not go to the stables (3 and 4). Do you think the conditional is consistent with either of them? Most people agree that the conditional is consistent with the third situation, in which Alicia did not go to the stables and she did not ride Starlight. The conditional can be true and situation 3 can be true at the same time. What do you think about the fourth situation, in which Alicia did not go to the stables and she rode Starlight? People differ in their opinions about it. Do you think it is ruled out by the conditional? Some people judge that when the conditional is true, situation 4 is false. Logicians call this interpretation *material equivalence* (Jeffrey 1981), and psychologists call it a *biconditional* interpretation (Evans, Newstead, and Byrne 1993). On

Table 2.1
Situations that are true and false when the conditional "if Alicia went to the stables then she rode Starlight" is true, for two interpretations

	Interpretations	
"If Alicia went to the stables then she rode Starlight"	Conditional	Biconditional
Alicia went to the stables and she rode Starlight	True	True
Alicia went to the stables and she did not ride Starlight	False	False
Alicia did not go to the stables and she did not ride Starlight	True	True
Alicia did not go to the stables and she rode Starlight	True	False

this interpretation the conditional means "if *and only if* Alicia went to the stables she rode Starlight." Alicia going to the stables is an antecedent condition that is necessary for the consequent to occur—that is, it must happen, for her to ride Starlight. Alicia going to the stables is also a sufficient condition—that is, it is enough, for her to ride Starlight, as table 2.1 shows.

But perhaps you interpreted the fourth situation to be consistent with the conditional? Some people judge that when the conditional is true, situation 4 could also be true. For example, Starlight sometimes may be at another location, say in Alicia's own field, or at a horse show. In other words, when Alicia goes to the stables she rides Starlight, and when she does not go to the stables but goes somewhere else, out to her field, or to a horse show, she also rides him. Logicians call this interpretation *material implication*, and psychologists call it the *conditional* interpretation. Alicia going to the stables is not a necessary condition for the consequent to occur; it need not happen, for her to ride Starlight. Alicia going to the stables is still a sufficient condition; it is enough, for her to ride Starlight. People come to different interpretations of conditionals, often depending on the conditional's content and context. The conditional and biconditional interpretations are the two more common interpretations. In fact, people can come to as many as ten different interpretations (Johnson-Laird and Byrne 2002). Later chapters return to some of the other interpretations.

Conditionals and Possibilities

What do people think about when they understand a conditional? One explanation is that they think about possibilities (Johnson-Laird and Byrne

2002). Consider again the four situations outlined in table 2.1. Do people think about all four possibilities whenever they understand the conditional? The answer is, they do not. There are several key principles that guide the possibilities that people consider. They understand a conditional such as "if Alicia went to the stables then she rode Starlight" (if A then B) by keeping in mind only the possibilities compatible with the conditional—for example, they think about "Alicia went to the stables and she rode Starlight" (A and B). (For clarity of exposition, the structure of the possibilities is denoted using A's and B's.) Generally, they do not think about false possibilities, such as "Alicia went to the stables and she did not ride Starlight" (A and not-B) (Johnson-Laird and Byrne 2002). The first principle is as follows:

1. Principle of true possibilities: *People keep in mind true possibilities*. They do not think about false possibilities.

Of course for most conditionals several possibilities could be true. For example, on the conditional interpretation, there are three true possibilities, "Alicia went to the stables and she rode Starlight" (A and B), "Alicia did not go to the stables and she did not ride Starlight" (not-A and not-B), and "Alicia did not go to the stables and she rode Starlight" (not-A and B). Do people think about all of these true possibilities? The answer once again is, they do not. Multiple possibilities tend to exceed working-memory capacity. People usually mentally represent the conditional by thinking about just a single true possibility, "Alicia went to the stables and she rode Starlight" (Johnson-Laird and Byrne 1991). They think first about the elements mentioned in the conditional (see table 2.2). For example, they understand a conditional such as "if Karl did not drive fast, then he did not arrive on time" by keeping in mind the possibility that Karl did not drive fast and did not arrive on time.

Their understanding of the conditional is not entirely akin to a conjunction. They know that there may be other true possibilities, but their thoughts about them remain unformed. An unformed thought is akin to a marker or a mental footnote, a reminder to yourself that you have not exhausted all of the relevant possibilities (Johnson-Laird and Byrne 1991). People are aware that there are alternative true possibilities that they have not thought through, but that they can return to and think about later (Johnson-Laird and Byrne 1991). They consider a single true possibility

Table 2.2
Possibilities people keep in mind when they understand a factual conditional

---

Factual conditional: "If Alicia went to the stables then she rode Starlight"
Initial possibilities
    <u>Alicia went to the stables and she rode Starlight</u>
    (There may be other possibilities but these remain unformed)
Possibilities for biconditional
    <u>Alicia went to the stables and she rode Starlight</u>
    Alicia did not go to the stables and she did not ride Starlight
Possibilities for conditional
    <u>Alicia went to the stables and she rode Starlight</u>
    Alicia did not go to the stables and she did not ride Starlight
    Alicia did not go to the stables and she rode Starlight

Note: The possibility people think about initially is underlined.
Source: Adapted from Johnson-Laird and Byrne 1991, 2002.

fully. In contrast, their thoughts about the other true possibilities remain unformed.

People think about as few alternatives as possible because of the limitations of their working memories. The second principle is as follows:

2.   Principle of few possibilities: *People keep in mind few possibilities.*

Accordingly, people do not keep in mind the full set of entries in a truth table, such as described in table 2.1. They do not think about the situation that is false. And they do not think about every situation that is true. Entries in a truth table represent the truth or falsity of an assertion, whereas possibilities are psychologically basic (Johnson-Laird and Byrne 2002). In some circumstances people try to consider more possibilities. They often develop their unformed ideas to think about other possibilities when they try to make inferences from a conditional.

Conditional Inferences
How do people make inferences from conditionals? They can readily make some inferences based on the possibilities they have kept in mind, but they find other inferences more difficult to make. Suppose you know "if Mark left at 9 a.m. then he caught the airplane" and you are told, "Mark left at 9 a.m." What, if anything, do you think follows from these premises? Most people find it easy to infer "he caught the airplane." They have understood

Table 2.3
Inferences from the conditional "if Mark left at 9 a.m. then he caught the airplane"

Modus ponens	*Affirmation of the consequent*
Mark left at 9 a.m.	Mark caught the airplane.
Therefore he caught the airplane.	Therefore he left at 9 a.m.
Modus tollens	*Denial of the antecedent*
Mark did not catch the airplane.	Mark did not leave at 9 a.m.
Therefore he did not leave at 9 a.m.	Therefore he did not catch the airplane.

the conditional by keeping in mind the single true possibility, "Mark left at 9 a.m. and he caught the airplane" (A and B). The information in the additional premise, "Mark left at 9 a.m." matches part of the information in the single possibility they have kept in mind, and they can readily conclude, "he caught the airplane." The inference is affirmative (it does not require you to negate any elements), and it is in a forward direction (from A to B). It is called *modus ponens* by logicians. Is there a counterexample to the inference? Consider the premises: "if Mark left at 9 a.m. then he caught the airplane. He left at 9 a.m.". Is it possible for the conclusion, "he caught the airplane" to be false? Most people judge that there are no counterexamples to it (except in special circumstances described in chapter 5).

Suppose you are told "Mark did not catch the airplane." What, if anything, follows from this premise and the conditional? Many people say nothing follows. They have difficulty making the inference to the conclusion, "he did not leave at 9 a.m." The fact, "he did not catch the airplane" denies the consequent, and does not match any possibility they have thought about. They have not yet thought through any of the other possibilities to be able to identify that it does match one of them. Many people do not make the inference because they are hampered by the fact that they have kept in mind just a single possibility. To make the inference, they need to remember that there are alternative possibilities, and provided they remember that there are alternatives, they must think through what they are. Only when they think about the alternative possibilities will they be able to make the inference. If people think about the true possibility, "Mark did not leave at 9 a.m. and he did not catch the airplane" (not-A and not-B), they can make the inference (see table 2.3). The inference is negative and it is in a backward direction (from B to A). It is called *modus tollens* by logicians. Most people judge that there are no counterexamples to it.

There are two other inferences that people sometimes make from a conditional (Evans, Newstead, and Byrne 1993). Suppose you are told "Mark caught the airplane." What, if anything, do you think follows from this premise and the conditional? Sometimes people infer "he left at 9 a.m." The information that "he caught the airplane" matches part of the possibility that they have thought about, "Mark left at 9 a.m. and he caught the airplane." The inference is known as the *affirmation of the consequent*. Is there a counterexample to it? Consider the premises: "if Mark left at 9 a.m. then he caught the airplane. He caught the airplane." Is it possible for the conclusion, "he left at 9 a.m." to be false? The answer depends on your interpretation of "if."

On the "biconditional" interpretation, there is no counterexample to the inference. There is no possibility in which it is true that Mark caught the airplane, and it is true that he did not leave at 9 a.m. But on the "conditional" interpretation, one true possibility is that "Mark did not leave at 9 a.m. and he caught the airplane" perhaps because he took a shortcut, or he got a taxi to the airport. On this interpretation there is a counterexample to the inference. People make the inference whenever they interpret "if" as a biconditional, and they do not make it when they consider as true the possibility that Mark did not leave at 9 a.m. and he caught the airplane.

The final inference that people sometimes make from a conditional is the *denial of the antecedent* inference. Suppose you are told "Mark did not leave at 9 a.m." What, if anything, do you think follows? Like the modus tollens (not-B therefore not-A) inference, the information "he did not leave at 9 a.m." does not match any information that people have thought about from the outset. Many people say nothing follows. Other people think about the possibility "Mark did not leave at 9 a.m. and he did not catch the airplane" and they infer "he did not catch the airplane." Is there a counterexample to the conclusion? Once again, it depends on the interpretation of the conditional. On a biconditional interpretation there is no counterexample. But on a conditional interpretation there is: the conclusion is not consistent with the possibility "Mark did not leave at 9 a.m. and he caught the airplane." People make the inference when they have interpreted "if" as a biconditional. But they do not make it whenever they keep in mind just a single possibility and fail to think about their unformed thoughts, such as the possibility that Mark did not leave at 9 a.m. and he did not catch the airplane. They also do not make it whenever they have interpreted "if" as a conditional—that is, they have thought about the possibility that Mark did not leave at 9 a.m. and he caught the airplane.

Inferences and Possibilities

Most people find the modus ponens (A therefore B) inference easier than the modus tollens (not-B therefore not-A) one (Evans, Newstead, and Byrne 1993). In fact, the difference is greater when people are given a conditional "if" than when they are given a biconditional "if and only if." They can make the modus tollens (not-B therefore not-A) inference more readily from the biconditional. It requires them to think about two possibilities to make the inference, whereas the conditional requires them to think about three possibilities. The greater number of possibilities increases the difficulty of the inference. The result supports the idea that people make inferences by thinking about possibilities (Johnson-Laird, Byrne, and Schaeken 1992).

People also tend to make the affirmation of the consequent (B therefore A) inference more often than the denial of the antecedent (not-A therefore not-B) one (Schroyens, Schaeken, and d'Ydewalle 2001). People make the affirmation of the consequent inference when they have thought about a single possibility, but they must think about the negative possibility to make the denial of the antecedent one. In general, the fewer possibilities that have to be thought about for an inference, the easier the inference is (for a review see Johnson-Laird 2001). Inferences based on one possibility are easier than those based on multiple ones, and systematic errors correspond to a subset of possibilities (Johnson-Laird, Byrne, and Schaeken 1992). When the inference depends on more than one conditional, people can sometimes follow their logical consequences, although they often fall into error (Byrne 1989a; Santamaría, García-Madruga, and Johnson-Laird 1998). People sometimes treat conditionals as conjunctions when they do not think about other possibilities that are consistent with the conditional. In fact, there is a developmental trend for children and adolescents to interpret a conditional as a conjunction, then as a biconditional, and then as a conditional (Barrouillet and Lecas 1998; Markovits 1984). This trend is consistent with the idea that people envisage a single possibility when they reason about a conjunction, two possibilities when they reason about a biconditional, and three possibilities when they reason about a conditional. People may mentally represent possibilities by constructing "mental models" (Johnson-Laird 1983). Their mental representation of possibilities may be akin to small-scale models of the world (Craik 1943; see also Wittgenstein 1922).

What does it mean to say that people keep in mind two possibilities? Some processes appear linear—for example, people can utter only one word at a time in serial order. Other processes appear parallel—for instance, people can walk and chew gum. Is thinking about two possibilities a parallel process, in which two possibilities are processed simultaneously? Or is it a linear process, by which attention is switched, perhaps rapidly, from one possibility to another? The idea that people mentally represent two possibilities by switching attention from one to the other makes sense, but the key point is that thinking about two possibilities is often harder than thinking about a single possibility because of the constraints of working memory (Johnson-Laird and Byrne 1991). As a result, people tend to think about few possibilities.

People rely on possibilities to make deductions in each of the main domains of deduction (Johnson-Laird and Byrne 1991). They can make many different sorts of deductions. For example, they can make inferences based on quantifiers such as *all*, *some*, and *none* (Johnson-Laird and Byrne 1989; Newstead 1990; Johnson-Laird, Byrne, and Tabossi 1989). They can make inferences based on relational terms such as *in front of*, *before*, and *better than* (Byrne and Johnson-Laird 1989; Schaeken, Johnson-Laird, and d'Ydewalle 1996). And they can make inferences based on propositional connectives other than *if*, such as *or*, *not*, and *and* (Johnson-Laird, Byrne, and Schaeken 1992). They can even make deductions about deductions (Rips 1989; Johnson-Laird and Byrne 1990; Byrne and Handley 1997; Byrne, Handley, and Johnson-Laird 1995). In each of these domains people rely on possibilities to make inferences. People may also rely on possibilities to make inferences in other domains, such as inferences about probabilities (Johnson-Laird et al. 1999), and risk judgments (Girotto and Gonzalez 2001; McCloy, Byrne, and Johnson-Laird 2004). Of course, the idea that people rely on possibilities to make inferences is not without criticism (Evans 1993; Greene 1992; Bonatti 1994; O'Brien, Braine, and Yang 1994; see also the commentaries following Johnson-Laird and Byrne 1993b; and for replies see Johnson-Laird, Byrne, and Schaeken 1994; Johnson-Laird, Byrne, and Tabossi 1992).

The possibilities people envisage can be influenced by the content of the conditional and the context in which it occurs (Griggs and Cox 1983; Newstead et al. 1997). Consider the following example: "If Joe is in Rio de Janeiro then he is in Brazil." What possibilities do you think about when you understand it? Suppose you are told that "Joe is not in Brazil." What, if anything, follows? More than 90 percent of people conclude "Joe is not in Rio de Janeiro" (Johnson-Laird and Byrne 2002). This modus tollens inference has exactly the same structure (not-B therefore not-A) as the one we examined earlier about Mark leaving at 9 a.m. and catching the airplane. For some topics, many people say nothing follows. But few people say nothing follows about Joe in Rio. The ease with which they make the inference provides a clue about the possibilities they have thought about. They think about the possibility that "Joe is in Rio and he is in Brazil." But they also have ready access to another true possibility: "Joe is not in Rio and he is not in Brazil." Their geographic knowledge of the spatial inclusion of cities in countries helps them to think about the second possibility. Phil Johnson-Laird and I have tested the idea that it is their knowledge that helps them (Johnson-Laird and Byrne 2002). In one experiment, we gave forty-one participants inferences based on familiar content and we compared them to unfamiliar content. Consider the following example: "If Agnes is in the Champagne Suite then she is in the Hotel LaBlanc." Suppose you know "Agnes is not in the Hotel LaBlanc." What follows? People do not say "she is not in the Champagne Suite" quite so readily. They make the modus tollens (not-B therefore not-A) inference reliably more often from the familiar content than from the unfamiliar one. The result shows that knowledge can help people think about more possibilities.

Knowledge can also block some possibilities. Consider another conditional about Joe in Brazil, this time "if Joe is in Brazil then he is not in Rio." What do you envisage when you understand it? Suppose you are told "Joe is in Rio." What will you conclude? Fewer than one-third of people conclude that "Joe is not in Brazil" (Johnson-Laird and Byrne 2002). Yet the inference has the same structure as the earlier one about Joe in Brazil. The information that "Joe is in Rio" denies the second part of the conditional, and the conclusion denies the first part of the conditional. Their reluctance to make the inference provides a clue about the possibilities they have kept in mind. They understand "if Joe is in Brazil then he is not in Rio" by keeping in mind the true possibility, "Joe is in Brazil and he is not in Rio." Their geographic knowledge this time leads them to reject the possibility that "Joe is not in Brazil and he is in Rio." Once again it is clear that it is their knowledge that blocks them constructing the extra possibility because it does not happen when the content is unfamiliar. Suppose you are told "if Agnes is in the Hotel LaBlanc then she is not in the Champagne Suite," and you are then given the information "Agnes is in the Champagne Suite." What do you think follows? Most people are not so reluctant to make the inference "she is not in the Hotel LaBlanc" (Johnson-Laird and Byrne 2002). They make the modus tollens (not-B therefore not-A) inference reliably more often from the unfamiliar content than from the familiar one. The result shows that knowledge can block people from envisaging possibilities.

When people think hypothetically—for example, when they understand and reason about conditional relations—they think about possibilities. They think about a limited set of possibilities. Two principles that guide the sorts of possibilities they think about are that they think about true possibilities, not false possibilities; and they think about only a few possibilities, not all the true possibilities. The inferences people make can be explained by the principles that guide the possibilities they think about when they understand conditional relations.

Rationality and Conditional Inferences

Are people capable of rational thought on this view? People are rational in principle but they err in practice (Johnson-Laird and Byrne 1993a). An analogy clarifies the distinction. Suppose John writes "I seen her do it." His sentence is ungrammatical. Does his mistake indicate that he is incapable of grammatical utterances? Perhaps not. His mistake may be confined to the verb *to see*. Does it indicate that he is unaware of the grammatical principles for this verb? It might. He may genuinely believe that *seen* is the past tense of *see*, perhaps because of vernacular usage. But his mistake may be a slip of the pen. He may have meant to write "I have seen her do it" or "I see her do it" and been interrupted, or hurried, or tired. John may be grammatical in principle but may have erred in practice. Suppose now that John makes an inferential error. When he knows that "if Alicia went to the stables then she rode Starlight," then is told that "Alicia did not ride Starlight," John says that nothing follows. Does his mistake indicate that he is incapable of rational thought? Perhaps not. His mistake may be confined to inferences of this sort. Does it indicate he is unaware of the rational principles for this inference? It might. He may genuinely believe that nothing ever follows from such premises. But his mistake may reflect a failure to think through all of the possibilities. He may have forgotten that his initial understanding of the conditional, as consistent with the possibility "Alicia went to the stables and she rode Starlight," was provisional, and that there are other possibilities consistent with the conditional. He may even have difficulty thinking about alternative possibilities for this topic. The point is that someone may have an underlying competence that is sometimes hidden because of performance factors.

What is rational thought on this view? Rational thought is thought that leads to reasonable conclusions—for example, deductive rationality is thought that leads to conclusions that must be true whenever the premises are true. There are no counterexamples to a good deductive conclusion. A conclusion is reasonable not in virtue of its form being sanctioned by a normative theory, such as a particular logical calculus, but because it corresponds to the way the world must be given the reasoner's interpretation of the premises. Rational thought depends on a coherent set of processes for considering possibilities. The principles for considering possibilities form a competent algorithmic procedure, and when it operates perfectly it produces accurate rational answers (Johnson-Laird and Byrne 2002). But there are limits to its operation, such as the constraints of working memory. These limits have the consequence that people rarely think systematically about the possibilities. Of course, there are also valid deductions that do not seem reasonable, such as a conjunction of the premises. Deductions may be constrained to assert something new that was not explicit in the premises (Johnson-Laird and Byrne 1991). Deductive reasoning is rational because people have the underlying competence to think of all the relevant possibilities so that they could search for counterexamples. Why then do people make mistakes? Their performance is sometimes not rational because of the limits to the possibilities they can consider. The principles that give rise to rationality can also explain instances of irrationality.

Human rationality depends on imagination. People have the capacity to be rational at least in principle because they can *imagine* alternatives (Johnson-Laird 1982). The possibilities they imagine are guided by several simple principles. The principles that guide the possibilities people think of are principles that underpin their rationality. These principles for rational thought also guide imaginative thought.

Rational Thought and Imaginative Thought

How do the principles that guide rational thought extend to imaginative thought? A bridge from rationality to imagination can be built on counterfactual conditionals. Conditionals are a good example of deductive rationality; counterfactual thoughts are a good example of everyday imagination. Counterfactual conditionals combine both rational and imaginative elements.

Counterfactual Conditionals

Counterfactuals are special. Consider the counterfactual conditional, "if Oswald had not killed Kennedy then someone else would have." It seems to mean something very different from the factual conditional, "if Oswald did not kill Kennedy then someone else did" (Lewis 1973). Perhaps the most noticeable difference superficially between the two conditionals is in the use of language such as "had not killed" instead of "did not kill" and "would have" instead of "did." Attempts to understand counterfactuals have led to important developments in linguistics (Athanasiadou and Dirvin 1997; Barwise 1986; Traugott et al. 1986). The counterfactual is in the *subjunctive mood* (sometimes referred to as the subjunctive mode). The subjunctive mood conveys wishes, conjectures, and uncertainties. It allows a speaker syntactically to cue a listener to consider counterfactual and hypothetical situations.

The subjunctive mood can be used to convey uncertainties such as "if James were to win the lottery next year, he would buy a yacht." It is also used to convey counterfactual conjectures about the past—for example, "if James had won the lottery last year, he would have bought a yacht." The subjunctive mood is sometimes used in indirect discourse, as in "he said that the meeting would be held indoors" (Adams 1975). When the subjunctive mood is used about the future, its function is often to introduce uncertainty. Consider Frank, who asserts that "if I were to become a movie star next month, I would move to Hollywood." Do you think it is probable that Frank will become a movie star next month? Suppose Frank had uttered the future conditional without the subjunctive mood: "If I become a movie star next month, I will move to Hollywood." Do you think it is probable that he will become a movie star next month? The use of the subjunctive mood in a conditional about the future may introduce greater uncertainty to the hypothetical conjecture (Byrne and Egan 2004).

The use of the subjunctive mood about the past and present does something even more interesting. A counterfactual conditional such as "if only he had been handsome, I would have married him" evokes two possibilities, an imaginary possibility in which the man is handsome and the speaker marries him, and a reality in which the man was not and she did not. Counterfactuals conjure up two possibilities. Subjunctive constructions about the present and the past often convey two possibilities—for example, "would that she were rich" conveys not only the wish that she were rich, but also the fact that she is not. Language has various devices that enable speakers to invite their listeners to consider two possibilities, the possibility mentioned and some alternative to it. The subjunctive mood invites people to hold in mind the possibility mentioned, and also its negation or another alternative.

People can express counterfactuality even in languages with no specific linguistic markers for the subjunctive mood (Au 1983). Mood is not a necessary component to convey counterfactuality, since context alone can cue it (Dudman 1988). Moreover, people can make counterfactual conjectures without using the subjunctive mood (Johnson-Laird 1986). Nor is linguistic mood sufficient, since conditionals in the subjunctive mood about the past are not always interpreted as counterfactual. As described in chapter 5, their interpretation depends on their content (Thompson and Byrne 2002). But it is crucial to be able to convey a counterfactual alternative by some means, and the subjunctive mood often helps a speaker accomplish this goal.

Attempts to understand counterfactual conditionals have also led to important developments in artificial intelligence (Ginsberg 1986). Computer programs that can understand and use counterfactual constructions have been developed (Isard 1974; Costelloe and McCarthy 1999), and programs that solve problems can rely on the counterfactual construction of subgoals (Ginsberg 1986). For example, the realization "I could have reached that block if I had been standing on the step" leads to the formulation of the subgoal to stand on the step.

Attempts to understand counterfactual conditionals have led to important developments most notably in philosophy (Jackson 1987; Lewis

1973; Stalnaker 1968). Philosophers have long been concerned with the meaning of counterfactual conditionals (Ayers 1965; Kvart 1986). There is something odd about counterfactuals. The way people interpret them goes beyond the truth of their components (Quine 1972). In the propositional calculus, the meaning of a conditional such as "if Oswald did not kill Kennedy then someone else did" is truth functional. The truth of the conditional depends on the truth value of its two components, the antecedent "Oswald did not kill Kennedy" and the consequent "someone else did." The conditional is true whenever the antecedent is false (Oswald did kill Kennedy) or whenever the consequent is true (someone else killed Kennedy). This succinct description of the truth value of the conditional captures the three situations in which "if" is true on the conditional interpretation, as a glance back at table 2.1 will confirm. But the counterfactual "if Oswald had not killed Kennedy then someone else would have" violates a truth functional account. The counterfactual seems to presuppose that its antecedent is false. It presupposes that Oswald *did* kill Kennedy. But in that case, the counterfactual must be true (because a conditional is true whenever its antecedent is false). In fact on a truth functional account, every counterfactual must be true. They all have false antecedents. But people do not judge all counterfactuals to be true (Miyamoto and Dibble 1986). Do you think that if Oswald had not killed Kennedy someone else would have? Some people may believe the counterfactual is plausibly true, taking into account conspiracy theories and the unpopularity of some of Kennedy's political decisions in certain circles. But other people may believe the counterfactual is not plausibly true, taking into account the lone-gunman suggestion or the view that Kennedy was moving toward a more positive phase of his presidency. The point is that the judgment of the truth of the counterfactual is not based on the truth of its components.

Philosophers have suggested instead that the truth of a counterfactual may depend on its truth in a "possible world" (Stalnaker 1968; Lewis 1973). The possible world depends on the real world, and it is the most similar possible world to the real world except that the antecedent of the counterfactual is true in it. If the consequent is also true in this possible world then the counterfactual as a whole is true, otherwise it is false (Stalnaker 1968). There is not always a single possible world most similar to the real world except that the counterfactual's antecedent is true. A counterfactual may be true if there is a possible world in which the antecedent and consequent are true and this possible world is closer to the real world than any world in which the antecedent is true and the consequent is false (Lewis 1973). The similarity of a possible world to the real world may depend on making minimal changes to the real one (Pollock 1986).

Of course, imagined possible worlds cannot be observed, and so the truth and falsity of a counterfactual cannot be observed. Instead, the critical psychological difference between factual and counterfactual conditionals may lie in the possibilities that people think about. Consider the conditional "if Iraq had weapons of mass destruction then the war was justified." It is consistent with three possibilities (on a conditional interpretation): Iraq had weapons of mass destruction and the war was justified, Iraq did not have weapons of mass destruction and the war was not justified, and Iraq did not have weapons of mass destruction and the war was justified. Most people mentally represent the factual conditional initially by thinking about just the single possibility that Iraq had weapons of mass destruction and the war was justified. Now consider the counterfactual conditional, "if Iraq had had weapons of mass destruction then the war would have been justified." It is consistent with the same three possibilities as the factual conditional (on a conditional interpretation). What possibilities did you think about when you understood it? You may think about more than one possibility. You may mentally represent the counterfactual by thinking about the conjecture mentioned in the counterfactual, Iraq had weapons of mass destruction and the war was justified. You may also think about the facts presupposed by the counterfactual, Iraq did not have weapons of mass destruction and the war was not justified. The factual and counterfactual conditionals are consistent with the same possibilities, but their difference hinges on the mental representation of different possibilities. The key difference is that people think about a single possibility when they understand a factual conditional, but they think about two possibilities when they understand a counterfactual, and they keep track of whether the possibilities are conjectures or presupposed facts.

Of course, counterfactuals about unknown situations may not convey the truth or falsity of their antecedents. Suppose you do not know whether or not Paul Newman won an Oscar for his role in the film *Cool Hand Luke*. You may say, "if Paul Newman had won an Oscar for *Cool Hand Luke* it would have been richly deserved." Your assertion may not convey as a presupposed fact that the antecedent is false, but only that its truth is unknown to you. And chapter 5 shows that just as people come to different interpretations of factual conditionals, so too do they come to different interpretations of counterfactuals (Johnson-Laird and Byrne 2002).

Dual-Possibility Ideas

In many situations people consider just a single possibility, because of the constraints of their limited working memories. However, certain ideas are "dual-possibility" ideas. When people understand such ideas, they need to keep in mind several possibilities from the outset. Choices are a good example of dual-possibility ideas. Suppose you have a choice about where to go on holidays. Having a choice implies that you consider an option—for example, you will go to France for your holidays, and you also envisage an alternative to it, or even several alternatives to it. The alternative may be specific (for instance, you will go to Florida), or general (you will go somewhere else). The alternative may be just the negation of the option, you will not go to France (Legrenzi, Girotto, and Johnson-Laird 1993). To make a choice between two options requires that you think about two possibilities. There are many examples of dual-possibility ideas. One good example is counterfactual conditionals: people tend to think about two possibilities from the outset when they understand them.

People understand the counterfactual "if Alicia had gone to the stables then she would have ridden Starlight" by imagining the "what might have been" possibility, "Alicia went to the stables and she rode Starlight" (A and B). But they also keep in mind the presupposed "what is" facts, "Alicia did not go to the stables and she did not ride Starlight" (not-A and not-B), as table 2.4 illustrates. The counterfactual requires a richer mental representation than the factual conditional (Johnson-Laird and Byrne 1991). A key principle about counterfactuals is as follows:

3. Principle of dual possibilities: *Some ideas require people to think about two possibilities*. For example, when people understand "if A had been then B would have been," they tend to think about two possibilities, A and B, and not-A and not-B.

One of the unique aspects of the way people understand a counterfactual conditional is that they often think about what is false, at least for counterfactuals about known past facts. A counterfactual can convey to them the presupposed facts—for example, "Alicia did not go to the stables and she

Table 2.4
Possibilities people think about when they understand a counterfactual conditional

---

Counterfactual: "If Alicia had gone to the stables then she would have ridden Starlight"

Initial possibilities
  <u>Alicia did not go to the stables and she did not ride Starlight (facts)</u>
  <u>Alicia went to the stables and she rode Starlight (imagined)</u>
  (There may be other possibilities but these remain unformed)

Possibilities for biconditional interpretation
  <u>Alicia did not go to the stables and she did not ride Starlight (facts)</u>
  <u>Alicia went to the stables and she rode Starlight (imagined)</u>

Possibilities for conditional interpretation
  <u>Alicia did not go to the stables and she did not ride Starlight (facts)</u>
  <u>Alicia went to the stables and she rode Starlight (imagined)</u>
  Alicia did not go to the stables and she rode Starlight (imagined)

Note: The possibilities people think about initially are underlined.
Source: Based on Johnson-Laird and Byrne 1991.

did not ride Starlight." When they think about the conjecture, "Alicia went to the stables and she rode Starlight," they know that it is false, because it is contradicted by the presupposed facts. But they may suppose temporarily that the conjecture is true.

A key principle is that people tend to keep in mind just true possibilities. How can they ever think about what might have been? The answer is that they keep track of the status of the different possibilities. Often in everyday thoughts, people temporarily suppose something to be true even though they know it is false. They do so to understand and create fantasy and fiction, in daydreams as well as in theater, film, and literature. They keep track of what is actually true and what is imagined. People think about two possibilities when they understand a counterfactual conditional, and they note one as the "facts" and the other as an "imagined" possibility (Johnson-Laird and Byrne 2002). The principle is as follows:

4. Principle of counterfactual possibilities: *People think about possibilities that once were true possibilities but can no longer be true.* They keep track of the status of possibilities. For example, when people understand "if A had been then B would have been" they keep in mind A and B, noted as "imagined," and not-A and not-B, noted as "facts."

Chapter 3 presents evidence to show that people tend to think about two possibilities when they understand a counterfactual conditional.

The Mutability of Dual-Possibility Concepts

The dual-possibility nature of some ideas is a significant factor in how people think about what might have been. It helps to explain why people mentally change only some aspects of their mental representation of reality. When people create a counterfactual alternative they tend to mentally alter a possibility if they have mentally represented it with a second possibility. A basic principle of mutability is that an event is mentally changed if it brings to mind not only the event but also an alternative to it. The answer to the question posed earlier about why some aspects of reality are mutable is that some aspects require several possibilities to be kept in mind. For example, suppose you go to a concert and you sit in seat 426. After a while you move to seat 739 to get a better view. During the intermission, an announcement is made that there is a prize of a trip around the world for the person seated in seat 426 (Johnson 1986). You may wish you had not changed seats. The prize seems to have been almost in your grasp. But suppose instead you had gone to the concert and you sat in seat 739 from the outset. During the intermission, an announcement is made that there is a prize of a trip around the world for the person seated in seat 426. You may wish you had won, but you are unlikely to believe that the prize was almost in your grasp. In the first scenario, there is a ready-made alternative.

Some ideas such as choices and counterfactual conditionals are dual-possibility ideas. They require people to think about two possibilities. The key principle of mutability is as follows:

5. Principle of the mutability of dual possibilities: *People readily imagine a counterfactual alternative to a possibility if it is mentally represented with a second possibility.* Dual-possibility ideas are more mutable than single-possibility ideas.

People are influenced by the availability of alternatives (Kahneman and Tversky 1982; Roese and Olson 1995). What determines how easy it is to think of an alternative to an event? One suggestion is that people may rely on an "availability" heuristic. They may base their judgments on the ease with which instances can be brought to mind (Kahneman and Tversky 1982). People may find it easier to alter elements present in their mental representation because these elements can recruit their own alternatives from memory (Kahneman and Miller 1986). Consider the story earlier about Paul who crashes at the intersection. Paul's choice of route home by the scenic road is mentioned in the story, and this element cues the alternative of Paul's regular route.

An important factor in how people create alternatives to reality is that they imagine alternatives to those aspects of reality that they have mentally represented (Byrne 1997; Kahneman and Tversky 1982; Legrenzi, Girotto, and Johnson-Laird 1993). Because some aspects of reality are represented explicitly, they can be manipulated directly—for example, Paul's route is mentally represented explicitly and it can be mentally altered. Events may be focused on when they are in the foreground (Kahneman and Tversky 1982). When the route is not mentioned at all, it may not be brought to mind spontaneously. An additional cognitive step is required to think explicitly about this aspect of reality, before it can be mentally altered. People may create a counterfactual by selecting a salient fact from their representation, and they may remove it (Legrenzi et al. 1993; Seelau et al. 1995). An infinite number of things could be changed in any situation, and the availability of alternatives is influenced by cognitive capacity (Byrne 1997).

A normal event may evoke representations that resemble it, whereas an abnormal event may evoke alternatives to it (Kahneman and Miller 1986). Nonetheless, people may be driven by their goals too—for instance, the goal of doing well in an examination. People create more counterfactuals after a goal failure—for example, they imagine that a student who fails an examination will say "if only ..." regardless of how normal the outcome is (the student usually fails) or how exceptional (the student rarely fails) (Roese et al. 2005).

The availability of alternatives is also distinct from expectations. Consider two travelers, Cathy and Linda, who share a taxi on their way to the airport. They run into a traffic jam and are delayed by 30 minutes. They each miss their flights. However, Cathy's flight departed on time, whereas Linda's was 25 minutes late (and so Linda missed it by 5 minutes). Who do you think feels worse? Most people judge that Linda will feel worse (Kahneman and Tversky 1982). Even though both women expected to miss their flights, the one who missed hers by 5 minutes is judged to feel worse. The availability of the alternative that she could have caught her flight does not depend on her expectation before arriving at the airport.

The Rationality of the Counterfactual Imagination

The claim that the counterfactual imagination is rational rests on the idea that the principles that guide the possibilities that people think about and that underlie rational thought also underlie imaginative thought. There are three steps to the conclusion that the counterfactual imagination is rational. The first step is that human reasoning is rational. People are capable of rational thought, despite the many mistakes and persistently inaccurate beliefs they exhibit. Just as ungrammatical utterances do not necessarily mean a person is incapable of grammatical utterance at all, so too do errors of reasoning not necessarily mean a person is incapable of rational thought. The second step is that the principles that guide the possibilities that people think about and that underpin reasoning are rational principles. They are rational in that they provide the competence to make rational conclusions, even though they may be constrained in their performance by factors such as working memory. The third step is that these principles underlie the counterfactual imagination. The chapters that follow provide evidence that the principles guiding the possibilities people think about when they engage in rational thought apply to imaginative thought. The perceived fault lines of reality reflect the operation of these principles. Each chapter examines different sorts of dual-possibility ideas and their mutability.

Of course, there are many different kinds of thinking, from working out the height of a tree to reflecting on what it means to be human. Most have been studied in isolation from one another in a fragmentary way (Eysenck and Keane 2000). But some sorts of thinking may be closely related. Rational thought and imaginative thought may be based on the same kinds of cognitive processes, processes that underpin thinking about possibilities.

The claim that the counterfactual imagination is rational raises several issues about what it means to say that a cognitive process is rational. Can the counterfactual imagination be considered rational by virtue of being underpinned by rational principles? In the scenario in which Linda and Cathy both miss their flights, is it rational to be able to imagine an alternative in which Linda makes up the 5 minutes and gets to her flight, more readily than an alternative in which Cathy makes up the 30 minutes to get to her flight? Perhaps. But now consider two individuals who each buy lottery tickets. Noel is assigned ticket number 5276 and Tony's is 3891. The winning ticket is 5277. Who do you think is more disappointed? Is it rational to be able to imagine an alternative in which Noel's ticket had one different number, more readily than an alternative in which Tony's ticket had four different numbers? Perhaps not. The lottery number assignment is random, after all (Miller, Turnbull, and McFarland 1990). The closeness of the imagined alternative in which Noel was assigned the winning ticket is illusory. The closeness of the imagined alternative in which Linda caught her flight or Noel was assigned the lottery ticket may both reflect a process by which people imagine alternatives by making minimal changes to their representation of reality. But in some instances the process leads to irrational judgments.

Does it matter whether the counterfactual imagination is rational or irrational? After all, much creative thought may be neither. When musicians compose, dancers improvise, or painters paint, the exercise may be neither rational nor irrational. But the counterfactual imagination may play a role in helping people solve problems and prepare for the future (Roese 1994). When someone imagines an "if only ..." alternative to an event in the past, they can use the counterfactual they create to work out how to avoid the same event in the future, whether the thought is about playing another game of blackjack or about flying an airplane safely (Markman et al. 1993; Morris and Moore 2000). What are the consequences of an irrational counterfactual imagination? One illustration of when the counterfactual imagination goes awry is as follows. Suppose a child is allowed to take a cookie from a jar but she must not peek. The cookie jar has 19 plain cookies and 1 chocolate one. The child gets the chocolate cookie. How suspicious would you be that the child had peeked? Now suppose the cookie jar contained 190 plain cookies and 10 chocolate ones. How suspicious would you be if the child got a chocolate cookie in these circumstances? People tend to be more suspicious in the first situation than in the second (Miller, Turnbull, and McFarland 1990). Yet the likelihood of getting a chocolate cookie by chance is exactly the same in each situation. What differs is that there are more ways to imagine the child getting a chocolate cookie in the second situation. If the counterfactual imagination is not rational, its usefulness and reliability in everyday life—and especially for learning from mistakes and preparing for the future—may be at best limited and at worse questionable. The counterfactual imagination may be little more than a particularly vivid way of musing about the past.

How compromised is the counterfactual imagination by evidence that people's creation of "if only ..." alternatives sometimes leads them to make irrational judgments? Just as the existence of grammatical mistakes does not mean that a person is incapable of grammatical utterances, and the existence of reasoning mistakes does not mean that a person is incapable of rational thought, the existence of irrational judgments based on the imagination of counterfactual alternatives does not necessarily mean that a person is incapable of rational imaginative thought. The final chapter returns to the question of what it means for the counterfactual imagination to be rational or irrational.

Summary

Just as rational thought has been found to depend on the imagination of alternatives, so too may imaginative thought depend on the operation of rational principles. It may depend on the operation of a small set of principles that guide the nature of the possibilities people consider. Two key principles from the study of rational thought are that people think about true possibilities, and they think about few possibilities (see table 2.5). Counterfactual conditionals are an important bridge from rational thought to imaginative thought. They illustrate two further principles: some ideas require people to think about dual possibilities, and to keep track of the status of the possibilities as real or imagined. The fifth principle is that people can readily imagine a counterfactual alternative to a possibility if it is mentally represented with a second possibility from the outset.

Table 2.5
Summary of principles thus far

---

1. True possibilities: *People keep in mind true possibilities.*

2. Few possibilities: *People keep in mind few possibilities.*

3. Dual possibilities: *Some ideas require people to think about two possibilities.*

4. Counterfactual possibilities: *People think about possibilities that once may have been true possibilities but can be true no longer.*

5. Mutability of dual possibilities: *People readily imagine a counterfactual alternative to a possibility if it is mentally represented with a second possibility.*

Each of the subsequent chapters falls into three parts: first the chapter outlines a core phenomenon of the human imagination that has eluded explanation, such as the action effect—that is, the tendency for people to imagine alternatives to their actions rather than to their failures to act. Next it identifies some clues from the study of rational thought that can help to explain the phenomenon. Then it shows how the principles guiding the possibilities that underlie rational thought can explain imaginative thought. The aim throughout the rest of the chapters in the book is to establish the principles that underlie how the mind creates counterfactual thoughts.

3 Imagining How Actions Might Have Been Different

The only thing necessary for the triumph of evil is for good men to do nothing.
—Edmund Burke (attributed)

Suppose you hear about a new disease, such as SARS. It can be fatal and you suspect you could be exposed to it. You hear about a vaccine being developed and you consider whether or not to take advantage of it. Suppose you have read reports in the newspaper about people who contracted SARS and died. They had not been vaccinated. But the vaccine can also have serious consequences. Suppose you have read news reports about people who were vaccinated and died. What will you decide to do? The decision is difficult. Many people choose to do nothing, even when the chances of death from a vaccine are less than death from a disease (Ritov and Baron 1990). Take a moment to imagine the families of the victims. Which families do you think are more likely to say "if only ...", the families of individuals who died from the disease, or individuals who died from the vaccine? Most people think the families who will feel worse are the families of the individuals who died from the vaccine. They will wish their loved one had not been vaccinated. The example illustrates that thoughts about what might have been often fall toward one side of the perceived fault line between action and inaction. In many situations, when people imagine "if only ..." alternatives, they focus on an action, such as taking a vaccine, far more than on a failure to act.

"If Only ..." Alternatives to Actions

Most people prefer to do nothing, especially if a harmful outcome will result from doing something. They are more concerned with harm caused by actions, such as death from a vaccine, than with harm caused by omissions, such as death from a disease that could have been vaccinated against. Their concern about actions is strong when they implicate values such as human life or civil rights (Ritov and Baron 1999). Omissions and commissions differ in lots of ways—for example, there are many ways of doing nothing. Doing something usually requires more effort and stronger intentions. Most people prefer to do nothing, even when doing nothing itself leads to change (Ritov and Baron 1992). But many people judge telling a lie to be worse than withholding information, even when the intention to deceive is the same.

Consider the following dramatic scenario. You have a choice of killing five people or letting ten people die. The people will all be taken at random from the same population. What is the right thing to do? You probably would not wish to kill five people, but if you do nothing, twice as many people will die. Which outcome will prey on your conscience more? The right thing to do (in the sense of harm to the least people) is to kill five people. But most people choose to do nothing (Ritov and Baron 1990). The scenario illustrates a key aspect of the imagination: people tend to regret actions that lead to a bad outcome more than inactions that lead to a bad outcome (Kahneman and Tversky 1982). This tendency has been demonstrated in a variety of situations, some of which are listed in table 3.1. Suppose you were given an opportunity to apologize to someone with whom you have had a falling out. Take a moment to imagine what you might apologize for. Participants on a Dutch TV show were given such an opportunity, to apologize on national television to individuals they had fallen out with. Most of them apologized for things they did rather than for things they failed to do (Zeelenberg, van der Pligt, and Manstead 1998). Moreover, when people were asked whether they tended to apologize for something they did but wished they had not done, or something they did not do but wished they had, most chose their actions. Many people focus on the actions of victims and perpetrators when they defend their roles in mock trials (Catellani and Milesi 2001).

The action effect has also been demonstrated in laboratory studies. Consider the following scenario (adapted from Gilovich and Medvec 1994, 360):

Sam and Jim do not know each other, but both are enrolled at the same elite university. Both are only moderately satisfied where they are and both are considering

Table 3.1

Situations in which most people imagine counterfactual alternatives to actions

Bad outcome for actor and nonactor, e.g., investments	Kahneman and Tversky 1982
Everyday risky decisions, e.g., vaccination	Ritov and Baron 1990
Outcomes are known, gains	Ritov and Baron 1995
Short-term perspective, e.g., college choice	Gilovich and Medvec 1994, 1995a
Apologize for actions	Zeelenberg et al. 1998
Mock jurors defend actions	Catellani and Milesi 2001
Good outcome for actor and nonactor, e.g., holidays	Landman 1987
Regardless of order of action/nonaction	Gleicher et al. 1990
Long-term matched outcomes, e.g., investments	Byrne and McEleney 2000
Matched outcomes without explicit counterfactuals	Avni-Babad 2003
Reasons for action with matched outcomes	Byrne and McEleney 2000
Intensity of retrospective autobiographical regrets	Feldman, Miyamoto, and Loftus 1999
Inaction leads to change	Ritov and Baron 1999
Inaction leads to more inaction (people avoid action)	Tykocinski and Pittman 1998
Rate actor first before nonactor	Feeney and Handley 2001a
Promotion failures (e.g., missed opportunities) and prevention failures (e.g., accidents, assaults)	Roese, Hur, and Pennington 1999

Note: See table 3.4 for situations in which many people imagine counterfactual alternatives to failures to act.

transferring to another prestigious college. Each agonizes over the decision, going back and forth between thinking he is going to stay and thinking he will leave. They ultimately make different decisions: Sam opts to stay where he is, and Jim decides to transfer. Suppose their decisions turn out badly for both of them: Sam still doesn't like it where he is and wishes he had transferred, and Jim doesn't like his new environment and wishes he had stayed.

Who do you think will feel more regret, Sam or Jim? Most participants in experiments judged that the actor, Jim, feels more regret than the non-actor, Sam (Kahneman and Tversky 1982; Gilovich and Medvec 1994). Of course the objective situation for each individual is the same—both are unhappy in their universities. But people judge their subjective situation to be different.

Actions and inactions can result in a bad outcome. A bad outcome may be the presence of something bad, such as a car crash, or the absence of something good, such as a good examination result (Roese, Hur, and

Figure 3.1
Calvin and Hobbes © 1991 Watterson. Reprinted with permission of Universal Press
Syndicate. All rights reserved.

Pennington 1999). But the tendency to imagine counterfactual alternatives
to actions is not confined to bad outcomes. When the outcome is good,
most people judge that individuals feel better about their actions than their
inactions (Landman 1987). Consider two families, the Smiths and the
Bradys. Both families are planning their holidays this year, and both are
concerned that their holidays not be marred by too much rain. For the
past few years the Smiths have spent their holidays in France for the last
fortnight of August. This year they considered going to Italy but decided
to return to France after all. The Brady family usually spend their holidays
in Italy at the end of August. This year they considered going to France and
decided to do so. Suppose the weather turned out to be sunny in France but
stormy for the entire two weeks in Italy. Who do you think feels most
relieved about their holiday choice? Many participants judge that the
Bradys will feel better about their action than the Smiths will feel about
their inaction (Landman 1987).

The action effect may depend on an assumption of causality between the
action and the outcome (N'gbala and Branscombe 1997). For example,
imagine that Noel went to a football game at a stadium and his car was
wrecked in the parking garage. Tony stayed at home and his car was
wrecked outside his house. Neither Noel's action nor Tony's inaction can
be seen as causally linked to the damage to their cars, and in this case,
both Noel and Tony are judged to feel equal regret (N'gbala and Branscombe 1997). Of course, failures to act can be real causes of outcomes
(Hart and Honore 1959). For example, the Herald of Free Enterprise passenger car ferry capsized off the Belgian port of Zeebrugge en route to the En-

glish port of Dover in 1987, ending on its side half submerged in shallow water. The death toll was almost two hundred people—the worst for a British ship in peacetime since the sinking of the Titantic in 1912. The cause of the tragedy was the failure of staff to close the bow doors (through which cars drove onto the ferry). However, people may tend not to view omission as a real cause (Ritov and Baron 1990).

Most people focus on actions regardless of whether the action is described before or after the inaction (Gleicher et al. 1990). But many people rate the regret a nonactor experiences just as highly as they rate the regret an actor experiences, when the actor and the nonactor are described in separate stories (N'gbala and Branscombe 1997). The comparison of an actor to a nonactor contributes to the action effect. Nonetheless, people judge that an actor will feel bad even when no direct comparison to a nonactor is made (Ritov and Baron 1995; Feeney and Handley 2001a).

Many experimental results indicate that actions are mentally mutable: people readily change them in their mental representation of reality when they imagine alternatives to the way a situation turned out. It is easier to imagine having done nothing in place of something that was done; it seems harder to imagine having done something in place of nothing. Deleting an action from a mental representation may require less mental effort than attempting to add one selected from myriad possibilities. Actions can seem to be a figure against the ground of inaction (Kahneman and Tversky 1982). Many actions call to mind the alternatives of not acting, or acting differently, whereas inactions do not readily call to mind actions. Actions seem to be mentally "rewound" in reminiscences and replayed differently (Hofstadter 1985). Of course, there are important exceptions to this pattern. But the basic phenomenon to be considered first is why people often imagine a counterfactual alternative to an action in which they had not acted or they had acted differently.

This chapter offers an explanation for why many people imagine alternatives to actions, rather than inactions. When people understand an action they must keep in mind not only the action but also its negation or complement, inaction. They think about two possibilities when they understand an action, but they think about just a single possibility when they understand an inaction. People can imagine a counterfactual alternative more readily when they have thought about two possibilities from the outset, rather than when they have thought about just a single possibility.

Table 3.2

Summary of principles thus far

1. True possibilities: *People keep in mind true possibilities.*

2. Few possibilities: *People keep in mind few possibilities.*

3. Dual possibilities: *Some ideas require people to think about two possibilities.*

4. Counterfactual possibilities: *People think about possibilities that once may have been true possibilities but can be true no longer.*

5. Mutability of dual possibilities: *People readily imagine a counterfactual alternative to a possibility if it is mentally represented with a second possibility.*

I. Actions: *People think about two possibilities when they understand an action.*

II. Single possibilities: *People can switch from thinking about one possibility to thinking about two possibilities e.g., for inactions.*

Clues from Reasoning: Counterfactual Conditionals

People imagine counterfactual alternatives by thinking about possibilities. As we saw in the previous chapter, the possibilities they think about are guided by a small set of principles. For example, people think about true possibilities, and they think initially about few possibilities (see table 3.2). Some ideas require people to think about two possibilities from the outset, and they keep track of the status of the possibilities, as facts or imagined possibilities. The next section illustrates the notion of dual-possibility ideas with reference to counterfactual conditionals. People think about two possibilities when they understand counterfactual conditionals. The two possibilities they envisage affect the way they reason about counterfactual conditionals. The section after next sketches the idea that people think about two possibilities when they understand actions. The two possibilities they envisage affect the way they imagine alternatives to actions. People can more readily imagine a counterfactual alternative to a possibility if it is mentally represented from the outset with a second possibility. The final section considers inactions. People usually understand inactions by thinking about just a single possibility. But sometimes people can switch from thinking about a single possibility to thinking about two possibilities for inactions.

Counterfactual Conditionals and Dual Possibilities

Experimental evidence indicates that many people keep in mind two possibilities when they understand a counterfactual conditional. For example, participants were given counterfactual conditionals such as "if Mark had left at 9 a.m. then he would have caught the airplane" and then given a surprise recognition test (Fillenbaum 1974). They mistakenly judged that they had been given the negated consequent (for example, "Mark did not catch the airplane") on 44 percent of occasions, and they mistakenly judged that they had been given the negated antecedent ("Mark did not leave at 9 a.m.") on 25 percent of occasions. The result is consistent with the suggestion that people understand the counterfactual by keeping in mind two possibilities, the conjecture, "Mark left at 9 a.m. and he caught the airplane" (A and B), and the presupposed facts, "Mark did not leave at 9 a.m. and he did not catch the airplane" (not-A and not-B) (see table 2.4). Studies of the comprehension and plausibility of counterfactuals are also consistent with this result (Carpenter 1973; Johnson-Laird 1986; Tetlock and Lebow 2001).

Further evidence that most people think about two possibilities comes from the inferences they make. Most reasoners make different inferences from the counterfactual conditional than from a factual one, such as "if Mark left at 9 a.m. then he caught the airplane." Suppose you are told "if Mark had left at 9 a.m. then he would have caught the airplane," and then you discover that Mark did not catch the airplane. What would you conclude? The theory predicts that people should be able to readily infer that Mark did not leave at 9 a.m. The modus tollens (not-B therefore not-A) inference is difficult to make from a factual conditional but it should be easier from the counterfactual because of the enriched representation.

Alessandra Tasso and I have corroborated this prediction (Byrne and Tasso 1999). In one experiment we allocated eighty participants to several groups. Half the participants were given factual conditionals in the indicative mood, such as "If Linda is in Galway then Cathy is in Dublin," and the other half were given conditionals in the subjunctive mood, such as "if Linda were in Galway then Cathy would be in Dublin." The conditionals were in the present tense. We gave the participants the minor premises corresponding to the two affirmative inferences, "Linda is in Galway" (modus ponens) and "Cathy is in Dublin" (affirmation of the consequent), as well as the two negative inferences, "Cathy is not in Dublin" (modus tollens) and "Linda is not in Galway" (denial of the antecedent). We asked them to say what, if anything, followed from the premises.

The participants made reliably more modus tollens (not-B therefore not-A) inferences (twice as many) from the subjunctive compared to the

indicative conditional. They also made reliably more denial of the antecedent (not-A therefore not-B) inferences (again twice as many) from the subjunctive compared to the indicative conditional:

Modus tollens (not-B therefore not-A):
   Subjunctive, 80 percent; indicative, 40 percent
Denial of the antecedent (not-A therefore not-B):
   Subjunctive, 80 percent; indicative, 40 percent

They made somewhat fewer modus ponens (A therefore B) inferences and
somewhat more affirmation of the consequent (B therefore A) inferences
from the subjunctive compared to the indicative, but neither difference
was reliable:

Modus ponens (A therefore B):
   Subjunctive, 90 percent; indicative, 100 percent
Affirmation of the consequent (B therefore A):
   Subjunctive, 50 percent; Indicative, 30 percent

The results corroborate the prediction that people think about two possibilities when they understand the subjunctive conditional and a single possibility when they understand the indicative conditional.

The subjunctive conditionals in the experiment were not strictly speak-
ing counterfactual, in the sense that they did not concern matters that
were no longer possible: the present tense ensures that the possibilities
can turn out to be true, whereas past possibilities are no longer possible. In
subsequent experiments we obtained the same results for past- and present-
tense conditionals such as "if Bert was in Madrid then Peg was in Venice"
and "if Bert had been in Madrid then Peg would have been in Venice." The
experiments replicated the reliable difference between factual and counterfactual conditionals for the negative inferences and the absence of any reliable difference between them for the affirmative inferences (Byrne and
Tasso 1999). Most people make the same frequency of inferences from conditionals in the past and present tense for counterfactuals (Byrne and Tasso
1999), just as they do for factual conditionals (Schaeken, Schroyens, and
Dieussaert 2001).

The experiments show that many people make more of the negative
inferences from counterfactuals than from factual conditionals (see also
Byrne and Tasso 1994). The negative inferences require access to the
negative possibility (not-A and not-B). This possibility corresponds to the

presupposed facts for the counterfactual. The result corroborates the suggestion that people consider the negative possibility when they understand counterfactuals. An alternative view is that participants make more of the negative inferences just because this possibility corresponds to the facts (Mandel 2003b). The data indicate not. The experiments show that people do not make reliably fewer affirmative inferences from counterfactuals than from factual conditionals. The affirmative inferences require access to the affirmative possibility (A and B) and this possibility corresponds to the imagined possibility for a counterfactual. The result corroborates the suggestion that most people think about the affirmative possibility as well as the negative one when they understand counterfactuals. Overall the experiments verify that many people think about the imagined possibility and the presupposed facts.

Although people think about two possibilities when they understand a counterfactual conditional, it does not make them any more or less logically rigorous in their reasoning from the counterfactual than from a factual conditional. Reasoners made more of the negative inferences from counterfactuals than from factual conditionals. But they did so regardless of whether the inference was one for which there were counterexamples. As chapter 2 outlined, the modus tollens (not-B therefore not-A) inference has no counterexamples on either a conditional or a biconditional interpretation. But there are counterexamples to the denial of the antecedent (not-A therefore not-B) inference on a conditional interpretation. Yet most participants made more of both sorts of negative inferences from counterfactuals.

Do people understand counterfactuals by keeping in mind just the two possibilities consistent with a biconditional interpretation, or can they can think about more possibilities? Chapter 6 shows that they can think about more possibilities. Most participants appear to consider both possibilities when they understand a counterfactual, but some may consider just a single possibility—for example, the negative one. Chapter 8 discusses such differences between individuals.

These data are difficult to explain on the view that people reason by accessing a mental logic of formal rules of inference. One view is that "if A then B" means that B is inferable from A (together with facts and laws indicated by the context)—that is, it requires adding A to your beliefs and arguing about B (Ramsey 1931). One formal inference-rule theory proposes that there is a rule for the modus ponens (A therefore B) inference: given if A then B and A, one can infer B. It also proposes that there is a "conditional-proof" rule: "To derive or evaluate if p then ... first suppose p; for any proposition q that follows from the supposition of p taken together with other information assumed, one may assert if p then q" (Braine and O'Brien 1991, 183). The conditional-proof rule is constrained in its application to ensure that suppositions are consistent with prior assumptions. In the case of a counterfactual supposition the assumptions are a record of an actual state of affairs (Braine and O'Brien 1998). But on this view, the modus ponens (A therefore B) inference should not be made from a counterfactual conditional. Instead it should be viewed as a contradiction. Given a counterfactual of the form "if p had been then q would have been," a formal derivation of a conclusion should include the conditional "if p then q" and also the presupposed facts "not-p and not-q." The minor premise "p" contradicts the fact "not-p," and so nothing can be concluded. Yet participants made the modus ponens (A therefore B) inference readily from the counterfactual. The result is difficult to explain for a formal inference-rule theory.

As these examples indicate, the evidence shows that people understand counterfactual conditionals by keeping in mind two possibilities: the facts and an imagined alternative. People think about two possibilities for some ideas. The evidence that people understand counterfactual conditionals by envisaging two possibilities provides an important clue that helps solve the puzzle of why people imagine counterfactual alternatives to actions more than inactions.

The Rational Imagination: Why People Imagine Alternatives to Actions

People think about two possibilities when they understand an action. When you understand the decision to act you think about the preaction possibility and the postaction possibility. When you take an action as a result of a reflex—for example, you move your hand away from a flame—you are unlikely to have thought about two possibilities, moving your hand and not moving your hand. But when you take an action as a result of a decision—for instance, you decide to move your shares from one company to another—you probably have thought about the two possibilities.

Actions and Dual Possibilities

To illustrate the two possibilities that people think about for actions, consider again the investment story described in chapter 1 (based on Kahneman and Tversky 1982):

Mary owns shares in company A. During the past year she considered switching to stock in company B, but she decided against it. She now finds out that she would have been better off by $1,000 if she had switched to the stock of company B. Laura owned shares in company B. During the past year she switched to stock in company A. She now finds out that she would have been better off by $1,000 if she had kept her stock in company B.

When people think about this situation, they think about some of the possibilities. For example, when they think about Laura's action they think about the preaction possibility, Laura owned shares in company B, and the postaction possibility, Laura owns shares in company A:

Laura owned shares in company B (preaction).
Laura owns shares in company A (postaction).

When they think about Mary's inaction they think about the shares she owns in company A:

Mary owns shares in company A (predecision and postdecision).

Inactions are mentally represented more economically than actions (Byrne 1997; Byrne and McEleney 2000). Of course, Mary might have owned shares in company B had she decided to switch, but people do not think about this possibility from the outset. There is no change in state for inactions, and so the preaction and postaction possibilities remain the same. People do not keep track of the decision process itself but only its outcomes, and so they often forget the reasons for inactions (Savitsky, Medvec, and Gilovich 1997). There are more things to keep in mind when someone does something than when they do nothing, and people need to keep more things in mind about the actor, Laura, than about the nonactor, Mary. As a result actions are thought about more fully than inactions (as table 3.3, part 1, shows). This difference in the possibilities that people keep in mind for actions and inactions may underlie the perception that actions are a departure from the status quo (Kahneman and Miller 1986).

Most people judge that Laura, the individual who acted, feels greater regret (Kahneman and Tversky 1982). Because people keep in mind more information for actions than for inactions, they can mentally change

Table 3.3
Possibilities people think about when they understand actions and inactions

---

1. Initial possibilities

Decision to act: *Laura owned shares in B ... she switched to stock in A*

    Laura owned shares in company B (preaction)

    Laura owns shares in company A (postaction)

Decision not to act: *Mary owns shares in A ... she considered switching to stock in B but decided against it*

    Mary owns shares in company A (predecision and postdecision)

2. Consequences

Decision to act: *Laura owned shares in B ... she switched to stock in A*

    Laura owns shares in A and she loses money (postaction)

    Laura owns shares in B and she makes money (preaction)

Decision not to act: *Mary owns shares in A ... she considered switching to stock in B*

    Mary owns shares in A and she loses money (predecision and postdecision)

    Mary owns shares in B and she makes money (imagined)

---

actions more easily than inactions. The postaction possibility (Laura owns shares in company A) can be replaced with the past, now counterfactual, preaction possibility (Laura owns shares in company B). This "subjunctive mental replay" (Hofstadter 1985) results in the counterfactual, "if only Laura had kept her shares in company B ...". Deleting information from a mental representation may be easier than adding new information (Dunning and Parpal 1989; Kahneman and Tversky 1982; Legrenzi, Johnson-Laird, and Girotto 1993).

People can readily imagine a counterfactual alternative to an intentional action because they have envisaged two possibilities when they understand the action, as the following corollary describes:

Corollary 1 for thoughts about actions: *People keep in mind two possibilities when they understand an action*. For an action, people think about the preaction possibility as well as the postaction possibility. They can imagine a counterfactual alternative by mentally changing the current possibility to be the same as the past possibility.

The rest of the chapter considers an important *exception* to this principle.

Failures to Act

In certain circumstances people imagine a counterfactual alternative to an inaction. They usually imagine a counterfactual alternative to an action, and say, for example, "if only I had not switched my shares ...". But this action effect can be reversed to an inaction effect, with people instead imagining a counterfactual alternative to a failure to act and saying, for example, "if only I had switched my shares ...". The reversal can seem puzzling, but the possibilities people think about shed light on it. The reversal depends on whether an imagined possibility is made prominent for the inaction. People usually think about a single possibility when they understand an inaction. But people can switch from thinking about one possibility to thinking about two possibilities for an inaction. The rest of this section considers some ways this transformation occurs, for instance, when people consider the consequences of an inaction over time. It considers evidence that people say "if only ..." about an inaction only when the imagined counterfactual alternative has a better outcome (if I had acted the outcome would have been better than it actually was) than the imagined alternative for the action (if I had not acted, the outcome would have been the same or worse than it actually was).

People can switch to thinking about two possibilities for the inaction instead of one possibility. An instance of the switch occurs when they adopt a long-term perspective. In the story about Sam and Jim, both are in college A and both are unhappy. Jim decides to transfer to college B, and Sam stays where he is, and their decisions turn out badly: they are both unhappy with their college choice. From the perspective of, say, 10 years later, who do you think would regret his decision more? Most participants judged that the nonactor, Sam, would regret his decision more than the actor, in the long run (Gilovich and Medvec 1995a). From a short-term perspective, most participants judged that the actor, Jim, would regret his decision more than the nonactor, on learning that it was a mistake. This temporal reversal is intriguing, and what is more, it occurs in several everyday situations.

Failures to Act in Everyday Life   When most people look back over their lives, it is their inactions that they tend to regret, the things they failed to do, such as failing to spend time with family and friends, failing to take advantage of educational opportunities, or failing to pursue hobbies. When people were asked to recall events they regretted, their regrets over the past week were evenly split between actions and failures to act, but their regrets over their lives were mainly for what they failed to do (Gilovich and Medvec 1994). One of the few actions that people regret from a

Table 3.4

Situations in which most people imagine counterfactual alternatives to inactions

Regrets from past life; long-run college choice	Gilovich and Medvec 1994, 1995a
Losses (e.g., health treatments)	Ritov and Baron 1995
Frequency of autobiographical regrets	Feldman, Miyamoto, and Loftus 1999
High self-esteem	Feeney, Gardiner, and McEvoy 2001
Reason to act, e.g., soccer-team failures	Zeelenberg et al. 2002
Obligation to act, e.g., organ donation	Feeney and Handley 2001b
Weak reason for inaction, strong for action	Zhang, Bonnefon, and Deng 2004

long-term perspective is what Gilovich and Medvec call "unwise romantic adventures." Otherwise, in general, people tend to regret inactions in the long term (see table 3.4).

Of course, every action implies a corresponding inaction: when someone regrets not going to college, they may mean they regret the inaction, failing to go, or the implied corresponding action, starting work instead. Most regrets of action fall into the category of rushing in too soon, and most regrets of inaction fall into the corresponding category of failures to seize the moment (Gilovich and Medvec 1994). In this respect, regrets can seem to have the flavor of "damned if you do and damned if you don't." Missed educational opportunities, and not spending enough time with friends and relatives, were two of the inactions people regretted highly, and no one regretted time spent developing a skill or hobby even when it was no longer pursued (Gilovich and Medvec 1994).

The focus on inactions may reflect a difference in the repair work carried out to remedy regrets for actions and inactions. People may try to put right their actions by apologizing or at least by rationalizing and justifying them, and so regret for actions decreases. Regret for inactions may increase over time because the fears and doubts that led to inaction fade (Savitsky, Medvec, and Gilovich 1997). Some inactions are missed chances, but for others a second chance is possible (Gilovich and Medvec 1995b).

Autobiographical regrets in retrospective recall are more often about inactions than actions, but the regrets for actions are judged to be more intense (Feldman, Miyamoto, and Loftus 1999). People may regret bad outcomes that result from changes (see also Connolly, Ordonez, and Coughlan 1997; Ordóñez and Connolly 2000; but see Ritov and Baron 1999). The emotion denoted by the term *regret* may be somewhat different for long-term and short-term regrets. Long-term regrets may be wistful (Kahneman 1995). Regret for actions and inactions is associated equally with hot emotions such as anger, disgust, embarrassment, and guilt, but regret for inactions is associated more with wistful emotions such as contemplation, nostalgia, and sentimentality, as well as with despair emotions, such as emptiness, helplessness, and unfulfilledness (Gilovich, Medvec, and Kahneman 1998).

The things people do not do far outnumber the things they do, and doing nothing leads to more instances of doing nothing (Tykocinski and Pittman 1998). The consequence of inaction is "inaction inertia," the tendency to forgo further action. Suppose there is a fitness club 30 minutes from where you live. You could have joined one 5 minutes from where you live but you missed the chance because you did not act quickly enough. Would you join the one 30 minutes away? Participants were less likely to judge that they would join it when they knew the missed club was 5 minutes away than when they knew the missed club was 25 minutes away (Tykocinski and Pittman 1998). Some people may avoid action to avoid thinking about what might have been.

Temporal perspective is not the only factor that leads people to imagine alternatives to inactions rather than actions. Knowledge of the outcome and of an alternative outcome can prompt people to imagine an alternative to an inaction (Ritov and Baron 1995). People also imagine an alternative to a failure to act when there were good reasons to act. Suppose two soccer coaches have each lost several matches and both must decide whether to change the composition of the team for the next match. The coach of team A decides to change some of the players and the coach of team B decides to leave the players the same. They both lose their next match. Who do you think feels worse? Most participants judge that the nonactor, coach B, will feel worse (Zeelenberg et al. 2002).

Why do people imagine a counterfactual alternative to an inaction when they adopt a long-term perspective ("if only Sam had transferred . . ."), or when they know about a good reason to act ("if only coach B had changed some players . . .")? These factors ensure that people think about two possibilities for the inaction, as the next section shows.

Dual Possibilities for Inactions

When people think about inactions they usually think about a single possibility, but in some circumstances they switch to thinking about two possibilities instead. Given a longer temporal perspective, people think about the *consequences* of actions and inactions. In certain cases, thinking about the consequences makes a difference to the counterfactual alternatives people imagine. In the college scenario Jim acts, moving from one college to another, and Sam does not act, staying in his first college, and both are unhappy. For the action, people have kept in mind two possibilities:

Jim was in college A (preaction).
Jim is in college B (postaction).

For the inaction, they have kept in mind just a single possibility:

Sam is in college A (predecision and postdecision).

Because people think about two possibilities for the action, they tend to say "if only Jim had not transferred . . .".

But from a long-term perspective, people think not only about the event in question, but also about its consequences, both real and imagined. What grows over time may not be the regret associated with the consequence but the realization that there is a large consequence to be regretted (Kahneman 1995). Over time, an event's consequences rather than the event itself may have an impact (Shafir and Tversky 1992). For the action, the consequences are known:

Jim was in college A and he was unhappy (preaction).
Jim is in college B and he is unhappy (postaction).

The consequences for the action are known for both the factual possibility (Jim is unhappy in college B), and the past, now counterfactual, possibility (Jim was unhappy in college A). But for the inaction, the consequences are known only for the factual possibility (Sam is unhappy in college A). The consequences are not known for the counterfactual possibility (if Sam had transferred to college B). And therein lies the crux. Suppose Sam had transferred to college B. What would the outcome have been? The answer is: we do not know. Sam might have been happy or he might have been unhappy had he moved:

Sam is in college A and he is unhappy (predecision and postdecision).
Sam is in college B and he is happy (imagined).
Sam is in college B and he is unhappy (imagined).

Table 3.5
Actions and inactions and their consequences

Action

Jim decides to transfer ... he doesn't like his new environment and wishes he had stayed

  Jim was in college A and he was unhappy (preaction)

  Jim is in college B and he is unhappy (postaction)

Inaction

Sam opts to stay where he is ... he still doesn't like it where he is and wishes he had transferred

  Sam is in college A and he is unhappy (predecision and postdecision)

  Sam is in college B and he is happy (imagined)

  Sam is in college B and he is unhappy (imagined)

In one of the counterfactual possibilities Sam is imagined to be happy. This imagined outcome is better than the factual outcome, Sam is currently unhappy (as table 3.5 shows).

When people think about the consequences, an asymmetry between the action and inaction becomes apparent. An imagined alternative to the inaction has a good outcome (if only Sam had transferred he might have been happy). But the imagined alternative to the action has a bad outcome (if Jim had stayed he would still have been unhappy just as he was originally). People regret the failure to act from a long-term perspective because (1) the long-term perspective makes them think about the consequences of the action and the inaction and so they think about two possibilities for the inaction as well as for the action, and (2) for the college story, when they think about the second possibility for the inaction the outcome is better than the actual one (if Sam had transferred he might have been happy), whereas when they think about the second possibility for the action the outcome is the same as the actual one (if Jim had stayed he would have been unhappy).

A key corollary is as follows:

Corollary 2 for thoughts about a single possibility: *In some circumstances people can switch from thinking about one possibility to thinking about two possibilities*. For example, they think about inactions by keeping in mind a single possibility; but they can think about two possibilities—for instance, when they think about the consequences of the inaction over time.

Of course they do not know for certain whether the imagined outcome would have been better than the actual one for the nonactor (if Sam had transferred he might have been happy or he might have been unhappy). But there is at least a possibility of a good outcome, whereas when they imagine an alternative to the action they know the outcome would have been the same as the actual one (if Jim had not transferred he would still have been unhappy). There is an asymmetry in the potential goodness of the imagined outcomes for the action and the inaction.

In other situations there is no such asymmetry. Consider the investment scenario again. When people imagine an alternative to the inaction they know that the outcome would have been better (if only Mary had switched to shares in company B she would have made $1,000). Likewise, when they imagine an alternative to the action they know that the outcome would have been better (if only Laura had kept her shares in company B she would have made $1,000). The imagined outcomes are matched for the investment story (Mary and Laura both would have been better off) but not for the college story (Sam might have been better off, Jim would not). The asymmetry for Sam and Jim in the college story is not apparent from a short-term perspective: most people concentrate on what is known about the action and inaction rather than on their imagined consequences. But from a long-term perspective, people consider the consequences and the discrepancy between the action and inaction becomes apparent.

Of course, when people imagine a counterfactual alternative (if only I had acted ...), it is not always possible to know what the outcome might have been. In the college story people cannot know the consequences for Jim or Sam with certainty, whereas in the investment story, they can know the consequences for Mary and Laura with certainty. Some situations in everyday life are like the college story in that you cannot know the consequences. Can you imagine what would have happened if you had pursued a different career after you left school, or if you had stayed with a partner you knew when you were younger? Would you be happier than you are now, or not? The imagined outcome of many sorts of actions and inactions seems unknowable (one individual's life has no control comparison). Things may have turned out better, or they may have turned out worse. But other situations in everyday life are like the investment story in that the imagined outcome of the actions and inactions seems knowable. Can you imagine what would have happened if you had bought a property

30 years ago near where you live now? Would you be richer than you are now, or not? You can probably work out how much money it would be worth to you now and establish with reasonable certainty whether you would have been better off or worse off. Whether people regret their actions or inactions is affected by the certainty of the outcomes (Tanner and Medin 2004). People regret a failure to act when a long-term perspective makes them think about the consequences of the action and inaction and so they think about two possibilities for each, and the imagined outcome is better than the actual one for the inaction but not the action.

Temporal perspective is not the only factor that can lead people to imagine counterfactual alternatives to inactions rather than actions. In the story about the soccer coaches who had each lost several prior matches, the coach of team A decides to change some of the players in his team, and the coach of team B decides to leave his players the same. They both lose their next match and most people judge that team B's coach will feel worse about his inaction than team A's coach will feel about his action (Zeelenberg et al. 2002). People regret the failure to act when there was a good reason to act, which the prior knowledge of lost matches provides. Once again, there is an asymmetry in the outcomes. A reason to act leads people to think about the consequences of the action and the inaction, just as a long-term perspective does. And once again, when people think about the consequences of the action and the inaction, they discover an asymmetry in the outcomes. The nonactor, coach B, had fielded a team of players in earlier matches and had lost; he fielded the same players in the current match and lost. When people imagine an alternative to the inaction the imagined outcome is better than the actual one (if coach B had changed some players they might have won). Coach A had fielded a team of players in earlier matches and had lost; he fielded a different set of players in the current match and also lost. When people imagine an alternative to the action the imagined outcome is the same as the actual one (if coach A had not changed any players they would still have lost). A good reason to act may ensure that people do not experience self-blame as well as regret (Connolly and Zeelenberg 2002). But a good reason to act ensures that people can imagine an alternative that has a good consequence—for example, "if only coach B had changed some players, they might have won."

In each of the examples considered earlier, people regret inactions because they can imagine a better outcome. For instance, people can think of the good that may have resulted had more time been spent with family and friends, had educational opportunities been seized, or had hobbies been pursued. In these situations, if only the person had acted a better outcome might have occurred. The impact of an imagined better outcome is illustrated in the example of Jane, who went to a travel agency to look for holidays in the Caribbean. There was a wonderful package deal at a very affordable price. She wondered whether to book it immediately but decided to think about it overnight. The next day when she returned to the travel agency the package was sold out and there were no other deals that looked as attractive. Jane is likely to regret her inaction. If she had acted, she would have been able to go on a fabulous holiday. The feedback from action is often the actual consequences, but the feedback from inaction is the imagined good outcomes that did not happen (Gilovich, Medvec, and Chen 1995).

People imagine a counterfactual alternative to an inaction more than to an action when they think about two possibilities for both—for example, because the temporal perspective or a reason to act ensures that they consider their consequences, and the imagined alternative to the inaction has a better outcome than the imagined alternative to the action. The next section considers evidence that corroborates this account.

The Inaction Effect

Recent evidence corroborates the proposal that people imagine a counterfactual alternative to an inaction only when they have thought about two possibilities for the inaction, and discovered an asymmetry in the goodness of the imagined outcomes for the action and the inaction. They do not imagine an alternative to an inaction when there is no asymmetry, even when they take a long-term perspective, or have a good reason to act.

Temporal Perspective and Inactions People say "if only ..." about a failure to act only when its imagined counterfactual alternative leads to a better outcome than the imagined alternative to the action. Alice McEleney and I tested this idea (Byrne and McEleney 2000). In one experiment we showed that temporal perspective does *not* lead people to say "if only ..." about their failures to act when the action and inaction lead to equivalent outcomes.

A long-term perspective on the investment story leads people to think about the consequences and so they think about two possibilities for the action and for the inaction (see table 3.3, part 2). Laura owns shares in company A and has lost money; she used to own shares in company B and would have made money if she had kept them:

Laura owns shares in company A and loses money (postaction).
Laura owns shares in company B and makes money (preaction, and imagined).

Mary owns shares in company A and has lost money; if she had moved to company B she would have made money:

Mary owns shares in company A and loses money (predecision and postdecision).
Mary owns shares in company B and makes money (imagined).

The real outcome is the same for both the actor and the nonactor: both have lost money in company A. The imagined outcomes are also the same for them: both would have made money in company B. There is no asymmetry in the investment scenario; the real and imagined consequences are equally matched (Kahneman 1995).

We showed that people say "if only ..." about the action not only in the short term but also in the long term when there is no asymmetry in the consequences (Byrne and McEleney 2000). In one experiment we allocated 112 participants to two groups; one group received a short-term version of the investment scenario and the second group received a long-term version. Suppose you were in the long-term group. Participants were given the following sort of information: "At the end of the first year she found out that she would have been better off by $1,000 if she had taken the offer and switched to shares in company B. After 10 years, she found out that her shares did not make up the lost ground in the meantime, and she would still have been better off by $1,000 if she had switched to shares in company B."

The participants answered three questions about the scenario: who did they think would imagine "if only ..." most often at the end of the first year of investment, how did they think she completed this thought, and who did they think would feel worse about her decision at the end of the first year of investment. Participants given the short-term version were told the outcome at the end of the first year only. Participants given the long-term version were asked the same questions but with regard to after 10 years of investment. The results showed that reliably more participants judged that the actor would think "if only ..." than that the nonactor would think "if only ...". There was no reliable difference between the short-term and long-term perspective in these judgments:

Short-term: actor, 71 percent; nonactor, 29 percent

Long-term: actor, 64 percent; nonactor, 36 percent

Reliably more participants also judged that the actor would feel worse than that the nonactor would feel worse. There was no reliable difference between the short-term and the long-term perspective in these judgments:

Short-term: actor, 87.5 percent; nonactor, 12.5 percent

Long-term: actor, 86 percent; nonactor, 14 percent

The experiment shows that people imagine a counterfactual alternative to an action rather than to an inaction. The action effect does not reverse to an inaction effect—that is, for the investment scenario they do not imagine a counterfactual alternative to an inaction more than to an action, even when they are given the long-term perspective (see also Byrne and McEleney 1997).

These results have been replicated even when the explicit counterfactual "she now finds out she would have been better off by $1,000 if she had switched to company B" is replaced it with "she does not know what would have happened had she not decided to switch" (Avni-Babad 2003). The results confirm that the critical feature is that both the real and imagined consequences for the actor and the nonactor are matched.

Reasons and Inactions A good reason to act may make inaction seem unjustifiable (Zeelenberg et al. 2002). But people imagine a counterfactual alternative to an inaction when there was a good reason to act because the imagined outcome is good (if coach B had changed some of the players he might have won). They do not imagine an alternative to the action because the imagined outcome is just the same as the actual one (if coach A had not changed any of the players he would still have lost). People think "if only ..." about the inaction in the soccer story because of the asymmetry in outcomes. A good reason to act does not lead people to say "if only ..." about a failure to act when the imagined outcomes are matched, as they are in the investment scenario.

We demonstrated this point by giving 50 participants an investment scenario that was bad from the outset instead of neutral (Byrne and McEleney

2000). We included the following preamble: "During her first year as a shareholder in company A the value of her shares fell considerably until they were worth only $1,000. Around that time there was a once-off offer to switch to shares in company B ...". The preamble ensures that there was a reason to act. Nonetheless, reliably more participants said "if only ..." about the action than the inaction (62 versus 38 percent), and reliably more judged that the actor would feel worse than that the nonactor would feel worse (70 versus 30 percent). The result shows that most people say "if only ..." about actions even when they have a good reason to act. They say "if only ..." about inactions when they have a good reason to act only when there is an asymmetry in the outcomes—that is, when they can imagine an alternative to the inaction that has a good outcome (if coach B had changed some of the players they might have won), but the imagined alternative to the action has a bad outcome (if coach A had not changed any of the players they would still have lost).

People can have strong or weak reasons for acting, or not acting. Consider a passenger who was booked on flight A but switched to flight B because taking flight B made onward connections easier. Another passenger was booked on flight B and considered switching to flight A, but stayed with B because the movie to be shown was better. When flight B experiences strong turbulence and both passengers are injured, who do you think will feel most regret for their flight choice, the first passenger or the second? Most people judge that the second passenger will feel worse (Zhang, Bonnefon, and Deng 2004). There is an asymmetry in the strength of reasons: the nonactor's reason is weak compared to the actor's strong reason. The social context can also provide ready-made reasons and expectations about acting or not acting. Consider an individual who decides whether to donate a kidney to his sick relative. He decides to do so, and some time later his relative dies. Consider another individual with a similar decision to make. He decides not to donate an organ to his relative, and some time later his relative dies. Who do you think feels worse? Most people judge that the nondonor will feel worse (Feeney and Handley 2001b). The next chapter examines the effect of different sorts of reasons, including obligations, on the counterfactual alternatives that people imagine.

People keep in mind a single possibility when they understand some ideas. Indicative conditionals are understood by keeping in mind a single possibility. But people can switch from thinking about a single possibility to thinking about two possibilities—for example, they think about two possibilities when they understand a counterfactual conditional. Even children as young as 2 years of age appreciate the meaning of *nearly* or *almost*, words that cue the imagination of two possibilities, the facts and a close alternative (Harris, German, and Mills 1996). The way people talk about an idea can convey whether a single possibility or dual possibilities must be kept in mind.

Summary

This chapter has focused on a key phenomenon of the human imagination: people tend to imagine a counterfactual alternative to an action rather than to an inaction. One perceived fault line of the human imagination is decisions to act. A clue to understanding the phenomenon is that in some circumstances people keep in mind two possibilities. Evidence that people think about some ideas by envisaging two possibilities comes from studies of counterfactual conditionals. People make different inferences from a counterfactual conditional ("if Mark had left at 9 a.m. then he would have caught the airplane") than from an indicative conditional. Their inferences indicate that they think about the conjecture, "Mark left at 9 a.m. and he caught the airplane," and the presupposed facts, "Mark did not leave at 9 a.m. and he did not catch the airplane."

The observation that people consider two possibilities when they understand counterfactual conditionals helps to explain why people imagine alternatives to actions. People understand actions by thinking about two possibilities. When people understand the action "Laura owned shares in company B and she decided to switch to company A," they think about the preaction possibility, "Laura owned shares in company B," and the postaction possibility, "Laura owns shares in company A." When they understand an inaction "Mary owned shares in company A, she considered switching to company B but she decided against it," they think about a single possibility, "Mary owns shares in company A." They imagine an alternative to the action ("if only Laura had not switched to company A") because they can mentally change the current possibility to be the same as the past possibility. A key principle is that people can readily imagine a counterfactual alternative to a possibility if it is mentally represented with a second possibility, and so people imagine "if only ..." alternatives to actions more than to failures to act.

In some circumstances people can switch from thinking about one possibility to thinking about two possibilities. For example, they think about two possibilities for an inaction when they adopt a long-term perspective or when there were reasons to act. People imagine counterfactual alternatives to inactions only in special circumstances: when the imagined alternative for the inaction (coach B's team might have won) has a better outcome than the imagined alternative for the action (coach A's team still would have lost).

Sometimes it can be difficult to act. Part of that difficulty is that you often do not know what the outcomes from your actions might be. And sometimes the consequences are nothing like you imagined them to be. When people decide to act they may be "caught between dread and witness," as Seamus Heaney described in his Nobel lecture in 1995:

One of the most harrowing moments in the whole history of the harrowing of the heart in Northern Ireland came when a minibus full of workers being driven home one January evening in 1976 was held up by armed and masked men and the occupants of the van ordered at gunpoint to line up at the side of the road. Then one of the masked executioners said to them, "Any Catholics among you, step out here." As it happened, this particular group, with one exception, were all Protestants, so the presumption must have been that the masked men were Protestant paramilitaries about to carry out a tit-for-tat sectarian killing of the Catholic as the odd man out, the one who would have been presumed to be in sympathy with the IRA and all its actions. It was a terrible moment for him, caught between dread and witness, but he did make a motion to step forward. Then, the story goes, in that split second of decision, and in the relative cover of the winter evening darkness, he felt the hand of the Protestant worker next to him take his hand and squeeze it in a signal that said no, don't move, we'll not betray you, nobody need know what faith or party you belong to. All in vain, however, for the man stepped out of the line; but instead of finding a gun at his temple, he was thrown backward and away as the gunmen opened fire on those remaining in the line, for these were not Protestant terrorists, but members, presumably, of the Provisional IRA.

4 Thinking about What *Should* Have Happened

All the woulda-coulda-shouldas layin' in the sun,
Talkin' 'bout the things they woulda-coulda-shoulda done ...
But those woulda-coulda-shouldas all ran away and hid
From one little *did*
—Shel Silverstein, *Falling Up*

When people think about what they might have done differently they sometimes think about what they *should* have done differently. Everyday judgments and decisions are often based on beliefs about obligations, and about what is permitted and what is forbidden. Should scientists be allowed to clone humans? Are you morally obliged to recycle your office wastepaper? Ought manufacturers to identify products containing genetically modified ingredients? People engage with many moral issues and ethical dilemmas in their daily lives. They consult their knowledge of obligation and permission to consider such moral questions. Their knowledge is derived not only from cultural mores, societal norms, and historical abstractions, but also from personal and familial principles and practices. This chapter aims to explain how people think about what they should and should not have done. The principles outlined in the previous chapters to explain how people think about what they *could* have done can be extended to give a new understanding of how they think about what they *should* have done.

People Say "If Only ..." about What Should *Not* Have Happened

Suppose an acquaintance's daughter suffers some minor injuries in a car accident after he failed to pick her up from school. He was delayed because he was chatting with friends, and some of the other parents you know are of the opinion that it was his fault that his daughter got hurt (N'gbala and Branscombe 1995). Would they blame him as readily if he had been delayed by something else, say, because he had stopped to help someone? It seems easier to imagine that "he should not have stopped to chat with friends" than to imagine that "he should not have stopped to help someone." Obligations, such as the moral imperative to help other people, can seem immutable. Conversely, people can readily imagine alternatives to socially unacceptable actions. This chapter aims to explain why.

Controllable Events and Acceptable Events

Consider Steven, who was delayed on his way home by a series of events and arrived too late to save his wife from dying of a heart attack (Girotto et al. 1991). The events that delayed Steven included a road blocked by a fallen tree, stopping at a bar for a drink, and having an asthma attack. When he considered what might have been, what do you think Steven's thoughts focused on after the death of his wife? When people were asked to complete his "if only ..." thoughts, they focused on his decision to stop at a bar for a drink, saying "if only I hadn't stopped for that drink" (Girotto et al. 1991). Of course, stopping for a drink is the only event in the series that was completely within Steven's control. Most people undid the controllable event whether it was framed as normal or exceptional (Steven always went to the bar for a drink or he rarely did), and regardless of what order it appeared in, in the scenario (see also Markman et al. 1995). But events within an individual's control differ in many ways, and one important way is whether they are socially acceptable. Drinking in a bar, the controllable event, may fit with social norms about how to celebrate with friends, but it seems inappropriate in the context of drinking alone while your spouse is ill at home.

In fact, most people focus their thoughts about what might have been on those controllable events that are forbidden or frowned-on events, more than on socially acceptable ones. Rachel McCloy and I demonstrated this effect in an experiment in which we gave seventy-six participants the story about Steven (McCloy and Byrne 2000). The events that delayed him included visiting his parents, stopping for a hamburger, buying a newspaper, and a traffic jam. One of the events was uncontrollable (the traffic jam) but the other three were all controllable. They had been judged by a separate set of participants in the context of being late as socially appropriate (visiting parents), socially inappropriate (stopping for a hamburger), or neutral (buying a newspaper). When the participants were asked to imagine Steven's thoughts after his wife's death, they focused on one of the four events (54 percent) or wished there had not been a delay at all (36 percent). Most revealingly, they focused on his decision to stop for a burger, the only event that was socially inappropriate in the context of a delay. They imagined an alternative to the inappropriate event reliably more often than to the appropriate one:

Socially inappropriate, 22 percent; appropriate, 12 percent

They imagined an alternative to the appropriate event (12 percent) and to the neutral one (11 percent) just as often as to the uncontrollable event (9 percent). The result shows that people can more easily imagine an alternative to some sorts of controllable events rather than others. They may be able to imagine an alternative to the other controllable events in other circumstances, but the nature of the outcome guides their tendency to imagine an alternative to the socially inappropriate event. The experiment shows that most people imagine an alternative to a socially inappropriate controllable event more than to an appropriate one. Other experiments have also shown that they imagine an alternative to a socially inappropriate event whether it leads to a bad outcome or a good outcome (McCloy and Byrne 2000). Consider for example an individual named Alan who attempts to get to a video shop to buy a stereo in a sale (Wells, Taylor, and Turtle 1987). Alan's progress is helped by several factors, some socially appropriate, such as taking a shortcut, and some inappropriate, such as ignoring a red light, and his progress is also hindered by several factors, some appropriate and some inappropriate (McCloy and Byrne 2000). Suppose the outcome is good, Alan succeeds in getting to the video shop on time, and he says "things would have been different if ...". Participants completed his thought by imagining an alternative to the socially inappropriate event, "things would have been different if he had not ignored a red light," more than to the socially appropriate one, "things would have been different if he had not taken a shortcut."

People imagine a counterfactual alternative to the prohibited possibility in many situations. Counterfactual thoughts are constrained not only by natural laws (Seeleu et al. 1995), but also by social laws such as social conventions and cultural regulations. Most people judge that individuals will regret their decision *not* to donate an organ to a relative who subsequently dies, more than they will regret their decision to donate one (Feeney and Handley 2001b). They also judge that individuals will regret their decision *not* to help a heart attack victim who subsequently dies, more than their decision to help one. The decision to donate an organ, or to help a stranger having a heart attack, adheres to social and personal obligations. People often regret their actions. But when their failure to act violates an obligation to act, as in these "good Samaritan" examples, they regret their inaction (Feeney and Handley 2001b; see also Tanner and Medin 2004). Obligations provide good reasons to justify action, and failure to meet obligations is frowned on. What should have been done affects people's sympathy and their judgments of fault (Green et al. 1999; Macrae 1992). When people violate an obligation they tend to think not only about what they did, but also about what they *should* have done.

There are many different sorts of obligations. Some derive from social and cultural conventions—for example, adults should take care of their elderly parents. Others derive from legal and historical precedents—for instance, children may inherit their parents' property. Still other obligations concern aesthetic or economic principles—for example, workers must pay taxes. Or they pertain to health and safety measures—for instance, social venues must have adequate fire-escape routes. People encounter many "deontic" situations—that is, situations concerning permission and obligation, as well as promises, threats, sacrifices, and so on (Legrenzi, Politzer, and Girotto 1996). Social mores delineate what you are obliged to do, and also what you are obliged *not* to do. A forbidden possibility is sometimes simply the mirror image of an obligation: you should not neglect your elderly parents, or you should not evade paying taxes. Forbidden possibilities spell out what a society outlaws or frowns on, again for many reasons, ranging from cultural and legal conventions to economic and health measures. Moral reasoning develops early, and children begin to understand what they are allowed to do and what they are obliged to do at a young age (Girotto, Light, and Colbourn 1988). Obligations vary from society to society. Some obligations seem to be present in most cultures—for example, that you should reciprocate by giving back to someone from whom you have received (Morris, Sim, and Girotto 1998). Within a society, its obligations can seem inalterable. They are the rock on which social interaction is built.

Because obligations can seem immutable, they make good excuses. Suppose a colleague makes a serious error at work because of inattention. He excuses his lapse by saying that he got very little sleep the night before because one of his children felt ill. Would you feel that this excuse was a reasonable one? Most people would probably be more understanding given this excuse, compared to if he said he got little sleep because he was out with friends all night. A reason based on parental obligation seems more acceptable than one based on personal gratification, perhaps because it is easier to think of alternatives to the latter—for example, he should not have stayed out with his friends all night. This point is discussed later in the chapter.

People may understand obligations by thinking about possibilities. As we have seen in earlier chapters, people usually think about true possibilities and not false possibilities, and they think initially about few possibilities (see table 4.1). Some ideas require people to keep in mind two possibilities, and to keep track of the status of the possibilities as imagined, or as the facts. People can more readily imagine an alternative to a possibility if they have mentally represented it from the outset with a second possibility, than if they thought about a single possibility. For example, they tend to imagine an alternative to an action rather than to a failure to act because they understand an action by mentally representing two possibilities, whereas they understand an inaction by thinking about a single

Table 4.1
Summary of principles thus far

1. True possibilities: *People keep in mind true possibilities.*

2. Few possibilities: *People keep in mind few possibilities.*

3. Dual possibilities: *Some ideas require people to think about two possibilities.*

4. Counterfactual possibilities: *People think about possibilities that once may have been true possibilities but can be true no longer.*

5. Mutability of dual possibilities: *People readily imagine a counterfactual alternative to a possibility if it is mentally represented with a second possibility.*

6. Forbidden possibilities: *People think about the forbidden possibility as well as the permitted one when they understand an obligation.*

I. Actions: *People think about two possibilities when they understand an action.*

II. Single possibilities: *People can switch from thinking about one possibility to thinking about two possibilities e.g., for inactions.*

III. Controllable events: *People think about two possibilities when they understand controllable events.*

possibility. When people think about an obligation they may think about what is permitted, and they may also think about what is forbidden. The next section examines how people reason about obligations. The section after it shows that the tendency to think about both the permitted possibility and the forbidden possibility sheds light on the counterfactual alternatives people imagine.

Clues from Reasoning: Inferences about Obligations

Knowledge of a regulation—for example, "hard hats must be worn on the building site"—ensures that most people know not only what is obligatory, wearing a hard hat, but also what is not permissible, not wearing a hard hat. People think about two possibilities when they think about an obligation. One of the possibilities they keep in mind is the forbidden possibility. The forbidden possibility influences the inferences people make, and the counterfactual alternatives they imagine.

Forbidden Possibilities

When people understand an obligation, such as, "if Jack's parents are elderly, he should look after them," they keep in mind two possibilities, "Jack's parents are elderly and he looks after them" (A and B), and "Jack's parents are elderly and he does not look after them" (A and not-B). They note that the status of this second possibility is that it is forbidden. People usually think about true possibilities. Even when they understand a counterfactual conjecture that contradicts known facts, they may temporarily suppose the conjecture to be true. But obligations are different. They require people to think about a forbidden possibility. They are unique in that they require people to consider the possibility that is explicitly ruled out by the conditional. This new principle is as follows:

6.   Principle of forbidden possibilities: *People think about a forbidden possibility as well as the permitted possibility to understand an obligation.* For example, when people understand "if A happens you are obliged to do B," they think about the permitted possibility, A and B, and the forbidden possibility, A and not-B, noted as "forbidden."

Consider a conditional that expresses an obligation, such as "if Paul rides a motorbike then he has to wear a helmet." The first part of the conditional

Table 4.2

The possibilities people think about for a conditional obligation "if Paul rides a motorbike he has to wear a helmet"

Initial possibilities

   Paul rides a motorbike and he wears a helmet (permitted)

   Paul rides a motorbike and he does not wear a helmet (forbidden)

Explicit possibilities

   Paul rides a motorbike and he wears a helmet (permitted)

   Paul does not ride a motorbike and he does not wear a helmet (permitted)

   Paul does not ride a motorbike and he wears a helmet (permitted)

   Paul rides a motorbike and he does not wear a helmet (forbidden)

"if Paul rides a motorbike" corresponds to a factual possibility. The second part of the conditional "he has to wear a helmet" expresses a deontic possibility, in this case, an obligation, well known in some jurisdictions from legal and safety considerations (Johnson-Laird and Byrne 2002). People think about the permitted possibility, "Paul rides a motorbike and he wears a helmet." But they also think about what is forbidden, "Paul rides a motorbike and he does not wear a helmet" (as table 4.2 shows). Their knowledge provides the complement of the permitted possibilities. Even 9-year-old children understand that an unfamiliar but plausible road-safety obligation such as "if you drive a car over 100 mph, it must have fluorescent body paint" means that it is forbidden to drive at high speed and not have fluorescent body paint (Girotto et al. 1989). Content and context can help people to consider what is not permissible as well as what is. For the obligation, they think about the permitted possibility, "you drive the car over 100 mph and it has fluorescent body-paint," and the forbidden possibility, "you drive the car over 100 mph and it does not have fluorescent body paint" (noted as forbidden). The forbidden possibility corresponds to the possibility that is ruled out as false for an indicative conditional.

What makes an obligation false? A conditional about an obligation is *not* false in the case that the forbidden possibility occurs. The conditional "if Paul rides a motorbike he has to wear a helmet" is not made false by the observation that Paul rode a motorbike and did not wear a helmet. The conditional's obligation is still true, but Paul violated it. The fact "Paul rode a motorbike and he did not wear a helmet" corresponds to the forbidden possibility. But the fact does not cancel the forbidden nature of the possibility. Most people reason differently when they must test whether a deontic conditional is obeyed or whether it is true (Girotto et al. 2001).

Of course, an obligation *can* be false in some circumstances—for example, in a country where it is not obligatory for motorbike riders to wear helmets. The conditional obligation "if Paul rides a motorbike then he has to wear a helmet" is false in such a country. The following permitted possibility in that country:

Paul rode a motorbike and he did not wear a helmet (permitted).

corresponds to the forbidden possibility of the conditional:

Paul rode a motorbike and he did not wear a helmet (forbidden).

Evidence that people keep in mind the forbidden possibility comes from their superior ability to make inferences about this possibility.

Forbidden Possibilities and Inferences

Most people reason well about obligations. Early research on conditional inferences focused on reasoning with factual conditionals, such as "if Paul rides a motorbike then he wears jeans." More recent research has focused on reasoning with conditionals about what should be done as well as conditionals about what is done (Manktelow and Over 1991). For example, in Wason's (1966) selection task, you are given a conditional such as "if Paul rides a motorbike then he must wear a helmet," and four cards corresponding to four instances, Paul rode a motorbike, Paul did not ride a motorbike, Paul wore a helmet, and Paul did not wear a helmet. Suppose you are asked to test whether the conditional is violated. Which cards would you choose to turn over? Most participants correctly select the cards "Paul rode a motorbike" and "Paul did not wear a helmet" (Manktelow and Over 1991; see also Johnson-Laird, Legrenzi, and Legrenzi 1972; Green and Larking 1995). These two cards effectively test the conditional: if you turn over the card corresponding to "Paul rode a motorbike" and find on the other side "he did not wear a helmet," you will know that the conditional was violated. Likewise, if you turn over the card corresponding to "Paul did not wear a helmet" and find on the other side "Paul rode a motorbike," you will also know that the conditional is violated. If you turn over the other cards, you will not know that the conditional was violated. For example, if the card corresponding to "Paul did not ride a motorbike" has on the other side "he wore a helmet," it does not violate the conditional.

Almost all participants in experiments with this sort of obligation content select the two correct cards (see Manktelow 1999 for a review). The result contrasts dramatically with their performance on abstract versions of Wason's selection task. Suppose you were given the conditional "if there is a vowel on one side of the card then there is an even number on the other side" and you were presented with four cards on which there is A, B, 4, and 7. What cards would you select to test the conditional? Most participants chose only the A, or the A and the 4. Very few select the 7 card, even though the 7 card could show whether the conditional was violated (for example, if you turn over the 7 card and find an A on the other side). The 7 card corresponds to the card "Paul did not wear a helmet," which participants select readily.

The improved performance on Wason's selection task when the conditional has an obligation content supports the idea that people have ready access to the forbidden possibility: they know it is not allowed for Paul to ride his motorbike and not wear his helmet. The obligation content makes a counterexample readily available. Familiarity can make the forbidden possibility available—for instance, from direct or vicarious experience stored in memory of an individual riding a motorbike without a helmet (Griggs and Cox 1983). Of course familiarity with the conditional is not essential: knowledge of the context or the linguistic expression (a modal auxiliary such as *must*) can cue the need to represent what is forbidden for unfamiliar obligations or permissions that are plausible (Girotto et al. 1989), and even for ones that are abstract (Cheng and Holyoak 1985; Girotto, Mazzocco, and Cherubini 1992; but see Jackson and Griggs 1990).

Because people think about the permitted possibility and the forbidden possibility, they can make certain inferences readily. Consider once again the modus tollens (not-B therefore not-A) inference (see table 2.3 for a summary of inferences). When a reasoner is told "if Paul rides a motorbike he must wear a helmet" and they are told that "Paul is not wearing a helmet," they can infer that it is not permitted for him to ride a motorbike. The inference highlights an important aspect of reasoning. There is more than one way to make an inference. The modus tollens (not-B therefore not-A) inference can be made in either of two ways.

A common route to making the modus tollens (not-B therefore not-A) inference is via the true possibilities. For a conditional based on neutral content, such as "if Nancy rides her motorbike she goes to the mountains," people envisage just a single possibility, "Nancy rides her motorbike and she goes to the mountains." Given the information "Nancy did not go to the mountains," some people infer that nothing follows, because the information does not match the single possibility they have thought about. To make the inference they must think about other true possibilities that are consistent with the conditional, such as "Nancy does not ride her motorbike and she does not go to the mountains." This route to making the inference may be most common for factual conditionals with neutral content, and it requires people to think about the other true possibilities.

But reasoning about obligations illustrates a second route for the inference via the mental representation of what is forbidden. For the conditional, "if Paul rides his motorbike he must wear a helmet," people think about two possibilities: "Paul rides his motorbike and he wears a helmet" and "Paul rides his motorbike and he does not wear a helmet (forbidden)." When they are told that Paul did not wear a helmet, they can match this information directly to the forbidden possibility, and infer that it is forbidden for him to ride his motorbike. This route to making the inference is available for conditionals about obligations because people envisage what is forbidden from the outset (see table 4.3).

The theory predicts that people should make more modus tollens (not-B therefore not-A) inferences from obligation conditionals because they can take advantage of the second route. Cristina Quelhas and I have tested the prediction in an experiment in which we gave 303 participants various sorts of inferences, including the modus tollens (not-B therefore not-A) one (Quelhas and Byrne 2003). The participants were assigned to different groups and our interest here is in two of them: one group who received a conditional with obligation content (for example, "if he rode a motorbike then he must have worn a helmet"), and a second group who received a factual conditional (for instance, "if Fred was in Paris then Joe was in Lisbon"). The obligation content was based on prudential obligations (Manktelow and Over 1990). Suppose you were told "if Paul rode a motorbike then he must have worn a helmet," and later you were told, "Paul did not wear a helmet." What would you infer: (1) he rode a motorbike, (2) he did not ride a motorbike, or (3) he may or may not have ridden a motorbike? The results showed that most participants selected (2) readily. They made reliably more modus tollens inferences (not-B therefore not-A) from the obligation than from the factual conditional:

Table 4.3
Two routes to the modus tollens (not-B therefore not-A) inference

Route 1: True possibilities Premises: "if A, B. Not-B"	Route 2: Forbidden possibilities Premises: "if A, B is obligatory. Not-B"

1. *Initial possibilities for first premise*
    A and B
	1. *Initial possibilities for first premise*
	    A and B (permitted)
	    A and not-B (forbidden)

2. *Attempt to add second premise fails (not-B cannot be added to A and B)*	2. *Attempt to add second premise eliminates first possibility and leaves second possibility (not-B can be added to A and not-B)*
3. CONCLUDE: Nothing follows	3. CONCLUDE: Not-A (A is forbidden)

4. *Think through unformed possibilities
for first premise*
    A and B
    Not-A and not-B
    Not-A and B	

5. *Attempt to add second premise eliminates all but second possibility (not-B can be added to not-A and not-B)*	
6. CONCLUDE: Not-A	

Obligation, 76 percent; factual, 61 percent

The result supports the prediction that reasoners have access to the forbidden possibility, which provides a second route by which they can make the inference.

Most participants made the same amount of modus ponens (A therefore B) inferences and affirmation of the consequent (B therefore A) inferences for the two sorts of conditionals: both sorts of conditionals provide access to the affirmative possibility (see also Manktelow and Fairley 2000). Consider now the denial of the antecedent (not-A therefore not-B) inference. Suppose you were told, "if Paul rode a motorbike then he must have worn a helmet," and later you were told, "Paul did not ride a motorbike." What would you infer: (1) he wore a helmet, (2) he did not wear a helmet, or (3) he may or may not have worn a helmet? The theory does not predict that people will make more of these inferences from the obligation compared to the factual conditional. They have kept in mind one permitted possibility and the forbidden possibility, and there is no direct match in these two possibilities to the information "he did not ride a motorbike." People have to think through the other possibilities, just as they have to for the factual conditional. And given that they have already envisaged two possibilities for the obligation, it may be difficult to juggle a third. The results show that participants did not make more of the inference from the obligation. In fact they made reliably fewer. The results support the view that people understand an obligation by keeping in mind the permitted possibility and the forbidden possibility.

Of course, a variety of modal auxiliaries can be used to convey the obligatory nature of the consequent—for example, it can be conveyed by an explicit modal, "he should wear a helmet," or by a modal that does not disambiguate between its deontic and epistemic status, such as "he must wear a helmet." It can even be left implicit, "he wears a helmet," in which case, an obligation interpretation depends on knowledge of the content or context. Obligations are often expressed using *must* or *should* or *ought*—for instance, "you must take care of your parents" or "you should take care of them" or "you ought to take care of them." In fact, the modal auxiliary *must* is ambiguous in English. It can mean epistemic necessity, as in "you must be tired," or deontic necessity, as in "you must look after your dog." Only the second use expresses an obligation. Likewise, permissions are often expressed using *may*—for example, "you may inherit your parents' property." *May* is also ambiguous; it can express epistemic possibility, as in "we may be lost," or deontic possibility, as in "she may leave now." Only the second use expresses a permission.

As these examples illustrate, obligation can be thought of as akin to necessity, and permission as akin to possibility (Johnson-Laird and Byrne 2002). Logicians have extended the ideas of necessity and possibility in "modal" logics to provide "deontic" logics to deal with obligation and permission (for an overview see Bucciarelli and Johnson-Laird, forthcoming). In our experiment we chose *must* because it is ambiguous about whether it concerns permission or possibility (see also Quelhas and Byrne 2000). It represents a strong test of our hypothesis: results found with *must* are sure to be found with *should*. Moreover, we found exactly the same results for a third group of participants who received a conditional with obligation content but no explicit modal auxiliary (for example, "If he rode a motorbike then he wore a helmet"), as we did for the group who received the obligation with an explicit modal. Knowledge of the content of the obligation is sufficient to ensure that people keep in mind the permitted possibility and the forbidden possibility. For instance, the advantage for the modus tollens (not-B therefore not-A) inference occurs for obligations even when there is no explicit modal auxiliary in the conditional:

Obligation (no *must*), 72 percent; factual, 61 percent

We also found the same pattern for the other three inferences for obligation content with no *must* as for obligations with *must*.

Overall, the experiment shows that most people make more of the modus tollens (not-B therefore not-A) inference from obligation conditionals than from factual conditionals. It supports the view that people make inferences from conditionals about obligations based not only on what is permitted, but also on what is forbidden. Before we consider how people imagine alternatives when they think about what they should do and should not do, it is worth considering two further aspects of obligations: some obligations outlaw more than one possibility, and obligations can be counterfactual—that is, the obligation once held but it no longer does.

Biconditional Obligations: Two Forbidden Possibilities

Some obligations outlaw one forbidden possibility, others outlaw two possibilities. Consider the obligation "if an envelope is sealed it must have a 40 cent stamp on it" (Johnson-Laird, Legrenzi, and Legrenzi 1972). How would you go about violating it? "One-way" conditionals of this sort have just one violating case: a person violates the obligation by sending a sealed letter that does not have a 40 cent stamp on it (A and not-B). Of course, the sender is not cheating in the case where an envelope is not sealed and it has a 40 cent stamp on it (not-A and B) (Gigerenzer and Hug 1992). As in the conditional about Paul and his helmet, these one-way obligations rule out one forbidden possibility: there remain three permitted possibilities. Many obligations can seem to be one-way (Fiddick, Cosmides, and Tooby 2000). When people list the possibilities consistent with "A obligates B" they most often list this interpretation (Bucciarelli and Johnson-Laird, forthcoming).

Consider now the following agreement between Meghan and her mother: "If Meghan watches TV, she must tidy her room." How can this agreement be violated? Suppose you are Meghan, how would you violate it? Now suppose you are Meghan's mother, how would you violate it? It can be interpreted to have two violating cases: Meghan cheats by watching

Table 4.4
Possibilities people think about for a biconditional obligation "if Meghan watches TV, she must tidy her room"

*Initial possibilities**
Meghan watches TV and she tidies her room (permitted)
Meghan watches TV and she does not tidy her room (forbidden)
Meghan does not watch TV and she tidies her room (forbidden)
Explicit possibilities
Meghan watches TV and she tidies her room (permitted)
Meghan does not watch TV and she does not tidy her room (permitted)
Meghan watches TV and she does not tidy her room (forbidden)
Meghan does not watch TV and she tidies her room (forbidden)

*People may keep in mind initially just one forbidden possibility depending on the perspective they take—for example, Meghan's perspective or her mother's.

TV and not tidying her room, and her mother cheats in the case where Meghan tidies her room but is not allowed to watch TV, as table 4.4 shows. These obligations are "biconditional" (Johnson-Laird and Byrne 1992, 1995). The first forbidden possibility is important from the point of view of a mother to see whether a child has failed to conform to the conditional, whereas the second forbidden possibility is important from the perspective of a child to see whether the mother has failed to conform. Even young children make this distinction when they test whether such obligations have been followed (Light, Girotto, and Legrenzi 1990). Most people choose one or the other of these possibilities to test whether such a conditional is violated in Wason's selection task when they are instructed to adopt the different perspectives (Manktelow and Over 1991), and they choose both from a neutral point of view (Politzer and Nguyen-Xuan 1992). Biconditional obligations are common, as any instance of a contractual obligation will illustrate, such as buying a car: "If the buyer pays 15,000 euro, the seller must sign over the car ownership." The two-way obligation ensures two forbidden possibilities; it is forbidden for the buyer to not pay and take the car, and it is forbidden for the seller to take the money and not give the buyer the car.

Obligations can be interpreted in different ways, just as permissions can. A biconditional obligation is understood by keeping in mind one of the permitted possibilities, and the two forbidden possibilities, noted as forbidden. In fact, people may envisage initially just one of the forbidden possibilities depending on their perspective. The theory predicts that perspective effects should arise for these two-way obligations just as they do for two-way permissions—for example, the perspective of a buyer or a seller. People make different sorts of inferences because they keep in mind the forbidden possibility, or possibilities.

Counterfactual Obligations

Consider the assertion "if Mary had lived in the 1700s, she would have had to have been chaperoned." The assertion expresses a counterfactual obligation—that is, an obligation that once held for women but that no longer applies. Counterfactual obligations communicate, through shared knowledge or context, information about what was once obligatory (a woman had to be chaperoned), and what was once forbidden (a woman not chaperoned), and it communicates that what was once forbidden is no longer forbidden.

Counterfactual obligations can be about past events such as the example about Mary, or about the present—for example, "if we were to arrive at the theater late, we would have to wait outside until the intermission." Obligations in the past and present can seem to mean something quite different from each other, even when they are not counterfactual. Most people understand factual conditionals in the past and present in the same way, for conditionals with neutral content (Schaeken, Schroyens, and Dieussaert 2001), and for counterfactuals with neutral content (Byrne and Tasso 1999). But obligations in the present tense, such as "if the nurse cleans blood then she has to wear rubber gloves," refer to repeated events and they can usually be rephrased using "every time ..." (Quelhas and Byrne 2003). Obligations in the past tense, such as "if the nurse cleaned blood then she had to wear rubber gloves," seem to pinpoint a specific event. Of course, obligations in the present tense can refer to a single unique event—for example, "if that man is dead the police must investigate the attack"—and obligations in the past can refer to repeated events, such as "if a landowner died in the nineteenth century, his land had to be inherited by his first son." Nonetheless, obligations in the past tense can seem evidential in that the consequent can seem to report an inference that the speaker has made, "if the nurse cleaned blood then I infer she wore rubber gloves," rather than an obligation that held, "if the nurse cleaned blood then she must have had to have worn rubber gloves."

Table 4.5

Possibilities people think about when they understand obligations and counterfactual obligations

---

Obligation: "If your parents are elderly you have to look after them"

Initial possibilities

   Your parents are elderly and you look after them (permitted)

   Your parents are elderly and you do not look after them (forbidden)

Counterfactual obligation: "If Mary had lived in the 1700s she would have had to have been chaperoned"

Initial possibilities

   Mary lived in the 1700s and she was chaperoned (imagined)

   Mary lived in the 1700s and she was not chaperoned (forbidden)

   Mary does not live in the 1700s and she is not chaperoned (facts)

Counterfactual obligations convey that the obligation itself no longer holds. What possibilities do you think about when you understand the counterfactual obligation, "if Mary had lived in the 1700s, she would have had to have been chaperoned"? A counterfactual obligation requires you to keep track of the counterfactual conjecture:

Mary lived in the 1700s and she was chaperoned (imagined).

and the forbidden possibility:

Mary lived in the 1700s and she was not chaperoned (forbidden).

But it also conveys to you the presupposed facts:

Mary does not live in the 1700s and she is not chaperoned (facts).

The facts correspond to a permitted possibility: Mary does not need to be chaperoned (see table 4.5).

   But the subjunctive mood is not sufficient to convey the counterfactuality of the obligation. Consider the counterfactual, "if Molly had andaped, she would have been torled." You may have no idea what "andaped" or "torled" are, but you may nonetheless grasp the presupposition that Molly did not andape and she was not torled. Consider now the counterfactual obligation, "if Molly had andaped, she would have had to have been torled." Do you consider the presupposition that Molly did not andape and she was not torled? Can you say whether it is still obligatory for her to be torled? The fact that an obligation once held but no longer holds is communicated largely through knowledge. Obligations recast in the subjunctive mood are not necessarily counterfactual, and we turn now to an experiment that demonstrates this point before we consider how people think about what they should and should not have done.

Subjunctive Obligations   Simply recasting a conditional about an obligation in the subjunctive mood does not render it counterfactual. Consider the obligation, "if the tourist goes deep-sea diving then she has to take a diving course." It is understood by keeping in mind one of the permitted possibilities and the forbidden possibility:

The tourist goes diving and she takes a diving course (permitted)
The tourist goes diving and she does not take a diving course (forbidden)

People also think about these possibilities when the obligation is phrased in the past tense, "if the tourist went deep-sea diving then she had to have taken a diving course." When it is recast in the subjunctive mood— "if the tourist had gone deep sea diving then she would have had to have taken a diving course"—it does *not* convey that in addition the real facts of the matter are as follows:

The tourist did not go diving and she did not take a diving course (facts)

It may convey that in fact the tourist did not go deep-sea diving. But it does not convey that in fact she did not take a diving course. Nor does it convey that she did not *have* to take a course. Accordingly, an obligation cast in the subjunctive mood may not be understood readily as a counterfactual obligation. Instead it may be understood in the same way as an indicative obligation—that is, by keeping in mind two possibilities, one corresponding to the permitted possibility, and one to what is forbidden.

The experiment described earlier tested this idea (Quelhas and Byrne 2003). We gave one of the further groups of participants subjunctive obligations with an explicit modal (for example, "If Paul had ridden a motorbike then he must have had to wear a helmet"), and we compared them to a group who received subjunctive conditionals with neutral content (for instance, "if Fred had been in Paris then Joe would have been in Lisbon").

Suppose you were told "If Paul had ridden a motorbike then he must have had to wear a helmet," and then you were told "Paul did not wear a helmet." What do you think follows, (1) he rode a motorbike, (2) he did not ride a motorbike, or (3) he may or may not have ridden a motorbike?

The theory proposes that people think about two possibilities for both the indicative obligation, "If Paul rode a motorbike then he must have worn a helmet," and the subjunctive obligation, "If Paul had ridden a motorbike then he must have had to wear a helmet." Accordingly it predicts that people should make as many of the modus tollens (not-B therefore not-A) inferences for subjunctive obligations as for indicative obligations.

The modus tollens (not-B therefore not-A) inference is made at a high rate for an obligation. The theory predicts it should be equally high for a subjunctive obligation and the results corroborated this prediction:

Indicative obligation, 76 percent; subjunctive obligation, 78 percent

The denial of the antecedent (not-A therefore not-B) inference is made at a relatively low rate for an obligation. The theory predicts it should be equally low for the subjunctive obligation and again the results corroborated this prediction:

Indicative obligation, 51 percent; subjunctive obligation, 58 percent

The moral of the experiment is simple: the subjunctive mood is not enough to render an obligation counterfactual.

What makes an obligation counterfactual? An obligation is counterfactual when the content or context conveys that the obligation once held but does so no longer, as the example about Mary being chaperoned illustrates. Suppose for example that it used to be obligatory to pay a property tax on houses that increased with increasing house size, but that the tax was abolished some years ago. Suppose your friend buys a large house. You might say, "if you had bought that house 10 years ago, you would have had to pay a very large tax bill." For a genuine counterfactual obligation, people may think about one of the permitted possibilities conjectured by the counterfactual conditional, your friend bought the house 10 years ago and paid a large tax bill (A and B). They may also think about the forbidden possibility, your friend bought the house 10 years ago and did not pay a large tax bill (A and not-B). And they may also think about the presupposed facts, your friend did not buy the house 10 years ago and did not pay a large tax bill (not-A and not-B). The theory makes the novel prediction that people who keep in mind these three possibilities should make a higher frequency of the modus tollens (not-B therefore not-A) inference from a counterfactual obligation than from a counterfactual conditional with neutral content because they have two routes by which to make the inference.

Studies of reasoning about obligations provide an important clue to understanding how people think about what should have been. People understand an obligation by keeping in mind not only the permitted possibility, but also what is forbidden. As a result they tend to make different inferences about obligations and facts. They can make more of certain inferences from the obligation, such as the modus tollens (not-B therefore not-A) one. The principle that people keep in mind forbidden possibilities when they understand an obligation helps to explain how they think about what they should have done and what they should not have done.

The Rational Imagination: Why People Focus on Forbidden Fruit

When you learn that manufacturers in Europe must identify genetically modified constituents in food, you understand what is forbidden: they are not allowed to conceal genetically modified constituents. When you know that scientists are obliged to restrict cloning attempts to nonhuman species, you understand what is forbidden: they are not allowed to clone humans. A conditional obligation is understood by thinking about one of the permitted possibilities, and also what is forbidden. This ready access to the forbidden possibility has a large impact on how people imagine events turning out differently. Because people keep in mind both the permitted possibility and the forbidden possibility, they can readily imagine a counterfactual alternative to the forbidden possibility.

Imagined Alternatives to Forbidden Possibilities

Steven, who did not return home in time to save his wife, is judged to say "if only ..." most often about his decision to stop for a beer. People imagine alternatives to controllable events more often than to uncontrollable events, because they think about two possibilities when they understand the controllable event, but only a single possibility when they understand the uncontrollable event. They imagine alternatives to socially unacceptable controllable events (stopping at a beer for a bar) more than acceptable controllable events (visiting parents), because they note that one of the possibilities they have thought about for the socially unacceptable controllable event is forbidden (stopping for a beer), and the other is permitted (not stopping for a beer). They imagine an alternative by mentally changing the forbidden possibility to be the same as the permitted possibility, and they say, "if only Steven had not stopped for a beer ...". The application of the principles to thinking about what should have been done is as follows:

Corollary 3 for thoughts about controllable events: *People think about two possibilities when they understand a controllable event.* They think about the voluntary intention to act, as well as the foregone option not to act.

They understand a socially unacceptable controllable event by noting that one of the two possibilities is forbidden and one is permitted.

They can imagine a counterfactual alternative by mentally changing the forbidden possibility to be the same as the permitted possibility; they tend not to change their mental representation of the permitted possibility to be the same as the forbidden possibility.

The forbidden possibility brings to mind its obligatory counterpart, just as an event that is exceptional for an individual brings to mind its normal counterpart (Kahneman and Miller 1986). Social regulations about what is permitted and what is obligatory are strong norms that guide behavior and thoughts. People imagine alternatives to events that depart from the norm because they keep in mind not only the event that departs from the norm but also the norm (Kahneman and Miller 1986). Norms have been examined for what a person habitually does, but equally important are the norms that govern what a person is expected socially to do (McCloy and Byrne 2000). Suppose Paul is injured in an accident when he is riding his motorbike without a helmet. There may be many possible counterfactual alternatives that could be imagined—for example, people could say, "if only he had not ridden home by that route," "if only the other driver had not been going fast," or "if only he had taken the bus that day." But these potential counterfactual alternatives may be overridden by the alternative, "if only he had worn his helmet." The forbidden possibility is represented from the outset, it is forbidden for Paul to ride his motorbike and not wear his helmet, and this possibility looms large when a bad outcome occurs. Conversely, when Paul does what he was obliged to do, he wears his helmet, people tend not to imagine a counterfactual alternative to it.

Imagined Alternatives and Obligations

People sometimes excuse their behavior by indicating that they were obliged to do what they did by social or moral or legal conventions (Markman and Tetlock 2000b). An obligation, such as a colleague's explanation that he had to stay up all night with his sick child, makes a good excuse because people consider two possibilities, the permitted possibility, the person stays up to help the child, and the forbidden one, the person does not stay up to help the child. Most people do not imagine counterfactual alternatives in which they change the permitted possibility to be the same as the forbidden possibility, and say, "if only he did not stay up to help the child." Instead the obligation seems immutable. Of course in extreme situations obligations may become mutable—for instance, someone may steal because they are starving, and the obligation not to steal may be overridden by the greater need to stay alive.

Consider another situation in which a friend of yours is bitterly disappointed: he had an important performance at a concert in front of thousands of people and it was not well received. You know he stayed out late at a preconcert party the night before, something he rarely does. He tells you he went to the party because he wanted to meet one of his orchestral heroes. You might be forgiven for thinking that his poor performance was his own fault and he should not have gone to the party. Just as Steven may berate himself for stopping for the beer that delayed his return to his dying wife, so too might you blame your friend for going out to a party the night before a big performance. But suppose instead your friend tells you he went to the party because it was a fund-raiser for his orchestra. You understand his obligation by keeping in mind two possibilities: "he went to the party" is a permitted possibility, and "he did not go to the party" is a forbidden possibility. Would you think he should not have gone to the party? Would you think his poor performance was his own fault? It is unlikely. Just as Steven's visit to his parents is not called into question when he is delayed, so too can your friend hardly be blamed for fulfilling his obligations. If you do what you should do socially, people do not tend to wish you had not done it.

Clare Walsh and I have tested the idea that obligations are immutable (Walsh and Byrne 2004a). In one experiment we gave 214 participants a scenario about a famous violinist about to perform at an important festival of classical music in Vienna (based on Klauer, Jacobsen, and Migulla 1995). He attended a festival ball the evening before the concert and had a late night. At the concert, his performance was poor, the audience did not respond well, and he was bitterly disappointed. We told some participants that the reason Bernard went to the ball was because "the ball is being run to help cover the festival expenses and therefore Bernard is obliged to attend." Suppose you were given this scenario. What do you imagine Bernard said "if only ..." about, after his disappointing performance? Do you think he wished "if only I hadn't gone to the ball"? We gave one group of participants the obligation reason, and another group no reason, just a descriptive filler, "the ball is being held in the Vienna City Ballroom." Participants generated reliably fewer "if only ..." sentence completions to describe Bernard's thoughts that focused on the ball when they were told he was obliged to go to it, than when they were not given a reason:

Obligation, 67 percent; no reason, 82 percent

We told a third group that he went because "he has a unique opportunity to meet a world-renowned violinist at the ball and this is his goal for attending." Participants' "if only ..." completions for Bernard focused on the ball just as often when they were told he would meet another violinist there, as when they were not given a reason:

Goal-based reason, 75 percent; no reason, 82 percent

The results show that people do not tend to imagine alternatives to obligations. Most people imagine a counterfactual alternative to an action (going to the ball) when they know of no reason for it, or when the reason is a goal (to meet another violinist). But they do not tend to imagine a counterfactual alternative to an action as often when the reason for it was that the individual was obliged to do it (he had to help raise funds). The results provide further support for the idea that people understand an obligation by keeping in mind two possibilities, the permitted one, Bernard helps raise funds by going to the ball, and the forbidden possibility, not helping with the fund-raising. Most people do not imagine an alternative to an action that is justified by a good reason, such as an obligation, compared to an action that is not justified, or one that is justified by a weaker reason. They do not tend to say "if only ..." about a decision when there is a good reason for it—for example, a losing streak for a soccer team, or a flight choice based on onward connections (Zeelenberg et al. 2002; Zhang, Bonnefon, and Deng 2004). But one of the strongest reasons for a decision is that it is based on an obligation.

Reasons can seem to cause actions. But there is an important difference between reasons and causes. Most participants tended to imagine an alternative to the action and said "I wish I hadn't gone to the ball" more than they imagined an alternative to the reason, as in "I wish I hadn't had to help with the fund-raising." In a sequence of events that includes a reason for an action, people tend to imagine an alternative to the action (Walsh and Byrne 2004a). But in a sequence of events that includes a cause for an effect, people tend to imagine an alternative to the cause (Kahneman and Miller 1986). Most people imagine the cause had not happened but do not imagine the reason had not happened, even for a reason as strong as an obligation. Why do people think differently about reason-action sequences than about cause-effect sequences? Consider the situation in which Bill is delayed by a series of events, this time a sequence of causally related events, on his way to a sale. Having a flat tire delays him. This delay causes him to get stuck in rush-hour traffic, this delay in turn causes him to be stopped at a crossing when a group of elderly people cross slowly, and this delay causes him to be stopped when he gets a speeding ticket for speeding to make up lost time. As a result of the delays, he arrives too late. When people imagine a counterfactual alternative to such a situation, they tend to change the first cause in the sequence of causes (Wells, Taylor, and Turtle 1987). They do so regardless of the order in which the four events are mentioned. It is as if mentally undoing the first cause prevents the entire sequence from occurring. Once a cause is known to have occurred its effects seem inevitable. But people do not seem to think this way about reasons. Comparisons of cause-effect sequences to reason-action sequences show that people tend to imagine counterfactual alternatives that focus on causes more than their effects, but not on reasons more than their actions (Walsh and Byrne 2004a).

Of course there are many sorts of reasons, and obligations are just one of them. Obligations exercise a very strong external constraint. But there are a great many different sorts of reasons, some good and some bad, including those based on external constraints such as obligations, rules, and orders, and those based on internal matters such as desires and goals (Von Wright 1983). Reasons enable people to distinguish intentional actions from unintentional ones, and they can be brief or enduring (Mele 1992). They can explain an action, but to understand fully why Bernard went to the party, say in the case where he says it was to meet his hero, it is necessary to know whether wanting to meet his hero was a sudden urge or whim, or part of an enduring strategy to advance his career. There is, of course, considerable philosophical debate on the similarities and differences between causes and reasons (Davidson 1963; Anscombe 1963). One important way they differ, according to our results, is that most people can more readily imagine alternatives to causes than to reasons. The next chapter returns to causal relations.

When people understand an obligation they consider two possibilities. They appreciate what is permitted and what is forbidden. A socially unacceptable event is understood by keeping in mind the choice to act, and its forbidden nature is noted. The more acceptable possibility is also kept in mind. When people imagine a counterfactual alternative, they change their mental representation of a forbidden possibility and they say, for example, "if only he had not stopped for a beer." It is easy to imagine a counterfactual alternative to a forbidden possibility. In contrast, it is difficult to imagine a counterfactual alternative to an obligation. People do not tend to change their mental representation of a permitted possibility and say, for instance, "if only he had not had to help with the fund-raising."

Obligations and Domain-Specific Possibilities

When people understand assertions about obligations, they think about one of the permitted possibilities and they also think about the forbidden possibility. There are of course alternative views about how people think about obligation and permission. Some theorists believe that the ease with which people reason about certain permissions or obligations shows that they store knowledge about social regulations in specialized "modules" (Cosmides 1989). The modules contain rules that are specific to reasoning about certain content, such as the domains of obligation and permission (Cheng and Holyoak 1985). On this view, content effects show that different contents (such as permission contents) are stored separately from other contents (such as causal contents), and they are operated on by different specialized procedures (Gigerenzer and Hug 1992; Holyoak and Cheng 1995; Fiddick, Cosmides, and Tooby 2000). Do people understand and reason about obligations and permissions by accessing a module that contains domain-specific knowledge and rules about how to reason with it? The next section addresses this question.

Permission Schemas and Social-Contract Modules
One recent suggestion is that there are domain-specific schemas to deal with obligation and permission that contain stored rules of inference

dedicated to such situations. The inference rules include ones such as 'if the action is to be taken then the precondition must be met," and "if the precondition is met then the action may be taken" (Cheng and Holyoak 1985). People reason well about conditionals that contain permissions and obligations when they are given Wason's selection task. They check accurately a conditional such as "if a person is drinking beer then they must be over nineteen," by seeing whether a person drinking beer is over nineteen and whether a person under nineteen is drinking beer (Griggs and Cox 1983). According to the permission-schema theory, the conditional is matched to a permission schema, activating a domain-specific rule corresponding to "if the action is to be taken then the precondition must be met." This rule guides the correct selections. People do well on the task even when relatively abstract content is given, such as "if the action is to be taken then the precondition must be met," provided the permission schema is activated (Cheng et al. 1986).

However, this view has been called into question by recent empirical evidence. For example, studies have shown that some permission rules do *not* facilitate good performance on the selection task. Consider this conditional: "If someone stays overnight in the cabin, they must bring a bundle of wood." People reason well with it only when additional information is given to encourage them to think of the violating case—that is, someone who stays overnight and does not bring a bundle of wood (Gigerenzer and Hug 1992). An alternative theory is that an innate reasoning module has evolved for violations of social contracts (Cosmides 1989). Social contracts are a subset of permissions and obligations. There are obligations that are not social contracts, but instead are based on health or aesthetics or other matters. According to the social-contract view, conditionals that specify a social contract—for example, "if a man eats cassava root he must have a tattoo on his face"—can guide people to make their choices in Wason's selection task (that is, someone who eats cassava root but does not have a tattoo) (Cosmides 1989). The effect occurs when the context makes clear that people must think about cheaters—that is, reasoners are given the context that all married men have tattoos and only married men may eat the desired but scarce cassava root.

One problem for this view is that facilitation in Wason's selection task occurs for conditionals that are not social contracts, such as precautions (Girotto, Blaye, and Farioli 1989; Manktelow and Over 1990; Cheng and

Holyoak 1989). Even children as young as 9 years are able to reason well about avoiding dangerous risks (Girotto et al. 1989). These data have led social-contract theorists to add an innate module for hazard management (Cosmides and Tooby 1992). Some conditionals concern both social contracts *and* hazard management—for example, "if you go hunting you wear these jackets to avoid being shot." Reasoners readily identify the person in danger as the person who goes hunting without wearing the jacket (Fiddick, Cosmides, and Tooby 2000). The implicit obligation in the rationale "to avoid being shot" clarifies that the situation requires the avoidance of risk. Of course obligations are not confined to social contracts, costs and benefits, or hazard management (Manktelow and Over 1990; Hiraishi and Hasegawa 2001). There are other kinds of obligations such as "if we are to take care of the planet, we must plant more trees," or "if you want spiritual enlightenment, you must meditate." Domain-specific accounts may be too restricted in their scope of explanation.

More damagingly, recent evidence shows that not all social-contract conditionals facilitate appropriate card selections (Liberman and Klar 1996; Love and Kessler 1995), and so it is not the case that a social-contract content is sufficient to help people reason well. In addition to social-contract content, such as, "if someone stays overnight in the cabin they must bring a bundle of wood," it is crucial to provide a "cheater-detection" framework (Gigerenzer and Hug 1992). But asking participants to check for cheaters, rather than to check whether the social contract has been followed, transforms the selection task into an easy categorization task (Sperber and Girotto 2002). The "check-for-cheaters" instruction requires people to indicate which of four cards could be an example of a category (cheater) defined by a combination of positive and negative traits. Most people are readily able to indicate potential instances of a category when they are told or know its defining traits, regardless of whether the category is evolutionarily significant (cheater) or not (hangglider) (Sperber and Girotto 2002).

And "checking for cheaters" is not sufficient in itself to improve selection-task performance either (Liberman and Klar 1996), even though instructions to check for violations can improve performance in some cases (Griggs and Cox 1983; Green and Larking 1995). Perhaps most damagingly to the social-contract view, conditionals that are neither social contracts nor precautions also facilitate good performance on the selection task (Sperber, Cara, and Girotto 1995; Sperber and Girotto 2002, 2003; Girotto et al. 2001; Hiraishi and Hasegawa 2001), and so it is not the case that a social-contract content is even necessary to help people to reason well. For example, people were told that a machine that produces cards according to the conditional "if A then 2" had gone wrong. They checked for cards that contained "A and no 2" to test the status of the conditional when it was uttered after the machine was repaired (which implies that cards containing A and no 2 are not produced any more) (Sperber, Cara, and Girotto 1995). The result shows that "checking for cheaters" is not necessary to improve selection-task performance. Instead it supports the idea that people can keep in mind two possibilities when they understand some conditionals such as obligations—that is, the permitted possibility and the forbidden possibility. In fact, they can even keep in mind these two possibilities when they understand a conditional that is not about an obligation, such as the machine example, when it is provided in a context that draws attention to the false possibility (a card containing an A and no 2), and indicates it should not occur (Sperber, Cara, and Girotto 1995).

Forbidden Possibilities, Permissions, and Social Contracts

The idea of schemas or modules for reasoning implies that there is no general mechanism but only fixed procedures leading from specific inputs to specific outputs. But people do *reason* about permissions and obligations rather than giving fixed responses to them. Their reasoning depends on their ability to think about permitted possibilities and especially about possibilities that are forbidden. The theory accounts for the evidence that has been gathered to support domain-specific views. The studies of Wason's selection task illustrate that what is essential is a clear understanding of what possibilities are forbidden. Consider the conditional "if a man has a tattoo, he may eat cassava root" (if A then B), in the context of a story that indicates that men without a tattoo (not-A) are not permitted to eat cassava root (forbidden: B) (Cosmides 1989). Obligations can have different interpretations, such as the conditional and biconditional interpretations, which ensure that different possibilities are noted as forbidden. The context ensures that in this instance, the conditional is interpreted as consistent with three permitted possibilities, a man with a tattoo eats cassava (A and B), a man with no tattoo does not eat cassava (not-A and not-B), and a man with a tattoo does not eat cassava (A and not-B) (Johnson-Laird and Byrne 2002). The next chapter describes this sort of "enabling" interpretation of a conditional in more detail. The important point to note here is that the one forbidden possibility indicated by the context is someone without a tattoo who eats cassava (not-A and B). As a result, the two possibilities that reasoners envisage initially include one of the permitted possibilities, a man with a tattoo who eats cassava, and the forbidden possibility, a man with no tattoo who eats cassava, noted as forbidden. Because they have kept in mind this forbidden possibility, they select the cards corresponding to "no tattoo" and "cassava" (Cosmides 1989; Fiddick, Cosmides, and Tooby 2000; Gigerenzer and Hug 1992). Importantly, without the context, people do not select these cards (Liberman and Klar 1996; Sperber and Girotto 2002, 2003). The result can be explained by the possibilities people keep in mind.

Contexts that ensure "checking for cheaters" essentially help people think about the forbidden possibilities and grasp their relevance. Most people can reason well about even unfamiliar conditionals such as "if there are xow there must be a force field," once they are given information that helps them think about the forbidden possibility (Liberman and Klar 1996; Sperber and Girotto 2002). The likelihood of instances of the forbidden possibilities is also crucial, as is the significance of their consequences (Love and Kessler 1995). Is there any evidence that any mechanism for any sort of thought has evolved? Human beings evolved, but it is not known which aspects of the brain resulted from selective pressures. Whatever reasoning prowess humans possess may have evolved, or it may be a by-product of something else that evolved. Even supposing that people have evolved to deal well with social regulations, what *processes* have evolved to reason with them? Evidence for content-specific errors may be evidence that certain *content* is connected in the mind, but it is not evidence that content-specific procedures operate on that content. Has a module with social-contract and hazard-management rules evolved, complete with a checking-for-cheaters strategy? Occam's razor suggests that if any sort of thinking did evolve, then what evolved is the ability to think about certain possibilities readily. Perhaps what evolved is the ability to understand obligations by thinking about not only the permitted possibility but also the forbidden possibility. This suggestion is more plausible, not least because it also explains why people keep these two possibilities in mind not only for obligations but also for indicative conditionals placed in contexts that elicit forbidden possibilities.

Summary

How do people imagine what they should have done or should not have done? Most people tend to imagine what should *not* have happened when they imagine a counterfactual alternative. They tend to imagine that events that are socially inappropriate or immoral or forbidden—rather than events that are appropriate or moral—had not happened. An important clue about why they do so comes from the study of reasoning: people understand the obligation "if Jack's parents are elderly he should look after them," by thinking about the permitted possibility, "Jack's parents are elderly and he looks after them," as well as the forbidden possibility, "Jack's parents are elderly and he does not look after them" noted as forbidden. As a result they can make certain inferences readily from conditionals about obligations, such as the inference from "Jack does not look after his parents" to "his parents are not elderly."

The suggestion that people envisage forbidden possibilities when they reason about obligations sheds light on their counterfactual thoughts. When people think about a socially unacceptable event, they envisage the choice to act, and the forbidden nature of the act is noted; they also consider the permitted possibility. Most people imagine a counterfactual alternative by mentally changing the forbidden possibility to be the same as the permitted possibility—for example, they say "if only he had not stopped for a beer." Forbidden possibilities are mutable. Conversely, obligations are immutable. Most people do not tend to imagine a counterfactual alternative by mentally changing a permitted possibility to be the same as the forbidden possibility—for instance, they do not say "if only he had not helped with the fund-raising." Most people tend to imagine a counterfactual alternative to an action less often when the reason for it was an obligation.

Sometimes it can be difficult to do the right thing. Throughout history there are many bleak examples of failures to act, such as when people have not helped others who were being persecuted during wars or genocide. Why do people allow terrible things to happen to others without trying to intervene? People often know what they should do, yet they fail to do it. There are probably many reasons why people fail to act in such situations; one may be that they anticipate they will regret their action. And they may be right. When you act you may draw attention to yourself, and the attention of others may be unwanted, particularly when it is malevolent attention. But it is also the case that people sometimes regret their failures to act. Regret for failure to do the right thing is conveyed starkly in the following quotation attributed to the German antifascist Martin Niemoller (of which there are various versions, this one attributed to *Time* magazine, August 28, 1989): "First they came for the Communists, and I didn't speak up, because I wasn't a Communist. Then they came for the Jews, and I didn't speak up, because I wasn't a Jew. Then they came for the Catholics, and I didn't speak up, because I was a Protestant. Then they came for me, and by that time there was no one left to speak up for me."

5 Causal Relations and Counterfactuals

... through the hole in reason's ceiling we can fly to knowledge.
—Patrick Kavanagh, "To hell with commonsense"

In the immediate aftermath of the September 11, 2001, attacks on the World Trade Center in New York, many media reports focused on the role of airport security in checking that passengers did not carry weapons on board aircraft. The tenor of many reports was that baggage handlers were not adequately monitoring weapons smuggling, and that their failure allowed the attack to occur. There seemed to be an irresistible allure to suggestions of "if only the hijackers had been prevented from getting on board ...". But why was media focus drawn so strongly to this factor? Presumably no sensible observer believed that the baggage handlers *caused* the attack. Nor presumably did anyone believe that even the most stringent security could be guaranteed to prevent a hijacking—after all, some of the September 11 hijackers were reported to have overcome resistance by convincing their victims that they had bombs on board. And other plausible causes could be selected instead: "If only the Al-Qaeda network did not exist ...", or "if only American and Middle East relations were harmonious ...", and many other antecedent events, such as "if only the hijackers had had second thoughts ...", or "if only the hijackers had been overpowered on board ...". But these counterfactual alternatives did not dominate coverage of the attack in the days that followed. The focus on the baggage handlers illustrates a curious feature of counterfactual thoughts: their relation to causal thoughts is not straightforward. My aim in this chapter is to explain why.

The Focus of Counterfactual and Causal Thoughts

One possible reason for the focus on the baggage handlers is that their role is one of the few events in the sequence of events that occurred on September 11 that can be considered fully *controllable*. When people imagine a counterfactual alternative, they tend to focus on what they can control. In the scenario in which Steven arrives home too late to save his wife after being delayed by a series of uncontrollable events and one controllable event, most people focus on the controllable event—that is, his stopping at a bar for a drink (Girotto et al. 1991). They focus in particular on socially unacceptable controllable events (McCloy and Byrne 2000), and perhaps it may be regarded as unacceptable to fail to fulfill the goals of a job, such as failing to prevent weapons from being taken onto an airplane. The behavior of airport baggage handlers may be more controllable (for example, measures can be introduced to improve their standard procedures), and it is also more specific and familiar than, say, the Al Qaeda network, or terrorist fanaticism. Nonetheless the curious phenomenon is that people often imagine a counterfactual alternative to a controllable event, even when the controllable event was not the cause of the outcome. Why do people wish an event had not happened—for example, "if only the baggage handlers had detected the hijackers' weapons ...", even when that event did not cause the outcome?

People are not simply confused when they focus on controllable events in their counterfactual thoughts: they do not mistakenly perceive the controllable event to be the cause of the outcome. A vivid example of the dichotomy between the focus of counterfactual and causal thoughts comes from a study in which participants read about a taxi driver who refused to give a couple a lift and the couple were subsequently killed in an accident in their own car as they drove across a bridge that collapsed (Wells and Gavanski 1989). Most people judge the taxi driver's decision to have had a causal role in the couple's death when they are told that he crossed the bridge safely, and so they are able to say "if only he had given them a lift they would still be alive." But they judge the cause, and the fault more generally, to be the collapsing bridge (N'gbala and Branscombe 1995). Clearly, people distinguish between what is the cause of the outcome and how the outcome could have been different.

Consider, as another example, that you were seriously injured in a car crash that happened on a route you do not usually take home, and that occurred when a careless driver crashed into you. What would you tend to say "if only ..." about most, "if only I'd gone home by my usual route ..." or "if only the other driver had been more careful ..."? Most people say "if only I had driven by my usual route ...," even though they identify the other driver as the cause of the accident (Mandel and Lehman 1996). In fact, this tendency has been verified in naturalistic studies of individuals who have sustained severe injuries, such as paralysis, as a result of a traumatic accident. They tend spontaneously to imagine counterfactual alternatives that depend on how they could have prevented their accident, without believing that they caused it (Davis et al. 1996). The evidence indicates that people imagine counterfactual alternatives to events within their control, even though they know these events were not the cause of the outcome.

The differences in the focus of counterfactual and causal thoughts can be explained by the possibilities people think about. The explanation advanced in this chapter has two main components. First, people mentally represent a causal claim and a counterfactual one by thinking about different possibilities. A causal claim can be readily paraphrased as a counterfactual conditional—for example, "Heating the water to 100 degrees centigrade caused it to boil" can be paraphrased by "if the water had not been heated to 100 degrees centigrade it would not have boiled." Many philosophers have supposed that to think counterfactually is to think causally (Hume [1739] 2000; Mill [1872] 1956). The causal assertion and the counterfactual differ in their syntactic form, but their meaning is the same. The strong causal relation is consistent with the possibility, "water was heated to 100 degrees and it boiled," and the possibility, "water was not heated to 100 degrees and it did not boil." The counterfactual is consistent with the same two possibilities. However, as we will see, people mentally represent a causal relation and a counterfactual conditional in different ways. For example, they keep in mind just a single possibility when they understand the strong causal relation. But they keep in mind both possibilities when they understand the counterfactual, one corresponding to the conjecture and the other to the presupposed facts (at least for counterfactuals about known events). As a result the counterfactual makes more information readily available to them from the outset than does the causal assertion.

Second, there are different sorts of causes, and people think about different possibilities when they understand them. A strong causal relation, such as the one about water boiling, is consistent with two possibilities and people initially think about just one of them. An enabling relation, such as "dry leaves made it possible for the forest fire to spread," is consistent with three possibilities: "dry leaves and the forest fire," "no dry leaves and no forest fire," and "dry leaves and no forest fire." People mentally represent the enabling relation by initially thinking about the possibility "dry leaves and the forest fire," and as we will see, they can readily access a second possibility, "no dry leaves and no forest fire." This second possibility provides a ready-made counterfactual alternative. They can imagine the situation turning out differently if the enabler had not occurred. They think about the strong causal relation by thinking about a single possibility and so it does not provide a ready-made counterfactual alternative. As a result people often focus on enabling relations more than on strong causal relations in their counterfactual thoughts.

The aim of this chapter is to show that the difference in the focus of counterfactual and causal thoughts arises because people think about different possibilities when they understand strong causal relations and enabling relations. In the rest of this section we consider the reciprocal relation between counterfactual and causal thoughts. In the next section we consider evidence that there are different sorts of causal relations—for example, strong causal relations and enabling relations. These different causal relations are consistent with different possibilities, people think about different possibilities when they understand them, and they make different inferences from them. The final section shows that people imagine counterfactual alternatives that mentally alter enabling relations more than other sorts of causal relations because enabling relations are mentally represented with a ready-made counterfactual alternative.

The Causal Chicken and the Counterfactual Egg

Causal thoughts can influence the counterfactual alternatives people imagine. Causal knowledge affects judgments about how plausible a counterfactual speculation is. Most people readily judge some counterfactuals to be more plausible than others (Miyamoto and Dibble 1986). They judge a counterfactual to be plausible or implausible depending on whether it fits their view of general causal laws (Tetlock and Lebow 2001). When experts in military and political history think about counterfactuals, such as "if Kennedy had listened to his hawkish advisers the Cuban missile crisis would have become nuclear," the more committed the expert is to the view that nuclear deterrence works, the more dismissive they are of counterfactuals that go against it. Experts committed to a causal law perceive less "wiggle room for rewriting history" (Tetlock and Lebow 2001, 838). The causal relation between the event and the outcome can also affect the subjective impression that some counterfactual alternatives are close to reality, and these "close-call" counterfactuals can seem to have "almost" happened (Kahneman and Varey 1990; McMullen and Markman 2002).

Causal thoughts can influence how people imagine counterfactual alternatives. And the relation is reciprocal: people sometimes imagine counterfactual alternatives to help them to work out causal relations. There are many situations in which our only clue to causality comes from imagined counterfactuals (Tetlock and Lebow 2001). Consider, for example, what caused the rise of the West. If Islamic armies had conquered France and Italy in the eighth century, would later European development have been sidetracked? Such counterfactual thoughts are an essential ingredient in historical reasoning, even if they are considered controversial (Tetlock and Lebow 2001). Working out the causes of complex multidetermined events is difficult for most people (Kuhn 1991; Brem and Rips 2000; Rips 2003). It may hinge on imagined counterfactual alternatives about how things might have been different or might have been the same.

The counterfactual thought that if an antecedent had not happened then the outcome would not have happened increases the judgment that the antecedent caused the outcome (Wells and Gavanski 1989). In the taxi-driver scenario, most people judge the driver's decision not to give the couple a lift to have had a causal role in the couple's death when they are told that the taxi driver crossed the bridge safely. They judge his decision to be less causally important when they are told that he was also killed as he drove across the collapsing bridge, and so they cannot say, "if only he had given them a lift they would still be alive" (Wells and Gavanski 1989).

Counterfactual conditionals can be about many different sorts of topics, such as people's actions or reasons and obligations. But they are often about causes. Counterfactual thoughts are so similar to causal thoughts that subjunctive conditionals about causal relations are understood as counterfactual more readily than subjunctive conditionals about other sorts of content. Valerie Thompson and I have shown this to be the case (Thompson and Byrne 2002). In one experiment we gave 151 participants counterfactuals with true causal content, such as "if the water had been heated to 100 degrees centigrade then it would have boiled," and counterfactuals with true noncausal content, including definitions such as "if the animal had been warm blooded then it would have been a mammal." Half of the conditionals were in the indicative mood and the other half were in the subjunctive mood. Suppose you were asked the following question: "John says that: If the car was out of petrol then it stalled. What, if anything, do you think that John meant to imply?" You can choose as many options as you think are appropriate from the following set: "(a) the car was out of petrol, (b) the car was not out of petrol, (c) the car stalled, (d) the car did not stall, and (e) nothing was implied." Which options would you choose? The logically accurate response is (e), nothing is implied: the indicative conditional does not imply that either of its components are true or false, only that there is a relation between them.

Suppose now you were asked, "John says that: If the car had been out of petrol then it would have stalled. What, if anything, do you think that John meant to imply?" We found that for subjunctive conditionals most participants tended to judge that John meant to imply (c) the car was not out of petrol, and/or (d) it did not stall. This judgment verifies that they have understood the subjunctive conditional by keeping in mind the presupposed facts, the car was not out of petrol and it did not stall (see Thompson and Byrne 2002 for details). They have come to a counterfactual interpretation of the subjunctive conditional.

Most interestingly, they reached the counterfactual interpretation reliably more often for subjunctive conditionals about causes than ones about definitions:

Causal subjunctive, 76 percent; definitional subjunctive, 59 percent

The result shows that most people judge a causal subjunctive to imply the negative possibility, more than a definitional subjunctive. For the definitional subjunctive most people (59 percent) keep in mind the two possibilities, "the animal was warm blooded and it was a mammal," and "the animal was not warm blooded and it was not a mammal," but some people (41 percent) do not think about the negative possibility. Chapter 8 returns to differences between individuals in the possibilities they think about for a subjunctive conditional. The important point to note here is that for the causal subjunctive most people (76 percent) keep in mind the two possibilities, "the car was out of petrol and it stalled," and "the car was not out of petrol and it did not stall," and fewer people (24 percent) do not think about the negative possibility.

Of course, people came to a counterfactual interpretation more often for subjunctive than for indicative conditionals, for conditionals that had a causal content and those that had a definitional content:

Causal subjunctive, 76 percent; indicative, 13 percent
Definitional subjunctive, 59 percent; indicative, 6 percent

Once they have come to these interpretations, they think about causal and definitional counterfactuals in a very similar manner. For example, they make the modus tollens inference from "the car did not stall" to "it was not out of petrol" and the denial of the antecedent inference, from "the car was not out of petrol" to "therefore it did not stall," more often from the counterfactual conditional than a factual conditional, for both causal and definitional conditionals (Thompson and Byrne 2002).

People reason by thinking about possibilities. As we have seen in the previous chapters, they think about true possibilities and not false possibilities, and they tend to think initially about few possibilities (see table 5.1 for a summary). Counterfactual conditionals are thought about more fully than factual conditionals. People mentally represent counterfactuals by thinking about two possibilities, and they keep track of the status of the possibilities as imagined, or the facts. People can readily create a counterfactual alternative to a possibility if it is mentally represented with a second possibility. For example, people mentally represent actions by thinking about two possibilities, the preaction possibility and the postaction possibility. They can readily imagine a counterfactual alternative to the action by mentally changing the current facts to be like the preaction possibility. When people understand an obligation, they think about the permitted possibility and the forbidden possibility, noted as *forbidden*. When they imagine a counterfactual alternative, they mentally change the forbidden possibility to be like the permitted possibility. And when people understand causal relations

Table 5.1
Summary of principles thus far

---

1. True possibilities: *People keep in mind true possibilities.*

2. Few possibilities: *People keep in mind few possibilities.*

3. Dual possibilities: *Some ideas require people to think about two possibilities.*

4. Counterfactual possibilities: *People think about possibilities that once may have been true possibilities but can be true no longer.*

5. Mutability of dual possibilities: *People readily imagine a counterfactual alternative to a possibility if it is mentally represented with a second possibility.*

6. Forbidden possibilities: *People think about the forbidden possibility as well as the permitted possibility when they understand an obligation.*

I. Actions: *People think about two possibilities when they understand an action.*

II. Single possibilities: *People can switch from thinking about one possibility to thinking about two possibilities e.g., for inactions.*

III. Controllable events: *People think about two possibilities when they understand controllable events.*

IV. Causes: People think about a single possibility when they understand a strong causal relation (*cause and outcome*). They can readily access a second possibility for an enabling condition (*enabler and outcome, no enabler and no outcome*).

---

they think about possibilities. But if counterfactual and causal thoughts are so clearly linked, why do people sometimes focus on one aspect of an event as the cause of an outcome, and a different aspect of it to mentally undo in their counterfactual thoughts? An important clue comes from research that shows that people readily distinguish between different sorts of causal relations.

Clues from Reasoning: Strong Causal and Enabling Relations

Although causal and counterfactual thoughts appear to be two sides of one coin, people often focus on one event to identify as the cause and a different event to imagine differently. The effect may arise because causal and counterfactual thoughts relate to different sorts of causal relations. There are several different types of causal relations, and a crucial distinction is between a strong causal relation and an enabling relation (Miller and Johnson-Laird 1976). This section considers evidence that there are different sorts of causal relations. The different causal relations are consistent with different possibilities, people mentally represent them by thinking about different possibilities, and they make different inferences from them.

Counterfactual Thoughts and Enabling Relations

Counterfactual thoughts can help people to work out causal relations, but the causal relations are of a special sort. Counterfactual thoughts often focus on *enabling* conditions (for example, "if only I had taken a different route home I would not have had the crash"), whereas causal thoughts often focus on strong causes (for instance, "the drunk driver caused the crash"). The reason that counterfactual and causal thoughts focus on different sorts of causal relations is that people think about different sorts of possibilities when they mentally represent a strong causal relation or an enabling relation.

Suppose lightning hits a forest and a devastating forest fire breaks out. The forest was dry after a long hot summer and many acres were destroyed. Suppose you wish the fire had not happened and you imagine how things might have been different. Perhaps you might say "if only there had not been that lightning ...". Or you might say "if only there had not been so many dry leaves on the forest floor ...". Of course, you probably would not think the dry leaves *caused* the forest fire. People can distinguish a causal relation, such as "lightning caused the forest fire," from an enabling relation, such as "dry leaves made it possible for the fire to occur." In fact, they distinguish these causal relations from many other irrelevant factors, too—for example, "there were stones on the forest floor." Enablers are sometimes called "allowing" relations (Goldvarg and Johnson-Laird 2001). When they are absent the effect does not occur despite the presence of the cause—for instance, when there are no dry leaves there is no fire even though there is lightning (Byrne 1989b). A missing enabler, no dry leaves, can prevent the fire, as can a disabler, wet leaves (Goldvarg and Johnson-Laird 2001; Cummins 1995; Dieussaert et al. 2000).

A distinction between two sorts of causal relations can be illustrated with reference to the standard contingency table for causal relations (see table 5.2). Perhaps the simplest and most common sort of causal relation people think about is a *strong* causal relation. Suppose you believe that "the lightning caused the forest fire" and you do not know about any other causal or enabling relations. The lightning is a strong cause, consistent with two possibilities: "the lightning happened and the fire happened" (cause and outcome), and "the lightning did not happen and the fire did not happen" (no cause and no outcome) (cells I and IV in table 5.2). (We can note in passing that the possibilities consistent with the strong causal relation are the same

Table 5.2
Presence and absence of causes and outcomes

	Outcome present	Outcome absent
Cause present	I	II
Cause absent	III	IV

Note: The individual cells of the contingency table are often referred to as A–D, but I use I–IV to avoid confusion with their description in the text.

as the biconditional interpretation.) Your causal assertion can be paraphrased as "if there had been no lightning the forest fire would not have happened."

Now suppose you also know about an enabling relation, such as the dryness of the leaves on the forest floor. You believe that "the dry leaves made it possible for the forest fire to happen." The enabler is consistent with three possibilities: "dry leaves and the forest fire" (enabler and outcome), "no dry leaves and no forest fire" (no enabler and no outcome), and "dry leaves and no forest fire," perhaps because there was no lightning (enabler and no outcome). The relation is consistent not only with cells I and IV, but also cell II in table 5.2. The single case that goes against an enabling cause is when the enabler does not occur and the outcome does—that is, there were no dry leaves and the forest fire occurred (no enabler and outcome) (cell III). Your causal assertion can be paraphrased as "if there had been no dry leaves the forest fire would not have happened." Counterfactual thoughts often focus on these enabling relations.

Of course, there are other sorts of causal relations, too, and the next chapter describes weak causal relations. When there are many causes available, the role of any one cause may be discounted (Kelley 1972). However, the mere presence of alternatives or disablers does not reduce reasoners' judgment of the causal strength of the relationship between a candidate cause and an outcome (Cummins 1995).

The Possibilities for Enabling Relations

Why do counterfactual thoughts, such as "if I had driven home by a different route I would not have been in the crash," and causal thoughts, such as "the drunk driver caused the crash," focus on different events? The difference is explained by the observation that counterfactual thoughts focus

Table 5.3
Different possibilities consistent with two different sorts of causes

Cause (strongly) causes outcome	
Cause and outcome	Biconditional, e.g., lightning*
Not-cause and not-outcome	Factor sufficient and necessary for outcome
Enabler enables outcome	
Enabler and outcome	Enabler, e.g., dry leaves
Not-enabler and not-outcome	Factor necessary but not sufficient for outcome
Enabler and not-outcome	

*When no other factors are considered.
Note: The full set of possibilities consistent with the causal relation is given.

on one sort of causal relation, enabling relations, whereas causal thoughts focus on another sort, strong causal relations (and in some cases, weak causes). The difference in the focus of people's causal and counterfactual thoughts arises because they think about different possibilities when they mentally represent enabling relations and strong causal relations (see table 5.3).

When people think about a strong causal relation—for example, "heating the butter caused it to melt"—they envisage initially just one possibility in which the strong cause and its outcome occurred (Goldvarg and Johnson-Laird 2001). A strong causal relation is consistent with two possibilities: "butter was heated and it melted," and "butter was not heated and it did not melt." But when people understand it they think initially about just a single possibility, "butter was heated and it melted" (cause and outcome). The meaning of the strong causal relation is consistent with two possibilities, but people mentally represent it initially by thinking about just a single possibility.

People can distinguish strong causal relations from other sorts of causal relations, and they do so by thinking about different possibilities. An enabling relation, such as "dry leaves caused the forest fire," is consistent with three possibilities: "dry leaves and the forest fire," "no dry leaves and no forest fire," and "dry leaves and no forest fire." When people understand the enabler they think initially about the possibility "dry leaves and the forest fire" (enabler and outcome), but they are able to think readily about a second possibility, "no dry leaves and no forest fire" (not-enabler and not-outcome). The second possibility emphasizes the *necessity* of the enabling condition, dry leaves are necessary for the forest fire to occur. The meaning of the enabler refers to three possibilities, but people mentally represent it initially by thinking about fewer possibilities.

These distinctions are captured in the following corollary for the different sorts of causes:

Corollary 4 for thoughts about causal relations: *People think about a single possibility when they understand a strong causal relation.* For example, they think about a strong causal relation by keeping in mind a single possibility, cause and outcome.

They are able to think readily about a second possibility when they understand an enabling relation. For example, they think about an enabling relation by keeping in mind the possibility *enabler and outcome,* and they can also think readily about the possibility *not-enabler and not-outcome.*

People understand a strong causal relation, "vitamin C deficiency causes scurvy," by thinking about a single possibility when they understand it, "vitamin C deficiency and scurvy" (Goldvarg and Johnson-Laird 2001). As a result, a strong causal relation can seem immutable. It may be difficult to imagine how the outcome could have been different *even though* the cause still occurred—for example, how scurvy might not have occurred even though there was a vitamin C deficiency. To imagine how a cause could have happened and the outcome did not, it may be easier to focus on an enabler instead. For instance, people can readily say, "if only there had been no dry leaves the forest fire would not have happened," or "if only I had not taken that route I would not have been in the crash." The outcome is undone despite the continued presence of other causes. Their thought is in essence that if there had been no dry leaves then *even if there had been lightning* there would have been no forest fire. People imagine alternatives to an enabling relation because they have mentally represented a second possibility in which the enabler does not occur and the outcome does not occur.

Evidence that most people keep in mind different possibilities for a strong causal relation and an enabling relation comes from studies of the inferences people make from conditionals about causal and enabling relations. The rest of this section examines these inferential studies and considers how people identify causal and enabling relations, and the next section considers evidence that people imagine counterfactual alternatives by thinking about enabling relations.

Different Interpretations Lead to Different Inferences

Suppose you are on another planet and an alien tells you "planet dust causes the larvae to grow." In the absence of any other information you might interpret this assertion to express a strong causal relation, consistent with two possibilities, "there is planet dust and the larvae grow" (cause and outcome), and "there is no planet dust and the larvae do not grow" (no cause and no outcome). Given the conditional "if there is planet dust, the larvae grow," you can make all four inferences. From the information "there was planet dust," you can make the modus ponens inference to "the larvae grew." Given the information "the larvae did not grow" you can make the modus tollens inference to "there was no planet dust," provided you think about the second possibility. Likewise, you can make the affirmation of the consequent inference from "the larvae grew" to "there was planet dust" and the denial of the antecedent inference from "there was no planet dust" to "the larvae did not grow" (see table 5.4). In the circumstances, coming to an interpretation that the cause is necessary and sufficient for the outcome is reasonable: you do not know any other information about how larvae grow on that planet. And in the circumstances, your interpretation supports all four inferences.

An enabling relation is consistent with different possibilities and so you can make just two of the inferences from it. Suppose your alien guide says

Table 5.4
The effects of different interpretations of a conditional on inferences (based on Byrne, Espino, and Santamaría 1999)

Interpretation	Inferences people make
Strong causal relation (biconditional)	
Planet dust and larvae grow	$A \therefore B$, $B \therefore A$
No planet dust and larvae do not grow	no $B \therefore$ no A, no $A \therefore$ no B
Enabling relation	
Planet dust (and still air) and larvae grow	$B \therefore A$
No planet dust and larvae do not grow	no $A \therefore$ no B
Planet dust (but no still air) and larvae do not grow	blocks $A \therefore B$ and no $B \therefore$ no A

"if there is planet dust, the larvae grow" but also adds "if there is still air the larvae grow" and explains that the still air allows the planet dust to settle on the larvae cocoons, whereas winds blow the planet dust out toward the seas. You may modify your interpretation of planet dust as a strong cause to an enabler: there are now additional conditions that you know about. The assertion is consistent with three possibilities, "there is planet dust and the larvae grow" (enabler and outcome), "there is no planet dust and the larvae do not grow" (no enabler and no outcome), and "there is planet dust and the larvae do not grow" (enabler and no outcome). In these circumstances, planet dust is necessary but not sufficient for the outcome. When you know "the larvae grew" you can make the affirmation of the consequent inference that "there was planet dust," and when you know "there was no planet dust" you can make the denial of the antecedent inference that "the larvae did not grow" provided you have thought about the second possibility. But you will resist the modus ponens inference: when you hear that there is planet dust, you do not know whether there is still air or winds, and so you do not know whether the larvae grow. The possibility that there was planet dust but there was no still air and so the larvae did not grow provides a counterexample (Byrne, Espino, and Santamaría 1999). Likewise when you hear that the larvae did not grow, you do not know whether there was no planet dust or whether there was but there was no still air, and so the modus tollens inference is blocked.

The information about still air suppresses the two inferences (Byrne 1989b). Still air is an additional condition and additional conditions are jointly necessary for the outcome (Byrne and Johnson-Laird 1992; Fairley, Manktelow, and Over 1999; see also Rumain, Connell, and Braine 1983; Staudenmayer 1975). The inferences can also be suppressed implicitly, by requiring people to generate additional background conditions in domains for which they have some knowledge (Cummins et al. 1991; see also Chan and Chua 1994; Fillenbaum 1993; Stevenson and Over 1995, 2001). The more additional conditions they can think of, the greater the suppression (Elio 1997; Vadeboncoeur and Markovits 1999; De Neys, Schaeken, and d'Ydewalle 2003; see also Thompson 1994; Markovits and Potvin 2001). Suppression occurs regardless of the order of the antecedents (Byrne, Espino, and Santamaría 1999; Dieussaert et al. 2000). Most people resist the inferences when they know about enabling conditions (see also Bonnefon and Hilton 2002, 2004; George 1999; Oaksford and Chater 1995; O'Brien 1993).

People come to these different interpretations of a conditional readily, and they make different inferences from them as a result, as Orlando Espino, Carlos Santamaría, and I have shown (Byrne, Espino, and Santamaría 1999). In one experiment we gave 135 participants arguments based on a variety of conditionals. Suppose you were given the following information: "if Rosa meets her friend then she goes to the cinema. Rosa meets her friend." Does it follow that (a) Rosa goes to the cinema, (b) Rosa does not go to the cinema, or (c) Rosa may or may not go to the cinema? Suppose instead you were given the following information: "if Rosa meets her friend then she goes to the cinema. If she has enough money then she goes to the cinema. Rosa meets her friend." What follows from these premises? Most participants who were given the single conditional chose (a), whereas most participants who were given the pair of conditionals containing an enabler chose (c). They made fewer modus ponens (A therefore B) and modus tollens (not-B therefore not-A) inferences given the pair of conditionals that contained an enabler, than the group who were given the single conditional:

Single conditional: modus ponens (A therefore B), 91 percent
                           modus tollens (not-B therefore not-A), 82
                           percent
Conditional and enabler: modus ponens (A therefore B), 41 percent
                           modus tollens (not-B therefore not-A), 40
                           percent

Even when we phrased the main conditional as a strong biconditional with an antecedent that was necessary and sufficient for the consequent, the inferences were suppressed. Suppose you were given the following information: "if and only if Rosa meets her friend then she goes to the cinema. If she has enough money then she goes to the cinema. Rosa meets her friend." What if anything follows? The third group made fewer inferences given the biconditional and an enabler than the group who were given the single conditional:

Biconditional and enabler: modus ponens (A therefore B), 43 percent
                           modus tollens (not-B therefore not-A), 46
                           percent

Their inferences show that people appreciate that for an enabling relation, it is possible for the antecedent to occur and the outcome not to occur.

Before considering how people imagine counterfactual alternatives based on their understanding of strong causal relations and enabling relations, it is worth considering how they identify whether an event is a cause or an enabler in the first place. The answer is the final piece of the puzzle that helps to explain why counterfactual and causal thoughts focus on different events.

How Do People Distinguish Causal and Enabling Relations?

People think about the different possibilities that are consistent with an event to help them distinguish causal and enabling relations (Goldvarg and Johnson-Laird 2001). Evidence that people keep in mind possibilities when they think about the causes of outcomes comes from studies that have examined causal relations of different sorts. For example, although an enabling relation is consistent with three possibilities, people mentally represent it by thinking about the possibility that the enabler occurs and the outcome occurs, and they are able to generate the second possibility readily, that the enabler does not occur and the outcome does not occur. The one possibility that goes against an enabling relation is the possibility that the enabler does not occur and the outcome occurs anyway (cell III of table 5.2). In fact, when it is a possibility that the enabler does not occur and the outcome occurs, people do not tend to say "if only the enabler had not occurred ..." (N'gbala and Branscombe 1995). When people are asked explanatory questions about what caused the outcome, they focus on information about the case in which the cause occurred and the outcome did not (McGill and Klein 1993). But when they are asked evaluative questions, such as whether something about the candidate caused the outcome, they focus on information not only about the case in which the cause occurred and the outcome did not, but also about the case in which the cause did not occur and the outcome did (cells II and III) (McGill and Klein 1993; see also Hilton 1990). Of course, in the absence of counterfactual information, people may rely on "proxies" such as covariation information or information about alternative explanations (Lipe 1991; see also Green 2001; Schustack 1988; Schustack and Sternberg 1981; White 2002).

There are several other views about how people distinguish strong causal relations from enabling relations, as table 5.5 shows. The problem is that a

Table 5.5
Some proposed ways to identify a causal relation as opposed to an enabling relation

Different possibilities brought to mind	Goldvarg and Johnson-Laird 2001
Normal vs. abnormal default	Kahneman and Miller 1986
Normal vs. abnormal obligation	Mackie 1974
Liklihood of covariation, constancy	Cheng and Novick 1991
Unknown condition vs. known	Hilton 1990

causal relation cannot be observed: events covary but whether one event caused the other must be inferred. One idea sometimes traced to Hume is that people identify the causes of outcomes by observing covariation or "constant conjunction," the presence or absence of the candidate cause and effect, as well as temporal and spatial relations. The problem with this idea is that covariation does not always imply causation (Cheng 1997). Another idea sometimes traced to Kant is that people identify causes by understanding the causal mechanism by which the candidate cause generates the effect. The problem with this idea is that it is unclear how the causal power of a candidate is detected (Cheng 1997). How then can people identify causes of outcomes?

One view is that people identify a causal relation by relying on the normality of the events. Abnormal events, such as lightning, are causes whereas normal events, such as dry leaves, are enablers (Kahneman and Miller 1986; Mackie 1974). Normality may be conceived in the statistical sense of what usually happens—that is, a default (Kahneman and Miller 1986; see also Hilton and Slugowski 1986) or a deontic sense of what ought to happen (Mackie 1974). However, people identify a factor as a cause provided it covaries with the effect—for example, nutrients caused the corn to grow, regardless of whether the factor is normal (nutrients are present in most of the farmer's fields) or abnormal (nutrients are present in few of the farmer's fields) (Cheng and Novick 1991; see also Cheng 1997). Hence normality does not seem to be the key.

People may rely on conversational conventions, and a cause is a condition assumed to be unknown to the hearer (they did not know about the lightning) whereas an enabler is one they already know about (they knew there were dry leaves in the forest). The conversational convention can be based on the maxim to be as informative as possible (Grice 1975), or that the information is relevant in that it allows new information to be inferred or old information to be strengthened or abandoned (Sperber and Wilson 1986). In fact, when people communicate their view of what caused an effect, they calibrate their answers to the knowledge they assume their hearer has—for example, they attribute their plants growing well to them being watered and being in sunlight more often when they must explain their growth to an alien then to their mother (Cheng and Novick 1991).

A third possibility is that normality may be conceived in the sense of what is constant and inconstant (Cheng and Novick 1991). People may rely on the likelihood that the factor (lightning) covaries with the effect (fire), within a relevant set of events (forest fires)—that is, the probability of the effect given the cause (cell I information in table 5.2) is greater than the probability of the effect given the absence of the cause (cell III information) (Cheng and Novick 1991). However, people identify a factor as a cause provided it covaries with the effect, even when a cause such as nutrients and an enabler such as sunlight are both described as inconstant (Goldvarg and Johnson-Laird 2001). Hence constancy does not seem to be the key either.

Philosophers have long suggested that the concept of causation depends on a contrast between reality and its alternatives. When people observe that one thing happens and another thing happens, the inference that one caused the other is not warranted. But the contrast between what was observed and what might have been observed enables people to infer causality (Mackie 1974; Mill [1872] 1956). Moreover, when people try to identify the causes of other people's behavior—such as that Paul gets embarrassed answering his cell phone in the theater—they attribute it to various causes. They attribute it to something about Paul (he gets embarrassed easily), something about his cell phone (its ring tone is loud and intrusive), or something about the theater (it is forbidden to have cell phones switched on). They must take into account various types of information—for example, consensus (whether other people get embarrassed answering their cell phone in a theater), distinctiveness (whether Paul gets embarrassed in theaters when called on to do other sorts of things, such as chatting with a friend), and consistency (whether Paul gets embarrassed answering his phone in other situations and places, such as restaurants) (Kelley 1972).

The "fundamental attribution error" is to attribute other people's behavior to their personality, actions, state of mind, and so on (Paul gets embarrassed when his phone rings because he is an easily embarrassed sort of person), but to attribute your own behavior to the circumstances (you got embarrassed because you thought you had turned your phone off before the play started). The error may arise because of the counterfactual alternatives available (Lipe 1991). You can think of more counterfactual alternatives for your own behavior than for Paul's. Counterfactual thoughts about what might have been may be one part of a more complex causal judgment process, or even a shortcut heuristic for assigning causality (Kahneman and Tversky 1982; Wells and Gavanski 1989). The relation between enabling relations and prevention is considered next, before a consideration of the imagination of counterfactual alternatives to enabling relations.

Enabling Relations and Prevention

People imagine a counterfactual alternative to an outcome such as a forest fire by mentally undoing enabling conditions such as dry leaves, and they say, for example, "if only there had not been dry leaves." The imagination of missing enablers ensures that counterfactual alternatives often focus on prevention (Mandel and Lehman 1996; see also Mandel and Lehman 1998).

The enabling condition, "dry leaves allowed the forest fire to start" (if there had not been dry leaves, the forest fire would not have started), is consistent with three possibilities, as we have seen, and its one false possibility is "no dry leaves and fire." A disabling factor can be a missing enabling cause—for example, "the absence of dry leaves disables fire." The disabling relation can be expressed with explicit negation (no dry leaves) or implicit negation (wet leaves), as in "wet leaves disable fire." The disabling relation can be expressed as prevention—for instance, "wet leaves prevent fire." Disablers or preventers are understood in the same way as missing enablers.

At least two kinds of bad outcomes have been identified (Roese, Hur, and Pennington 1999). Prevention failures result in the occurrence of a bad outcome, such as a forest fire or a car crash. People can imagine a counterfactual alternative in which the bad outcome, the forest fire, was prevented, by mentally deleting the enabler, dry leaves. Promotion failures result in the absence of a good outcome, such as a healthy green forest, or a good examination result. People can imagine a counterfactual alternative in which the good outcome, the healthy forest, was promoted, for example, by mentally adding a disabler, wet leaves. Counterfactual thoughts focus not only on prevention but also on promotion (Roese, Hur, and Pennington 1999), and enablers and disablers can provide counterfactual alternatives in each case. Of course, just as there are several different sorts of causal relations based on strong causal relations, weak causal relations, and enabling relations, so too are there several different sorts of prevention, based on strong prevention, weak prevention, and hindering conditions.

Strong causal relations and enabling relations are consistent with different possibilities, and people distinguish between them by keeping in mind different possibilities. The different possibilities influence the inferences people make from conditionals about strong causal relations and enabling relations, and the different possibilies also influence their imagination of how an outcome could have turned out differently.

The Rational Imagination: Why Counterfactual and Causal Thoughts Differ

It is a puzzle that people imagine how an outcome could have turned out differently "if only ..." by mentally undoing a factor, such as their choice of route home, even though they identify that the key cause of the outcome was something else, such as a careless driver swerving into their path. Why do people not imagine a counterfactual alternative in which the careless driver did not swerve into their path, and say "if only there had not been a careless driver on the road ..." or "if only the careless driver had not swerved into my path ..."? Experiments have shown that people tend to identify the cause of the event as the careless driver, but they think counterfactually about other antecedents, "if only I had driven home by a different route ..." (Mandel and Lehman 1996; N'gbala and Branscombe 1995). And naturalistic studies with people injured in accidents shows the same phenomenon: people identify the cause of their accident accurately (for example, another driver), but they imagine a counterfactual alternative in which their own actions could have prevented the accident (Davis et al. 1995).

The clue from reasoning about causes that helps solve the puzzle is the crucial distinction between a strong causal relation and an enabling relation. People mentally represent the strong causal relation by thinking initially about just one possibility, the co-occurrence of the cause and its outcome, whereas they mentally represent the enabling relation by thinking about the enabler and its outcome, and they can readily think about the absence of both. Accordingly most people focus on enablers (and disablers) in their thoughts about what might have been because the second possibility provides a ready-made counterfactual alternative.

Causes can seem immutable because people keep in mind just a single possibility. Enablers seem mutable because people can readily think about two possibilities. Moreover, the additional possibility that people envisage—for example, no dry leaves and no fire—effectively undoes the outcome. Counterfactual thinking is goal directed to focus on possibilities that undo the outcome (see Byrne 1997; Seeleu et al. 1995). Causes occur—lightning strikes, careless drivers swerve, and terrorists formulate campaigns of destruction—and wishing the cause did not occur may be a remote and implausible hope. But enablers can be mentally deleted in an imagined alternative: dry leaves removed, alternative routes home taken, airport security improved. Wishing that whatever could have been done had been done to prevent the outcome or promote a better one may be a plausible alternative.

When people create a counterfactual thought about how an outcome could have turned out differently by mentally undoing an enabling condition, and saying, for example, "if only there had been no dry leaves the forest fire would not have happened," they do not consider that the dry leaves caused the forest fire in any strong sense. They appreciate that the lightning caused the forest fire. Causal knowledge allows not only prediction but also control, and since there are many enablers for any outcome, people can focus on enablers that fall within their control. Of course, people can create counterfactual alternatives that focus on other sorts of causes, but often they will think about how an outcome could have been different if one of the events that enabled it to happen had not occurred.

People Generate More Causal Than Counterfactual Thoughts

It is easier to think about one possibility than about several possibilities. The theory predicts that people should produce more causal thoughts than counterfactual thoughts, because they mentally represent a strong causal relation by thinking about a single possibility, and they mentally represent a counterfactual by thinking about two possibilities. Alice

McEleney and I tested this prediction. We found that most people tend to think spontaneously more often about why a situation turned out the way it did, than about how it might have turned out differently (McEleney and Byrne 2000).

In one experiment we compared spontaneous causal and counterfactual thoughts by giving 248 students a story to read about "moving to a new town to start a new job." The story began, "the night before you leave, you write down your thoughts about the move in your diary.... I've got mixed feelings about moving.... My friends and social life are so important to me ...". The participants were then told about the events that happened during the first six weeks after moving: they were invited to a staff dinner, they decided whether to go a neighbor's party or the cinema, they were shown around the town by an old friend, and they decided whether to join a sports club or buy a new stereo. They were then told that six weeks after the move "things have turned out nothing like you had expected.... You haven't made any real friends.... You are very upset and very surprised." Their task was simple: they were asked to jot down "what you might write in your diary about your current situation and the events leading up to it." They were *not* told that thinking about what might have been, or about what caused outcomes, was the subject of the experiment. Causal and counterfactual thoughts were never mentioned to them at all. The study aimed to examine *spontaneous* counterfactual and causal thoughts.

Most people generated many causal thoughts in their diary entries—for example, "I haven't made friends because I didn't go to that party." The causal thought focuses on the facts, no friends made and no party. Most people also generated many counterfactual thoughts in their diary entries, such as "if only I had gone to that party I would have made friends." The counterfactual thought refers to an alternative possibility, one in which there are friends and a party attended. And in line with the prediction, most people generated more causal thoughts than counterfactual thoughts. The 248 participants generated 599 thoughts that were either causal or counterfactual thoughts. They jotted down more than twice as many causal thoughts as counterfactual thoughts:

Causal thoughts, 67 percent
Counterfactual thoughts, 33 percent

The participants jotted down on average 1.62 causal thoughts per person, and on average 0.79 counterfactual thoughts per person. The result shows that people think more often about causes than imagined alternatives. It provides some initial support for the view that people think about a single possibility for causes, whereas they think about two possibilities for counterfactual alternatives.

This view is also consistent with findings on the priming of causal thoughts by prior counterfactual thoughts. Consider a simple event, a red ball hits a lever and a blue light comes on (Roese and Olson 1997). Suppose you were asked the following causal question: "Did the red ball hitting the lever cause the blue light to come on?" To think about the strong causal relation you consider just a single possibility: the red ball hits the lever and the blue light comes on. Now suppose you were asked instead a counterfactual question: "If the red ball had not hit the lever, would the blue light have come on?" To think about the counterfactual, you consider two possibilities, the red ball hits the lever and the blue light comes on, and the red ball does not hit the lever and the blue light does not come on. There is an interesting asymmetry in the length of time it takes most people to answer causal and counterfactual questions. They answered the causal question more quickly when they had previously been asked the counterfactual question (Roese and Olson 1997). But they did not answer the counterfactual question more quickly when they had previously been asked the causal question. The result supports the suggestion that people think about the possibility "the red ball hit the lever and the blue light came on" when they understand both the causal and the counterfactual question. As a result, first answering the counterfactual question helps people answer the causal question because they have already thought about the affirmative possibility. It also supports the suggestion that people think about the possibility "the red ball did not hit the lever and the blue light did not come on" when they understand the counterfactual question only. As a result, first answering the causal question does not help people answer the counterfactual question because they still have more work to do to understand it; they must think about the negative possibility.

Because of the difference in the possibilities that people think about when they understand causal and counterfactual assertions, counterfactual assertions are harder to think about: they require more processing and take longer. Of course, because counterfactuals render otherwise implicit information explicit, people may learn more from imagining counterfactual alternatives than from thinking about causal relations (Kahneman 1995). For example, consider the suggestion "if China had been sympathetic to economic and technological development, it would have emerged as the world's first superpower." People think about two possibilities when they understand it, and the contrast between them may in turn suggest that not being sympathetic to such development *caused* China to miss being an early superpower (Roese and Olson 1997). In this way, counterfactual thoughts can help people work out their understanding of a causal relation (Tetlock and Lebow 2001).

Further support for the idea that a strong causal relation requires people to think about a single possibility and that a counterfactual requires people to think about two possibilities comes from the observation that causal assertions are made earlier by children than counterfactual assertions (Harris 2000). One of the important developments of childhood cognition is the ability to keep more information in working memory (Oakhill and Johnson-Laird 1985). It follows that children should be able to think about strong causal relations, which require them to consider initially a single possibility, before they can imagine counterfactuals, which require them to consider two possibilities.

Children engage in imaginative pretend play from about 2 years of age— for example, they can climb into a large brown box and pretend it is a boat at sea (Riggs and Peterson 2000). Pretense and counterfactual thinking are closely related (Harris 2000). But counterfactual thinking requires a comparison of the facts with the imagined alternative. From 2 or 3 years children begin to also think about what has not happened but might have happened, and they can use *nearly* and *almost* (Harris, German, and Mills 1996). Children can imagine counterfactual alternatives to bad outcomes that occur, but they find it difficult to think accurately about counterfactual alternatives to a bad outcome that occurred because of an impossible event such as someone wanting to stay awake forever (Sobel, forthcoming). By the age of 3 or 4 they consider alternatives when they think about how an outcome could be prevented (Harris, German, and Mills 1996). Even at the age of 3 and a half years children were accurate at answering prevention questions. By the age of 3 or 4 years, children can answer questions not only about why something happened—for example, why did Laura's fingers get wet ink on them (because she used the pen)—but also about what should have been done instead so it would not have happened (she should have used the pencil). Children refer to an alternative not only when they are asked about prevention, but even when they are asked why something happened (Harris, German, and Mills 1996). They are able to make conditional inferences about the hypothetical future, such as "if I draw on this piece of paper, which box will it go in?" (in a situation in which blank sheets go in a different box from used sheets), before they can make inferences about counterfactuals such as "if I had not drawn on the paper, which box would it go in?" (Riggs et al. 1998; see also Perner 2000). Thinking about causal relations may emerge developmentally earlier than thinking about counterfactual alternatives.

What Makes People Think about a Cause or Imagine an Alternative?

People tend spontaneously to imagine an alternative after a bad outcome—for example, when a college student does badly on an examination (Roese and Olson 1997). They also tend spontaneously to think about what caused a bad outcome (Bohner et al. 1988; Weiner 1985). In the experiment with Alice McEleney, we gave half of the participants a story with a happy ending (they made lots of friends) and the other half a story with a sad ending (they had not made any friends). The 248 participants generated 197 counterfactual thoughts and 402 causal thoughts. But the participants given the sad story produced reliably more counterfactual thoughts than the participants given the happy story. And they produced reliably more thoughts about what caused the sad outcome than the happy outcome:

Counterfactual thoughts:

After bad versus good outcomes, average per person 1.22 versus 0.38

Causal thoughts:

After bad versus good outcomes, average per person 1.91 versus 1.34

Most people feel the need to identify the causes of situations that turned out badly, and to imagine how they could have turned out differently (see also McEleney and Byrne 1999). But our results also showed that causal and counterfactual thoughts can be evoked by different triggers.

One trigger for causal thoughts is an unexpected outcome (Bohner et al. 1988; Weiner 1985). Most people think about the cause of an event more often after unexpected outcomes, such as when a college student performs differently on an examination—that is, a poor student performs well or a good student performs badly (Sanna and Turley 1996). In the experiment, we gave half of the participants a story with an ending in line with their expectations, "I've never had any trouble making new friends" or "I've always had trouble making new friends," and the other half of the participants a story with an ending that was not in line with these expectations. Participants given the unexpected outcome generated reliably more causal thoughts than participants given the expected outcome, and they did so regardless of whether the outcome was good or bad. Their expectations about the outcome did not affect their counterfactual thoughts:

Causal thoughts:
  Expected versus unexpected, average per person 1.47 versus 1.79
Counterfactual thoughts:
  Expected versus unexpected, average per person 0.86 versus 0.76

Unexpected outcomes violate the connection between the cause and the outcome, and assert instead the cause occurred and the outcome did not—for instance, "I joined the gym and yet I did not make any friends." Unexpected outcomes seem to be a special trigger for causal thoughts but not for counterfactual thoughts. They tend to indicate a failure of prediction, and causal knowledge may be important for prediction. An unexpected outcome may lead people to question whether the cause is a strong cause.

One trigger for counterfactual thoughts is the controllability of the events (Girotto, Legrenzi, and Rizzo 1991; Markman et al. 1993; Roese 1997). Most people imagine alternatives to controllable events more than uncontrollable ones. In the experiment, we gave half of the participants a story with events that fell within their control (for example, you called your old friend and asked to be shown around town). We gave the other half of the participants the story with the same events described to imply they were uncontrollable (for instance, you bumped into an old friend who insisted on showing you around). We found that participants given the controllable events tended to generate more than twice as many counterfactual thoughts compared to those given the uncontrollable ones. The controllability of the events did not have any effect on the number of causal thoughts participants generated:

Counterfactual thoughts:

Controllable versus uncontrollable, average per person 1.1 versus 0.5

Causal thoughts:

Controllable versus uncontrollable, average per person 1.72 versus 1.6

Controllable antecedents seem to be a special trigger for counterfactual thoughts, and people say, for example, "if I had not decided to join the gym I would not have made friends."

One function of causal and counterfactual thoughts may be to help people prepare for the future (Roese 1997; Markman et al. 1995). Thinking about how one thing causes another may increase the ability to predict and control events (Einhorn and Hogarth 1986; Mandel and Lehman 1996). Counterfactual thoughts may be useful for helping to prevent bad outcomes or promote better ones, based on what is within one's control.

Causal and counterfactual thoughts differ in their focus in several ways (see table 5.6). Causal claims can be about unknown future outcomes, as in "heating cryptonite will cause it to expand" (Cummins 1995; McGill and Klein 1993), whereas counterfactual claims are about past events that are no longer possible. People sometimes generate subjunctive conditionals about the future, such as "if the cryptonite were to be heated tomorrow it would expand," but these subjunctive conditionals are not interpreted as conveying any counterfactual presuppositions (Byrne and Egan 2004).

Table 5.6
Some proposed differences in focus of causal and counterfactual assertions

Counterfactual	Causal	
Controllable events	Covarying events	Mandel and Lehman 1996
Necessary antecedents	Sufficient antecedents	N'gbala and Branscombe 1995
Focus on not-A e.g., not-A and B (III cell)	Focus on not-B e.g., A and not-B (II cell)	McGill and Klein 1993
Evaluate candidate Did something about x cause y?	Identify candidate What caused y?	McGill and Klein 1993
Bad outcome	Unexpected outcome	Sanna and Turley 1996
Prevention	Prediction	Mandel and Lehman 1996
Past inference	Future inference	Einhorn and Hogarth 1986
Outcome known	Outcome known or unknown	

Counterfactual thoughts may often be based on inferences about past events, whereas causal thoughts may more often be based on inferences about future events (Einhorn and Hogarth 1986; see also Yarlett and Ramscar 2002; Sloman and Lagnado 2003; Spellman and Mandel 1999). Causal and counterfactual claims can be made readily about known past outcomes—for example, "heating the cryptonite caused it to expand" and "if the cryptonite had not been heated it would not have expanded." They can be about general universal matters, as in "heating metal causes it to expand" and "if metal were not heated it would not expand." They can be about specific individual events—for instance, "heating this piece of metal causes it to expand" and "if this piece of metal were heated it would expand" (Goldvarg and Johnson-Laird 2001). Nonetheless a causal assertion and a counterfactual assertion mean the same thing and are consistent with the same possibilities. The key difference between them is that people mentally represent them by thinking about different possibilities. A strong causal relation "A caused B" is consistent with two possibilities (A and B, not-A and not-B). People think about it by mentally representing a single possibility (A and B). They think about the corresponding counterfactual "if A had not happened then B would not have happened" by mentally representing the two possibilities, and they note that one corresponds to the conjecture and the other to the presupposed facts (at least for counterfactuals about known events). An enabling relation "A allowed B" is consistent with three possibilities (A and B, not-A and not-B, A and not-B). People think about it by envisaging the possibility, A and B, but they can also readily envisage the second possibility, not-A and not-B. They think about the corresponding counterfactual by envisaging the same two possibilities. People imagine counterfactual alternatives to enabling relations most readily because they understand enabling relations by thinking about the possibility in which the enabler does not occur and the outcome does not occur and this possibility provides a ready-made counterfactual alternative.

Summary

One mystery about thoughts about what might have been is that people sometimes wish an event had not happened, even when they know it was not the cause of the outcome. For example, they imagine the September 11 attack had not occurred and they say "if only the baggage handlers had detected the hijackers weapons . . .''. They appreciate that the real cause of the outcome was not the baggage handlers' failure, but some other cause, such as the existence of the terrorists and their plans. But counterfactual and causal assertions mean the same thing and are consistent with the same possibilities. When people imagine a counterfactual alternative, it can help them work out a causal relation. And conversely, causal beliefs influence people's judgments of the plausibility of counterfactual conjectures. Why then do counterfactual thoughts focus on a controllable event, even when the controllable event was not the cause of the outcome?

The clue from reasoning to help solve this mystery is that there are different sorts of causes. The difference in focus can be explained by the possibilities that people think about to represent causal relations and counterfactuals. A key distinction is between a strong causal relation and an enabling relation. A strong causal relation is consistent with two possibilities and people envisage just one of them from the outset, *cause and outcome*. An enabling relation is consistent with three possibilities, and people think about the possibility, *enabler and outcome*, and they are also able to think readily about a second possibility, *not-enabler and not-outcome*. The second possibility provides a ready-made counterfactual alternative. As a result, people can more readily mentally change enabling relations, counterfactual thoughts focus on them whereas causal thoughts focus on strong causal relations, and people spontaneously generate more causal thoughts than counterfactual thoughts.

The way people think about causal relations has important implications for their everyday lives. For example, in 2003 the Irish government announced its intention to ban smoking in all workplaces, including pubs and restaurants. The vintners' association immediately launched a campaign against the proposal. They lobbied hard against the introduction of the ban, and their main concern was that if the smoking ban was introduced, smokers would stop going to pubs, pubs would do less trade, and workers would lose their jobs. The government's concern was that if the smoking ban was not introduced, workers would be exposed to the hazards of passive smoking, they would experience ill-health, and some would lose their lives. Most people can appreciate the causal relation between passive smoking for a nonsmoker and lung cancer. When a nonsmoking bartender dies of lung cancer, people understand that the passive smoking led to his lung cancer. They think about the possibility that he was exposed to cigarette smoke and he contracted lung cancer, and they can also think about the possibility that he was not exposed to cigarette smoke and he did not contract lung cancer. The enabling relation provides access to a ready-made counterfactual alternative, "if he had not been exposed to cigarette smoke, he would not have contracted lung cancer." But the causal relation between not being allowed to smoke and job losses does not provide a ready-made counterfactual alternative. The government held out against the vintners, and the nonsmoking ban went into effect in Irish pubs in March 2004. A vivid counterfactual alternative may be worth a thousand causal arguments.

6 "Even If . . ."

What might've happened, is what I usually think. How would life be different? And my feeling is, given the swarming, unforeseeable nature of the world, things could've turned out exactly as they have.

—Richard Ford, *The Sportswriter*

Suppose a survivor from an airplane crash with severe injuries struggles for days through the jungle but dies just before reaching a village. It is tempting to think "if only he had managed to walk to the village, he would have been rescued" (Miller and Turnbull 1990). But suppose you must try to console the victim's relatives. What might you say? Or suppose you wish to defend the rescue team who got as far as the village but no further. Your motivation to console or defend may influence the alternative you imagine (Seelau et al. 1995; Roese, Sanna, and Galinsky 2005). You may decide to emphasize the severity of the victim's injuries and suggest "even if he had managed to walk to the village, he still would have died." Sometimes thoughts about what might have been change an antecedent event (the victim walked to the village) but leave the outcome unchanged (he still died). "Even if . . ." conditionals have been called "semifactual" by philosophers because they combine a counterfactual antecedent and a factual consequent (Chisholm 1946; Goodman 1973). Imagined semifactual alternatives are intriguing because, unlike other thoughts about what might have been, they suggest that the outcome is inevitable. People can imagine semifactual alternatives in many contexts. For example, you may believe that even if the baggage handlers had detected the hijackers with weapons on September 11, the attacks would still have occurred (because the other unarmed hijackers would have escaped detection and continued with their plan). You may think that even if Kennedy had moved to make a nuclear strike against Cuba during the missile crisis, nuclear war would still have been averted (because Russia would have drawn back).

Previous chapters have explored the counterfactual alternatives that people tend to imagine most readily—for example, they tend to mentally change intentional decisions, controllable actions, socially unacceptable events, and enabling causal relations. Their imagined counterfactual alternatives mentally change the outcome and also mentally change one of its antecedents. As a result, people judge that the antecedent contributed causally to the outcome. Imagined semifactual alternatives have the opposite effect. For instance, the semifactual alternative about the baggage handlers diminishes the contribution of their failure to detect the weapons. My aim in this chapter is to explain how people create semifactual alternatives, and why these imagined alternatives diminish judgments of causality.

People Imagine Semifactual Alternatives

Imagine you read an account of a bank robbery in which a bank teller sets off the alarm and the bank robber grabs her. The bank teller is accidentally shot by the police who were attempting to capture the robber. You could create an alternative by mentally changing the antecedent that the bank robber grabbed the bank teller, and you could mentally change the outcome that the bank teller was shot. In your counterfactual alternative the bank robber did not grab the bank teller and she was not shot. The counterfactual conditional, "if only the bank robber had not grabbed the bank teller, she would not have been shot" emphasizes the causal relation between the antecedent and the outcome. Alternatively, you could create an alternative by mentally changing the antecedent, but you could leave mentally unchanged the outcome that the bank teller was shot. In your semifactual alternative the bank robber did not grab the bank teller but she was shot anyway. The semifactual conditional, "even if the bank robber had not grabbed the bank teller, she would still have been shot," denies a causal relation between the antecedent and the outcome.

Semifactual Conditionals and Possibilities

"Even if ..." is an interesting construction linguistically and logically (Konig 1986). What does someone mean when they utter an "even if ..." semifactual, such as "even if the police had not followed all their leads, the killer would still have been caught"? "Even if ..." and many adverbs and adverbial phrases such as "anyway," "nonetheless," "regardless," and "all the same" can be used to convey the possibility of the truth of the consequent (the killer was caught) in the context of the falsity of the antecedent (the police followed up all their leads). A subjunctive conditional often conveys that the presupposed facts are that the consequent is false. For example, the counterfactual "if the police had not followed up all their leads the killer would not have been caught" conveys the conjecture that the police did not follow up all their leads and the killer was not caught, and the presupposed facts that the police followed up all their leads and the killer was caught. But the subjunctive "even if" conditional cancels the presupposition of the falsity of the consequent. It conveys the conjecture that the police did not follow up all their leads and the killer was caught, and the presupposed facts that the police followed up all their leads and the killer was caught.

Suppose you are describing a friend of yours to a colleague. Your friend does not like mathematics and became a scientist. You assert "even if Nora had liked mathematics, she would still have become a scientist." Your semifactual conditional is consistent with at least two possibilities, "Nora liked mathematics and she became a scientist" (A and B), and "Nora did not like mathematics and she became a scientist" (not-A and B). People understand the semifactual by mentally representing these two possibilities initially, the conjecture, "Nora liked mathematics and she became a scientist" (A and B), and the presupposed facts, "Nora did not like mathematics and she became a scientist" (not-A and B). They keep track of whether the possibilities are conjectures or presupposed facts. Your semifactual denies a link between liking mathematics and choosing science as a career. It suggests it is possible to become a scientist (and not a mathematician), despite liking mathematics (see table 6.1).

Compare the semifactual conditional to a counterfactual one. Suppose your friend does not like mathematics and she did not become a scientist and you assert "if Nora had liked mathematics, she would have become a scientist." The counterfactual conditional is consistent with at least two possibilities, "Nora liked mathematics and she became a scientist," "she did not like mathematics and she did not become a scientist." People understand the counterfactual by thinking about these two possibilities initially. Your counterfactual emphasizes the relation between liking

Table 6.1

Possibilities that people mentally represent for counterfactual and semifactual conditionals

---

Counterfactual conditional: "If Nora had liked mathematics, she would have become a scientist"

Initial possibilities

Nora did not like mathematics and she did not become a scientist (facts)	<u>not-A and not-B</u>
Nora liked mathematics and she became a scientist (imagined)	<u>A and B</u>

Semifactual conditional: "Even if Nora had liked mathematics, she would still have become a scientist"

Initial possibilities

Nora did not like mathematics and she became a scientist (facts)	<u>not-A and B</u>
Nora liked mathematics and she became a scientist (imagined)	<u>A and B</u>

---

mathematics and choosing science as a career, and suggests it is possible to become a scientist because of liking mathematics.

The semifactual alternative invites you to suppose that Nora liked mathematics (when in fact she did not) and to suppose she became a scientist (and in fact she did). Of course, semifactuals about unknown situations may not convey a presupposition about the truth or falsity of their antecedents. Suppose you do not know whether Iraq had weapons of mass destruction. You may say, "even if Iraq had had weapons of mass destruction, the war still would not have been justified." But many semifactuals do presuppose the falsity of their antecedents, and as we will see, they have a profound impact on people's judgments of causality. And just as people come to different interpretations of factual conditionals (as many as ten different interpretations), and they come to different interpretations of counterfactuals, so too can they come to different interpretations of semifactual conditionals.

Semifactual Alternatives Deny a Causal Link

When people imagine a counterfactual alternative about a causal relation their judgment that the antecedent caused the outcome increases. For example, the counterfactual conditional "if only the airplane survivor had made it to the village he would have been rescued" emphasizes that not getting to the village was a crucial factor. When people imagine a semifactual alternative, the judgment that the antecedent caused the outcome may *decrease* (Mill [1872] 1956). For example, the semifactual conditional "even if the airplane survivor had made it to the village he still would have died" emphasizes that not getting to the village was not a crucial factor. Semifactual conditionals can be about many different sorts of topics, such as people's actions or reasons and obligations. But they are often about causal relations. People may make judgments about causality, that the antecedent caused the outcome, by imagining that the antecedent had not happened and thinking about whether the outcome would not have happened. But their judgments about causality may also depend on imagining that the antecedent had not happened and thinking about whether the outcome would still have happened (Mill [1872] 1956). An event may appear inevitable when people imagine how a change to an antecedent might have resulted in the same outcome (Sherman and McConnell 1995; Mandel and Lehman 1996).

When people can imagine a semifactual alternative in which an antecedent is mentally undone and the same outcome occurs, their judgments of causality are affected dramatically. Consider a student who did badly on an examination. Shortly after she began the examination, she had a panic attack. There is a drug to combat panic that often makes her feel better but she forgot to take it. Do you think that forgetting to take the pill caused her to do badly on the examination? Most participants judged that it did (Roese and Olson 1996). Presumably they could imagine a counterfactual alternative in which she took the pill and she did better on the examination. But suppose instead that the drug rarely makes her feel better. In that case, do you think forgetting to take it caused her to do badly? Most participants judged it did not. Presumably they could imagine the semifactual alternative in which she took the pill and she still did badly on the examination (Roese and Olson 1996; see also Boninger, Gleicher, and Strattman 1994).

Imagined semifactual alternatives affect judgments of causality, and as a result they affect judgments of fault and responsibility and blame. Suppose your task is to rewrite the account of the bank robbery described earlier, but you are to change only the actions of the bank robber, and you are to make sure the outcome is different—that is, the teller does not get shot (Branscombe et al. 1996). You might imagine that the bank robber did not grab the teller and the teller did not get shot. Now suppose instead that your task is to rewrite the story, again changing only the actions of the bank robber, but this time you are to make sure that the outcome remains the same. You might imagine that the bank robber did not grab the teller but she still got shot. People ascribe more blame to the bank robber when they imagine his actions were different and the outcome was different, compared to when they imagine his actions were different but the outcome remained the same (Branscombe et al. 1996). Blame presumably attaches to a causal role. When people are invited to think about a counterfactual or semifactual alternative, their judgments of cause and blame are affected in many everyday situations, such as jury decision making.

Thinking about how the outcome could have turned out the same even if antecedents to it had been different affects other everyday tendencies, such as the "hindsight bias" (Nario and Branscombe 1995). The hindsight "knew it all along" bias is the tendency to think an outcome was inevitable once it is known (Fischhoff 1977). For example, suppose you did not know that the bankteller got shot in the bank robbery described earlier. How likely do you think it was that she would get shot? Your judgment of the likelihood will be higher than one made by someone who genuinely does not know the actual outcome. People tend to view things that actually happened as more inevitable when they know they occurred compared to when they do not know they occurred. The tendency can be "debiased" when people imagine counterfactual alternatives (Roese and Olson 1996). The debiasing can backfire, however, when people are asked to imagine many alternatives: the difficulty of thinking of more and more alternatives leads people to judge the outcome was inevitable after all (Sanna, Schwarz, and Stocker 2002).

Such thought experiments may be important in situations where real experiments are not possible, for example in historical analyses. Suppose you have a hunch that Western societies were better adapted to prevail in competition with other civilizations. To check your hunch it may be useful to think about other important factors. You might compare the semifactual conditional, "even if the Black Death had killed a majority of the European population, Western society would still have risen," to the counterfactual conditional, "if the Black Death had killed a majority of the European population, other civilizations would have come to the fore instead" (see Tetlock and Lebow 2001).

Semifactual Alternatives and Weak Causal Relations

Why do imagined semifactual alternatives influence judgments of causality? The answer lies in the different sorts of causal relations. The previous chapter outlined two sorts of causal relations, strong causal relations and enabling relations. Semifactual alternatives often focus on a third sort of causal relation—that is, a weak causal relation.

A strong causal relation such as "heating the butter caused it to melt" is consistent with two possibilities: "the butter was heated and it melted" and "the butter was not heated and it did not melt." People mentally represent the strong causal relation by initially thinking about a single possibility, "the butter was heated and it melted." The strong causal relation can be paraphrased by the counterfactual conditional, "if the butter had not been heated it would not have melted." The counterfactual about the strong causal relation is also consistent with two possibilities: "the butter was heated and it melted" and "the butter was not heated and it did not melt." People mentally represent the counterfactual by thinking about these two possibilities from the outset. The strong causal assertion and the counterfactual have the same meaning, but people mentally represent them in different ways.

An enabling relation, such as "Mark driving home by an unusual route made it possible for the crash to occur," is consistent with three possibilities, "Mark drove home by an unusual route and the crash occurred," "Mark did not drive home by an unusual route and the crash did not occur," and "Mark drove home by an unusual route and the crash did not occur" (perhaps because there were no careless drivers on that route). People mentally represent the enabling relation by thinking about the possibility "Mark drove home by an unusual route and the crash occurred," and they can also readily access the second possibility, "Mark did not drive home by an unusual route and the crash did not occur." The enabling relation can be paraphrased by the counterfactual conditional, "if Mark had not driven home by an unusual route the crash would not have occurred." The enabling and counterfactual assertions have the same meaning, and people mentally represent them in the same way. Their mental representation of the enabling relation provides them with a ready-made counterfactual alternative. As a result, counterfactual thoughts tend to focus on enabling relations.

Imagined counterfactual alternatives can help people to work out causal relations, and causal beliefs guide judgments of the plausibility of counterfactuals. Yet, as we saw, a curious feature of counterfactual and causal thought is that people sometimes wish an event had not happened, even when they know it was not the cause of the outcome. For example, they imagine that the September 11 attack on the New York twin towers had not occurred by wishing the baggage handlers had detected the hijackers' weapons. Yet they realize that the real cause of the attack was not the baggage handlers' failure. Counterfactual and causal thoughts may focus on different aspects of an event because they focus on different sorts of causal relations. Causal thoughts tend to focus on strong causal relations, whereas counterfactual thoughts tend to focus on enabling relations.

This chapter examines a third sort of causal relation, weak causal relations such as "a careless tourist lighting a campfire caused the forest fire." Weak causal relations are consistent with three possibilities, "a careless tourist lit a campfire and the forest fire occurred" (A and B), "no careless tourist lit a campfire and no forest fire occurred" (not-A and not-B), and "no careless tourist lit a campfire and the forest fire occurred" (perhaps because there was lightning, or someone dropped a cigarette) (not-A and B). In the contingency table introduced in the previous chapter, the relation is consistent not only with cells I and IV, but also III (see table 5.2). The single case that goes against a causal relation of this sort is when the cause occurs and the outcome does not, a campfire and no forest fire (cell II). Accordingly we can call it a weak causal relation (Goldvarg and Johnson-Laird 2001). (We can note in passing that the possibilities consistent with the weak causal relation are the same as the conditional interpretation examined in previous chapters.)

People mentally represent the weak causal relation by thinking about the possibility "a careless tourist lit a campfire and the forest fire occurred" (A and B) and they can also readily access a second possibility, "no careless tourist lit a campfire and the forest fire occurred" (not-A and B). The second possibility emphasizes that the weak cause is not *necessary* for the outcome to occur—that is, the campfire is not necessary for the forest fire to occur. The weak causal relation can be paraphrased by the semifactual conditional, "even if a careless tourist had not lit a campfire, the forest fire would still have occurred." People mentally represent the weak causal and semifactual assertions in the same way. Their mental representation of the weak causal relation provides them with a ready-made semifactual alternative. As a result, semifactual thoughts tend to focus on weak causal relations. The next section shows that people mentally represent a semifactual conditional by thinking about these two possibilities, and the section after it shows that when people imagine a semifactual alternative, their judgments that the antecedent caused the outcome decrease.

Clues from Reasoning: "Even If ..." Conditionals and Inferences

People think about a semifactual conditional such as "even if the airplane crash victim had made it to the village he still would have died" by thinking about two possibilities, the conjecture, "he made it to the village and he died," and the presupposed facts, "he did not make it to the village and he died." As we saw in previous chapters, people may reason and imagine by thinking about possibilities (see table 6.2). They think about true possibilities and they generally do not think about false possibilities. They tend to think initially about very few possibilities, because of the constraints

Table 6.2
Summary of principles thus far

1. True possibilities: *People keep in mind true possibilities.*
2. Few possibilities: *People keep in mind few possibilities.*
3. Dual possibilities: *Some ideas require people to think about two possibilities.*
4. Counterfactual possibilities: *People think about possibilities that once may have been true possibilities but can be true no longer.*
5. Mutability of dual possibilities: *People readily imagine a counterfactual alternative to a possibility if it is mentally represented with a second possibility.*
6. Forbidden possibilities: *People think about the forbidden possibility as well as the permitted possibility when they understand an obligation.*
I. Actions: *People think about two possibilities when they understand an action.*
II. Single possibilities: *People can switch from thinking about one possibility to thinking about two possibilities, e.g., for inactions.*
III. Controllable events: *People think about two possibilities when they understand controllable events.*
IV. Causes: People think about a single possibility when they understand a strong causal relation (*cause and outcome*). They can readily access a second possibility for an enabling condition (*enabler and outcome, no enabler and no outcome*).
V. Semifactual alternatives: When people mentally represent a semifactual assertion they think about two possibilities, A and B, and not-A and B. When they mentally represent a weak causal relation they can readily access the same two possibilities.

of working memory. Some ideas are dual-possibility ideas—that is, they require people to keep in mind more than one possibility. People keep track of the status of the possibilities, as corresponding to an imagined possibility, or to the facts. They can more readily imagine a counterfactual alternative to a possibility when they have mentally represented it with a second possibility from the outset. For example, most people think about actions by considering the preaction possibility and the postaction possibility. They can imagine a counterfactual alternative to the action by mentally changing the postaction possibility to be the same as the preaction possibility. Most people understand an obligation by thinking about the permitted possibility and the forbidden possibility, noted as forbidden, and they mentally change the forbidden possibility to be like the permitted possibility.

These principles that guide the possibilities that people think about help to explain why most people tend to imagine counterfactual alternatives about actions, controllable events, and socially unacceptable actions. They explain the relation between imagined counterfactual alternatives and enabling relations. They also explain the relation between imagined semifactual alternatives and weak causal relations. The corollary for semifactual alternatives and weak causal relations is:

Corollary 5 for semifactual alternatives and weak causal relations: When people mentally represent a semifactual assertion "even if A had been then B would have been" they think about two possibilities, A and B, and not-A and B. When they mentally represent a weak causal relation they think about the possibility *weak cause and outcome*, and they can also think readily about the possibility *not-weak cause and outcome*.

Semifactual Conditionals and Inferences

The possibilities that reasoners consider when they understand a counterfactual have a dramatic effect on the inferences that they make. For example, they make the inferences that require access to the possibility "Nora did not like mathematics and she did not become a scientist" far more often from the counterfactual, "if Nora had liked mathematics then she would have become a scientist," than from the corresponding factual conditional. They readily make the modus tollens inference (from "she did not become a scientist" to "she did not like mathematics") and the denial of the antecedent (from "she did not like mathematics" to "she did not become a scientist") from the counterfactual. They also make the inferences based on the possibility "Nora liked mathematics and she became a scientist" equally from both conditionals. They make the modus ponens inference (from "she liked mathematics" to "she became a scientist") and the affirmation of the consequent (from "she became a scientist" to "she liked mathematics"). Their inferences corroborate the view that people mentally represent the counterfactual by thinking about two possibilities, whereas they think about a single possibility for the factual conditional.

The theory predicts that people's mental representation of a semifactual should also affect the inferences they make from it. People understand a semifactual conditional, such as "even if Nora had liked mathematics she would have become a scientist," by thinking about the conjecture, "Nora liked mathematics and she became a scientist," and also the presupposed facts, "Nora did not like mathematics and she became a scientist." Their mental representation affects the inferences that require access to the possibility "Nora did not like mathematics and she became a scientist"—that is, the affirmation of the consequent (from "she became a scientist" to "she liked mathematics") and the denial of the antecedent (from "she did not like mathematics" to "she did not become a scientist").

First consider the affirmation of the consequent (B therefore A) inference. Suppose you are given the factual conditional "if Nora liked mathematics, she became a scientist" and you find out that in fact Nora became a scientist. What would you infer: (a) she liked mathematics, (b) she did not like mathematics, or (c) nothing follows? Some people infer (a) she liked mathematics. The inference is made when people think only about the initial possibility, "Nora liked mathematics and she became a scientist." It also follows even when people consider some of the other possibilities, such as "Nora did not like mathematics and she did not become a scientist." But people do not make the inference when they envisage the possibility "Nora did not like mathematics and she became a scientist" (perhaps because she did not want to become a mathematician). The possibility provides a counterexample to the inference. It ensures that the premises can be true, "if Nora liked mathematics then she became a scientist" and "Nora became a scientist," but the conclusion "she liked mathematics" can be false. When someone makes the inference that "she liked mathematics," it is a strong clue that they have not considered the possibility

"Nora did not like mathematics and she became a scientist," or they have dismissed it as inconsistent with their interpretation of the conditional.

The possibility "Nora did not like mathematics and she became a scientist" is the very one that is made prominent by a semifactual conditional. Suppose you are given the semifactual assertion, "even if Nora had liked mathematics then she would have became a scientist" and then you find out that Nora did in fact become a scientist. What would you infer this time: (a) she liked mathematics, (b) she did not like mathematics, or (c) nothing follows? The theory predicts that people should not choose (a) this time. When they are told that "Nora became a scientist," they should be able to resist the inference that "she liked mathematics." The information that she became a scientist matches the information in both of the possibilities they have thought about, in one she liked mathematics and in the other she did not, as table 6.3 shows. The theory predicts that most people should realize that they cannot infer whether she liked mathematics and so they should choose (c).

Table 6.3
Inferences from a semifactual conditional based on the initial possibilities that people think about

---

"Even if Nora had liked mathematics she would have become a scientist"
Initial possibilities

Nora did not like mathematics and she became a scientist (facts)	not-A and B	(1)
Nora liked mathematics and she became a scientist (imagined)	A and B	(2)

Inferences (from the initial possibilities)
Affirmation of the consequent

Nora became a scientist	B (matches 1 and 2)
Therefore nothing follows	

Denial of the antecedent

Nora did not like mathematics	not-A (matches 1)
Therefore she BECAME a scientist	B

Modus ponens

Nora liked mathematics	A (matches 2)
Therefore she became a scientist	B

Modus tollens

Nora did not become a scientist	not-B (no match)
Therefore nothing follows	

Sergio Moreno-Ríos, Juan García-Madruga, and I have tested this idea (Moreno-Ríos, García-Madruga, and Byrne 2004). In one experiment we gave thirty-two participants semifactual conditionals and factual conditionals. We asked them to evaluate several sorts of inferences, including the affirmation of the consequent (B therefore A). As predicted, they made fewer inferences from the semifactual compared to the factual conditional:

Semifactual, 47 percent; factual, 84 percent

Instead almost half of the participants (44 percent) who were given the semifactual choose the (c) option "nothing follows." The experiment shows that many people resist the inference from the semifactual conditional.

Now consider the denial of the antecedent (not-A therefore not-B) inference. Many people resist it too. Suppose you are given the factual conditional, "if Nora liked mathematics then she became a scientist," and then you find out that in fact Nora did not like mathematics. What would you infer: (a) she became a scientist, (b) she did not become a scientist, or (c) nothing follows? Some people choose (c) because they envisage just the initial possibility, "Nora liked mathematics and she became a scientist." The information that Nora did not like mathematics does not match the contents of this possibility and so they believe that nothing follows. Some people infer (b) she did not become a scientist. They consider some of the other possibilities, such as "Nora did not like mathematics and she did not become a scientist." A third subset of people do not make the inference because they envisage another possibility, "Nora did not like mathematics and she became a scientist." The possibility provides a counterexample to the inference. It ensures that the premises can be true, "if Nora liked mathematics then she became a scientist" and "Nora did not like mathematics," but the conclusion "she did not become a scientist" can be false.

Because the possibility "Nora did not like mathematics and she became a scientist" is the one made prominent by a semifactual conditional, on this account they should not make the denial of the antecedent (not-A therefore not-B) inference. Suppose you are given the semifactual conditional, "even if Nora had liked mathematics she would have become a scientist" and then you find out that Nora did not in fact like mathematics. What would you infer this time: (a) she became a scientist, (b) she did not become a scientist, or (c) nothing follows? The theory predicts that people should not choose (b) this time. When participants are told that "Nora did not like mathematics," they should be able to resist the inference "she did not become a scientist." The information that Nora did not like mathematics matches the information in one possibility, and she became a scientist in this possibility (as table 6.3 shows). Some people should realize that they cannot infer whether she became a scientist and so they should choose (c). In fact, the theory also makes an otherwise counterintuitive prediction. Because people think about the possibility "Nora did not like mathematics and she became a scientist," it predicts that when they are given "Nora did not like mathematics," some people should conclude "she became a scientist."

The results corroborated the predictions. Reasoners made fewer denial of the antecedent (not-A therefore not-B) inferences from a semifactual compared to a factual conditional:

Semifactual, 48 percent; factual, 83 percent

Instead over one-third of them (34 percent) made the inference from "Nora did not like mathematics" to the conclusion that "she became a scientist." The experiment shows that many people resist the denial of the antecedent inference from semifactual conditionals (Moreno-Ríos, García-Madruga, and Byrne 2004).

The experiment also shows that the participants took more time to make inferences from semifactual compared to factual conditionals. We presented the inferences on computers and besides measuring their inferences, we measured the time they spent reading the sentences and the time they spent deciding on their conclusions. They took 7.9 seconds on average to make an inference from a factual conditional, and they took reliably longer—8.1 seconds on average—to make an inference from a semifactual. The result corroborates our suggestion that people must think about more possibilities when they understand a semifactual conditional.

Philosophers have debated the best expression of semifactual conditionals: some champion "even if ..." (Bennett 1982; Goodman 1973) and others "if ... still" (Barker 1991). There may be subtle differences between "even if ..." and "if ... still"—for example, "if it had been sunny, the picnic would still have been awful" may emphasize the enduring truth of the consequent, the picnic was in fact awful, and it would have been so despite differences in antecedent events. The construction "even if it had been sunny, the picnic would have been awful" may emphasize the falsity of the antecedent, that in fact it was not sunny. In the experiment, we used "if ... still," such as "if Nora had liked mathematics she would still have become a scientist," and in another experiment we relied on "even if ..." (see Moreno-Rios, García-Madruga, and Byrne 2004 for details). We found broadly similar results for inferences from them.

"Even if ..." conditionals may have the communicative intent to steer people away from making some inferences. In particular, "even if ..." conditionals may be effective in ensuring that listeners do not make the affirmation of the consequent (B therefore A) inference or the denial of the antecedent (not-A therefore not-B) inference. "If ..." conditionals may "invite" such inferences (Geis and Zwicky 1971). But "even if ..." conditionals are an antidote to that invitation.

There is a wide range of conditional connectives aside from "if ...," such as "only if," "unless," "whether," and "supposing" (Byrne, forthcoming). Some of these connectives may have the same meaning, and they may be consistent with the same possibilities, but their pragmatics may be different. People may mentally represent them by thinking about different possibilities. These different representations lead people to make different inferences. When people choose between different connectives that have similar meanings, they may select a connective to invite their listeners to make certain inferences. The inferences people make from "even if ..." conditionals support the view that people initially think about two possibilities when they understand them. Further support for the theory comes from priming studies.

Conditionals as Primes

Suppose someone describes a flower shop's stock by saying to you "even if there had been lilies there would still have been roses." You may understand their assertion by mentally representing two possibilities from the outset, "there were lilies and there were roses" and "there were no lilies and there were roses." When you are subsequently told that in fact "there were no roses and there were lilies" you can process this information rapidly. It matches one of the possibilities you have thought about from the outset. The semifactual conditional "primes" you to read the conjunction very rapidly. The theory predicts that people should be able to read the conjunction "there were no roses and there were lilies" more quickly after they have mentally represented a semifactual conditional "even if there had been roses there would have been lilies" than after they have mentally represented a factual conditional.

Orlando Espino, Carlos Santamaría, and I have tested this idea (Santamaría, Espino, and Byrne 2004). In one experiment we examined various conditionals as primes for reading subsequent conjunctions. We gave thirty-two participants stories to read in which, for example, Miguel was going to a flower shop with his sister. The participants were told that Miguel's sister told him that in this shop, even if there had been lilies there would have been roses. When they arrived at the shop they saw that there were no lilies and there were roses. The story continued by describing where Miguel and his sister went after the flower shop. The participants did not have to make any inferences from the conditionals. Their task was to read the short stories and answer some simple comprehension questions, such as, "did Miguel and his sister go to a flower shop?" The story was presented to participants on a computer screen one sentence at a time. They pressed the space bar to see each next sentence in the story.

We measured the length of time it took participants to understand the target conjunction, "there were no lilies and there were roses." We gave one group of participants an "even if ..." semifactual in the story prior to the target conjunction. We gave another group of participants an "if ..." conditional in the story prior to the target conjunction. The participants should be able to read the conjunction "there were lilies and there were roses" quickly after either conditional, but they should be able to read the conjunction "there were no lilies and there were roses" more quickly after the "even if ..." conditional compared to the "if ..." conditional.

The participants took about 2 seconds on average to read the conjunctions (see Santamaría, Espino, and Byrne 2004 for details). As expected they read the target conjunction "there were no lilies and there were roses" reliably faster (104 milliseconds faster) when it appeared after a semifactual "even if ..." than after a factual "if ..." conditional:

Semifactual, 1,822 milliseconds; factual, 1,926 milliseconds

They took about the same length of time to read the conjunction "there were lilies and there were roses" after a semifactual and after a factual:

Semifactual, 1,626 milliseconds; factual, 1,594 milliseconds (only a 32-millisecond difference), and there was no reliable difference between them. They also took about the same length of time to read the other conjunctions when they appeared after either conditional. There were no differences in the length of time it took them to read the conjunction "there were no lilies and there were no roses" (just a 52-millisecond difference), and they took the same length of time to read the conjunction "there were lilies and there were no roses" after the semifactual and the factual conditionals (just a 12-millisecond difference). The results show that people understand the conjunction "there were no lilies and there were roses" more quickly when they have first mentally represented a semifactual conditional, "even if there had been lilies there would have been roses" than when they have mentally represented a factual conditional.

In the experiment the participants did not have to make inferences or evaluate possibilities, so they were not prompted by additional information to think further about the possibilities. The priming methodology provides a direct measure of what possibilities people have thought about. It shows that people mentally represent a semifactual conditional "even if there had been roses there would have been lilies" by thinking about two possibilities, "there were roses and there were lilies" and "there were no roses and there were lilies." The finding that people think about these two possibilities when they imagine semifactual alternatives helps to explain why imagined semifactual alternatives affect their judgments of causality.

The Rational Imagination: Imagined Semifactuals and Causality

When people understand a semifactual such as, "even if the police had not followed up all their leads the killer would have been caught" they judge that the police following up all their leads was not a cause of the killer being caught. People understand the semifactual by thinking from the outset about two possibilities, the conjecture and the presupposed facts. This clue helps to explain why imagined semifactual alternatives affect judgements of causality.

Semifactual Alternatives and Causality

An imagined counterfactual alternative may help people to work out the cause of an outcome. When people imagine a counterfactual alternative and say, "if only there had been no dry leaves, the forest fire would not have happened," they think about the possibility, "there were dry leaves and the forest fire occurred" (A and B), and the possibility, "there were no dry leaves and no forest fire occurred" (not-A and not-B). These possibilities emphasise that the antecedent is necessary for the outcome, and they correspond to the possibilities that people can access readily when they understand an enabling causal relation, "dry leaves allowed the forest fire to occur."

In contrast, when people imagine a semifactual alternative and say "even if there had been no campfire, there would still have been the forest fire," they think about the possibility "there was a campfire and the forest fire occurred" (A and B), and the possibility "there was no campfire and the forest fire occurred" (not-A and B). These possibilities emphasize that the antecedent is not necessary for the outcome, and they correspond to the possibilities that people can access readily for a weak causal relation, "the campfire caused the forest fire." Imagined semifactual alternatives may serve to deny that the antecedent was a strong cause of the outcome.

Rachel McCloy and I examined the effect that imagining semifactual alternatives has on causal judgments (McCloy and Byrne 2002). In one experiment we asked 367 participants to think about what might have been after reading a scenario about a runner competing in the Olympics (based on a scenario in Boninger, Gleicher, and Strathman 1994, 301):

On the day before the 400 meter race, in a freak accident during training, you sprain your left ankle.... Your trainer recommends that you choose between two drugs, both legal according to Olympic guidelines. One is a well-known painkiller that has been proved effective but also has some serious side effects including temporary nausea and drowsiness. The other painkiller is a newer and less well-known drug.... the newer drug might be a more effective painkiller [but] its side effects are not yet known.... After considerable thought, you elect to go with the more well-known drug. On the day of the race, although there is no pain in your ankle, you already begin to feel the nausea and find yourself fighting off fatigue. You finish in fourth place.

In the days after the race the runner thought "even if ...". How do you think she completed this thought? People completed the "even if ..." sentence stem by saying, for example, "even if I had taken the newer drug, I still would have lost the race." They think about two possibilities, the conjecture, "she took the newer drug and she lost the race," and the presupposed facts, "she did not take the newer drug and she lost the race." To what extent do you think the runner's decision to take the older, well-known drug led to her failure to obtain an Olympic medal in the 400 meter race? The two possibilities imagined for the semifactual alternative emphasize that the antecedent, taking the well-known drug, was not necessary for the outcome, and they correspond to the possibilities that people consider for a weak causal relation. The theory predicts that judgments of the strength of the causal relation between the antecedent and the outcome should be weaker when people imagine a semifactual alternative.

Imagine instead that in the days after the race the runner thought "if only ...". How do you think she completed this thought? People completed the "if only ..." sentence stem by saying, for example, "if only I had taken the newer drug, I would have won the race." They think about two possibilities, the conjecture, "she took the newer drug and she won the race," and the presupposed facts, "she did not take the newer drug and she lost the race." To what extent do you think the runner's decision to take the older drug led to her failure? The two possibilities for the counterfactual alternative emphasize that the antecedent, taking the well known drug was necessary for the outcome, and they correspond to the possibilities that people consider for the relation.

The experiment examined whether completing "even if ..." and "if only ..." sentence stems affected judgments of the strength of the causal relation between the antecedent, taking the well-known drug, and the outcome, losing the race. We allocated participants to three groups. They were asked to imagine they were the runner, and to complete ratings of causality in response to the question "to what extent do you think your decision to take the well-known drug led to your failure to obtain an Olympic medal in the 400 meter race?" They marked their judgment on a 9-point scale where 1 meant "not at all causally related." One group was first asked to imagine that in the days and weeks following the race they thought "even if ...," and their task was to complete this sentence. They completed the "even if ..." sentence before they gave their causal rating. A second group was asked to complete an "if only ..." sentence before they gave their causal rating. The third group was a control group who were given no sentence completion task, but carried out the causality rating task directly after reading the story.

The experiment showed that when participants completed an "even if ..." sentence stem and said for example, "even if I had taken the newer drug I still would have lost the race," their ratings of the well-known drug as the cause of losing were reliably lower compared to the control group:

"Even if ...," mean rating 4.8; control, mean rating 5.7

When participants completed an "if only ..." sentence stem and said for example, "if only I had taken the newer drug I would have done better in the race," their ratings of the well known drug as the cause of losing were similar to the control group:

"If only ...," mean rating 5.2; control, mean rating 5.7

The experiment shows that completing an "even if ..." sentence decreased most people's judgement that the antecedent caused the outcome (see also McCloy and Byrne 1999).

The second tack in the experiment was to examine whether causal judgments were affected by knowing about other antecedents that could lead to similar or different outcomes. Suppose you were told that other athletes in other events suffering similar injuries used the newer drug and they felt no pain but experienced the same side effects. To what extent do you think the runner's decision to take the well-known drug led to her failure now? Suppose instead you were told that the other athletes who took the newer drug felt no pain and experienced no side effects. To what extent do you think the runner's decision to take the well-known drug led to her failure in this case? The theory predicts that participants' judgments that the antecedent caused the outcome will be affected when they are told about possibilities corresponding to a semifactual alternative or a counterfactual alternative. In the experiment we told one group of participants about a semifactual alternative—that is, a different antecedent (the newer drug) with the same intermediate outcome (bad side effects). We told a second group of participants about a counterfactual alternative—that is, a different antecedent (the newer drug) with a different intermediate outcome (no side effects). The third group were not given any information about other alternatives (the control condition).

The experiment showed that when participants knew about a semifactual alternative, they did not rate the runner's choice of drug as highly causally linked to her loss, compared to when they were not given any information:

Semifactual, mean rating 4.3; control, mean rating 5.3

But when participants knew about a counterfactual alternative, they rated her drug choice as reliably more causally linked to her loss, compared to when they were given no information:

Counterfactual, mean rating 6.2; control, mean rating 5.3

The results show that knowing about a semifactual alternative decreased people's judgement that the antecedent caused the outcome.

When people complete an "even if ..." sentence-completion task, or when they know about a semifactual alternative, they judge the causal relation between the antecedent and outcome to be weaker than when they do not. The results corroborate the view that people envisage two possibilities when they imagine a semifactual alternative. They understand the semifactual conditional, "even if she had taken the newer drug she still would have lost" by mentally representing the conjecture, "she took the newer drug and she lost," and the presupposed facts, "she did not take the newer drug and she lost." These two possibilities correspond to their understanding of a weak causal relation, and so they interpret the causal relation to be weak. We have considered one interpretation of semifactual and counterfactual conditionals. The next section considers other interpretations.

The Hidden Possibility

A semifactual such as "even if the runner had taken the newer drug she would have lost the race" is consistent with at least two possibilities, "the runner took the newer drug and lost the race," and "she did not take the newer drug and she lost the race." People mentally represent it initially by thinking about these two possibilities, the conjecture, "the runner took the newer drug and lost the race," and the presupposed facts, "she did not take the newer drug and she lost the race." Do people ever think about a third possibility, such as, "she did not take the newer drug and she did not lose the race"? This section examines evidence that they do. Likewise, a counterfactual conditional such as "if the car had been out of petrol it would have stalled" is consistent with at least two possibilities, "the car was out of petrol and it stalled," and "the car was not out of petrol and it did not stall." People mentally represent it initially by thinking about these two possibilities, the conjecture, "the car was out of petrol and it stalled," and the presupposed facts, "the car was not out of petrol and it did not stall."

Do people ever think about a third possibility, such as, "the car was not out of petrol and it stalled"? This section also examines evidence that they do.

Counterfactuals Are Not Biconditionals

Just as factual conditionals can be interpreted in many different ways, so too counterfactuals and semifactuals can be interpreted in different ways. For example, a counterfactual is consistent with three possibilities on a conditional interpretation, but it is consistent with just two possibilities on a biconditional interpretation. It is consistent with a different set of three possibilities on an enabling interpretation. For all of these interpretations, people mentally represent the counterfactual by thinking about just two possibilities from the outset, the conjecture and the presupposed facts. But people can distinguish between counterfactuals that have antecedents that are necessary for the consequent to occur (that is, biconditionals), and those that have antecedents that are not necessary for the consequent to occur (that is, conditionals).

Consider first a factual conditional that has an antecedent that is necessary for the consequent to occur, such as "if the water was heated to 100 degrees centigrade then it boiled." There are few if any alternative causes of water boiling. The conditional is a biconditional, consistent with two possibilities, "water was heated to 100 degrees centigrade and it boiled," and "water was not heated to 100 degrees centigrade and it did not boil." A factual conditional can have an antecedent that is not necessary for the consequent to occur, for example, "If the car was out of petrol then it stalled." There are many alternative causes of a car stalling—for example, faulty spark plugs, no water, and so on (Thompson 1994). The conditional is consistent with three possibilities: "the car was out of petrol and it stalled," "the car was not out of petrol and it did not stall," and "the car was not out of petrol and it stalled." For both sorts of conditional, people envisage just a single possibility at the outset. As a result they readily make the modus ponens (A therefore B) and the affirmation of the consequent (B therefore A) inferences, but they make fewer of the modus tollens (not-B therefore not-A) and denial of the antecedent (not-A therefore not-B) inferences. A strong clue to whether people have come to a conditional or biconditional interpretation is that they make more denial of the antecedent (not-A therefore not-B) and affirmation of the consequent (B therefore A) inferences from biconditionals than conditionals (Evans, Newstead, and

Byrne 1993). For the biconditional, these inferences are valid; no possibility contradicts them. But for the conditional, there is a counterexample to the inferences. Likewise for counterfactuals, when people have interpreted a counterfactual as a biconditional, the theory predicts that they should make the denial of the antecedent (not-A therefore not-B) and affirmation of the consequent (B therefore A) inferences but when they have interpreted a counterfactual as a conditional, they should not make these inferences as often.

In an experiment with Valerie Thompson, half of the counterfactuals we gave to participants were based on antecedents that were necessary for the consequent to occur (biconditional counterfactuals), and half on antecedents that were not necessary for the consequent to occur (conditional counterfactuals) (see Thompson and Byrne 2002 for details). We found that people made different inferences from the two sorts of counterfactuals. The key test is the denial of the antecedent (not-A therefore not-B) inference. Given "if the car was out of petrol then it stalled" and "the car was not out of petrol" people make the inference "the car did not stall" more often when they have thought about the possibility that the car was not out of petrol and it did not stall. As a result, they make it more often when they have understood a counterfactual compared to a factual conditional. They also make the inference more often when they have ruled out the possibility that the car was not out of petrol and it stalled, for example, when they have understood a biconditional. Most importantly for our purposes, these two factors are additive. On this account, people should make the inference from a counterfactual biconditional, such as "if the water had been heated to 100 degrees centigrade then it would have boiled." Their mental representation of the counterfactual biconditional includes the possibility that the water was not heated to 100 degrees and it did not boil (because it is a counterfactual), and they have ruled out the possibility that the water was not heated to 100 degrees and it boiled (because it is a biconditional). They should make more of the inference from a counterfactual biconditional than from a counterfactual conditional. In fact, the theory makes the even stronger prediction that they should make more of the inference from a counterfactual than a factual, even when they are both biconditionals. Even though the inference is naturally elevated for the factual biconditional, this account predicts that the counterfactual should elevate it even more.

The experiment corroborated these predictions (see Thompson and Byrne 2002 for details). For a counterfactual biconditional, such as "if the water had been heated to 100 degrees then it would have boiled" people made more of the inference than from a counterfactual conditional such as "if the car had been out of petrol then it would have stalled":

Counterfactual biconditional, 88 percent; counterfactual conditional, 43 percent

They also made more of the inference from a counterfactual biconditional than from a factual biconditional, such as "if the water was heated to 100 degrees then it boiled":

Counterfactual biconditional, 88 percent; factual biconditional, 61 percent

They also made more of the inference from the counterfactual conditional compared to the factual one:

Counterfactual conditional, 43 percent; factual conditional, 29 percent

The experiment shows that the usual increased frequency of the denial of the antecedent (not-A therefore not-B) inference from counterfactuals is not because they are interpreted as biconditionals.

When people understand a counterfactual, they envisage two possibilities from the outset, A and B, and not-A and not-B. For counterfactual biconditionals these two possibilities exhaust the possibilities consistent with them. For counterfactual conditionals a third possibility can be recovered, not-A and B. For counterfactuals about enabling relations the third possibility is, A and not-B. These three interpretations of counterfactuals may be the most common.

"Even If . . ." Conditionals and the Third Possibility

People understand a semifactual conditional such as "even if Nora had liked mathematics she would still have become a scientist" by thinking about just two possibilities from the outset, the conjecture, "Nora liked mathematics and she became a scientist," and the presupposed facts, "she did not like mathematics and she became a scientist."On a "relevance" interpretation the semifactual is consistent with just these two possibilities (Johnson-Laird and Byrne 2002). It is consistent with another possibility as well on a conditional interpretation, "she did not like mathematics and she did not become a scientist." On a "disabling" interpretation, it is con-

Table 6.4
Different interpretations of an "even if . . ." semifactual conditional

"Even if Nora had liked mathematics, she would have become a scientist"	Even if A, B
Relevance	
Nora did not like mathematics and she became a scientist (facts)	<u>not-A and B</u>
Nora liked mathematics and she became a scientist (imagined)	<u>A and B</u>
Conditional	
Nora did not like mathematics and she became a scientist (facts)	<u>not-A and B</u>
Nora liked mathematics and she became a scientist (imagined)	<u>A and B</u>
Nora did not like mathematics and she did not become a scientist (imagined)	not-A and not-B
Disabling	
Nora did not like mathematics and she became a scientist (facts)	<u>not-A and B</u>
Nora liked mathematics and she became a scientist (imagined)	<u>A and B</u>
Nora liked mathematics and she did not become a scientist (imagined)	A and not-B

Note: The possibilities people think about initially are underlined.

sistent with the third possibility, "she liked mathematics and she did not become a scientist" (see table 6.4). People do not think about a third possibility from the outset: the priming data show that there is no difference in the reading times for any other possibility, such as "Nora did not like mathematics and she did not become a scientist" and "Nora liked mathematics and she did not become a scientist," when participants read the conjunctions after a semifactual conditional compared to a factual conditional (Santamaría, Espino, and Byrne 2004).

But people may think about a third possibility when they try to make an inference from the semifactual conditional. The additional prompt of some extra information, such as "Nora did not become a scientist" may help them to think through other possibilities that did not come to mind immediately. In the experiment described earlier, Sergio Moreno-Ríos, Juan García-Madruga, and I discovered a strong clue that people consider a third possibility. The key test is the modus tollens inference, from "Nora did not

Table 6.5
The modus tollens (not-B therefore not-A) inference from "even if" on several interpretations

"Even if Nora had liked mathematics, she would have become a scientist"	Even if A, B	
Relevance		
Nora did not like mathematics and she became a scientist (facts)	<u>not-A and B</u>	(1)
Nora liked mathematics and she became a scientist (imagined)	<u>A and B</u>	(2)
Nora did not become a scientist, therefore nothing follows	*not-B (no match)*	
Conditional		
Nora did not like mathematics and she became a scientist (facts)	<u>not-A and B</u>	(1)
Nora liked mathematics and she became a scientist (imagined)	<u>A and B</u>	(2)
Nora did not like mathematics and she did not become a scientist (imagined)	not-A and not-B	(3)
Nora did not become a scientist therefore she did not like mathematics	*not-B ∴ not-A (matches 3)*	
Disabling		
Nora did not like mathematics and she became a scientist (facts)	<u>not-A and B</u>	(1)
Nora liked mathematics and she became a scientist (imagined)	<u>A and B</u>	(2)
Nora liked mathematics and she did not become a scientist (imagined)	A and not-B	(3)
Nora did not become a scientist therefore she liked mathematics	*not-B ∴ A (matches 3)*	

Note: The possibilities people think about initially are underlined.

become a scientist." What do you think follows? Your answer will depend on your interpretation of the semifactual conditional. Anyone who reaches the "relevance" interpretation, which is consistent with just two possibilities, "Nora liked mathematics and she became a scientist" and "Nora did not like mathematics and she became a scientist," should conclude that nothing follows (see table 6.5). Anyone who reaches the conditional interpretation which is consistent with three possibilities, "Nora liked mathematics and she became a scientist," "Nora did not like mathematics and she became a scientist," and "Nora did not like mathematics and she did not became a scientist" should conclude that "Nora did not like mathematics." Anyone who reaches the "disabling" interpretation which is consistent with three possibilities, "Nora liked mathematics and she became a scientist," "Nora did not like mathematics and she became a scientist," and "Nora liked mathematics and she did not became a scientist" should make the inference that Nora *liked* mathematics. It is possible to distinguish which of these three interpretations people have reached by examining their response to this inference. The results suggest that people tend to interpret the semifactual as either a "relevance" interpretation or as a conditional. They made fewer of the inferences from semifactual conditionals compared to factual conditionals (50 versus 75 percent). Instead, they often said that nothing followed (42 percent). But half of the participants made the inference, "Nora did not like mathematics" (50 percent).

Of course, different content and context may lead people to come to different interpretations (Johnson-Laird and Byrne 2002). It is possible to construct semifactual conditionals that correspond to each of the three interpretations. Counterfactuals and semifactuals can be interpreted in many different ways. In fact, a counterfactual such as "if Joe had been in Brazil he would not have been in Rio" does not even convey the usual presupposed facts based on the falsity of the antecedent (Joe was not in Brazil) and the falsity of the consequent (Joe was in Rio). As chapter 2 showed, knowledge of the content and context rules out the possibility that Joe was not in Brazil and he was in Rio.

Summary

Imagined semifactual alternatives have an important influence on judgments of causality: when people imagine that even if the antecedent event had not happened, the outcome would still have happened, they judge that the antecedent was not a strong cause of the outcome. A clue from reasoning is that people mentally represent a semifactual conditional such as "even if the runner had taken the newer drug she would still have lost the race" by thinking about two possibilities, the conjecture, "the runner took the newer drug and she lost the race" (A and B), and the presupposed facts "the runner did not take the newer drug and she lost the race" (not-A and B). As a result people readily resist the denial of the antecedent inference (from "the runner did not take the newer drug" to "she did not lose the race"), and in fact they tend to infer "she lost the race." They also resist the affirmation of the consequent inference (from "she lost the race" to "she took the newer drug"), and instead they infer that nothing follows. Readers can also read the conjunction "the runner did not take the newer drug and she lost the race" more quickly when they have first read a semi-factual conditional rather than a factual one. They read the conjunction, "the runner took the newer drug and she lost the race" as quickly after either conditional. The clue helps to explain why an imagined semifactual alternative affects people's causal judgments.

An imagined semifactual alternative makes available the possibility "the runner did not take the newer drug and she lost the race," and this possibility ensures that people judge that the runner not taking the newer drug was not a strong cause of her losing the race. When people complete an "even if …" sentence or when they are told about the possibility of the antecedent not happening and the outcome happening (for example, other runners took the newer drug and they experienced the same side effects), they judge that the antecedent was not a strong cause of the outcome. The possibilities that people think about when they imagine a semifactual alternative correspond to the possibilities that they think about when they understand a weak causal relation. A semifactual conditional is consistent with several interpretations, just as a counterfactual conditional is. People mentally represent a semifactual by thinking about two possibilities. They may be able to recover a third possibility, depending on their interpretation of the semifactual.

When people imagine an alternative to reality in which the outcome turns out the same even though they acted differently, the outcome may seem inevitable. The idea that an outcome was inevitable can be comforting. A semifactual alternative can seem to absolve people of blame and responsibility for what happened. Some religions and cultures value the ideas of fate and destiny and preordination, ideas that hinge on the possibility that the outcome would have occurred regardless of any individual's attempted intervention. In fact, the ideas of perfection and advancement became popular only a few hundred years ago. We can speculate that people may not have been so inclined to imagine alternatives that are better than reality in other historical epochs.

7 The "Last Chance"

What would I do without this world
Where to be lasts but an instant ...
—Samuel Beckett, "Six Poemes"

During the World Cup soccer tournament in Japan in 2002, the match between Ireland and Germany went into several minutes of extra "injury"
time. The score was 1–0 to Germany, and Ireland's hopes of getting into
the semifinals seemed to be finished. Then at the eleventh hour, Robbie
Keane scored a goal. For every Irish fan who watched the match there could
be no doubt: the striker had saved Ireland's World Cup hopes. The previous
hour and a half of skill and luck, good or bad, of a team of trained profes-
sionals seemed as nothing compared to the single final strike. Did Keane
really save the day? The question illustrates a curious feature of human
thought. In a temporal sequence of events, people zoom in on the most
recent one. This "last chance" focus in counterfactual thought is pervasive
in everyday life. My aim in this chapter is to explain why.

People Focus on Recent Events

Imagined counterfactual alternatives in the sports domain provide many
compelling instances of the effect of the temporal order of events (Sanna
et al. 2003). Fans tend to dwell on a teams' most recent performance in a
basketball league (Sherman and McConnell 1996). People judge a skier
to be lucky when they complete a good ski jump after a poorly rated one
(Tiegen et al. 1999). In fact, the emphasis on the most recent event extends
beyond the sporting domain. Counterfactual thoughts about how major
events in history could have turned out differently also tend to focus on

the "last chance" juncture, for example, in conjectures about why the West rose to dominance (Tetlock and Parker 2005). The most recent or precipitating event is usually the one chosen as the cause (Mill [1872] 1956).

Even in noncausal sequences of independent events, people focus on the most recent one. Consider a game in which two individuals, Lisa and Jenny, each toss a coin. If both tosses come up the same, heads or tails, they will each win $1,000. But if they come up different neither wins. Lisa goes first and tosses a head, Jenny goes next and tosses a tail, and so neither wins. How do you think things could have turned out differently, if only ...? Who do you think feels more guilt? And who do you think will blame the other more? When people are asked to think about how things could have turned out differently, almost all of them think, "if only Jenny had tossed a head ..." (Miller and Gunasegaram 1990). What is more, they judge that Lisa will blame Jenny more, and that Jenny will feel more guilt than Lisa.

The focus on the recent event occurs in many everyday sequences, for example, people imagine a counterfactual alternative to the most recent event in a sequence in which the teacher sets examination questions first and then the students study assigned topics, and also when the students study assigned topics first and then the teacher sets the examination questions (Miller and Gunasegaram 1990). It occurs for games based on the color of cards, marbles in a sack, or throws of a dice (Byrne et al. 2000). Even when people are given an ordered sequence of letters, for example, xf, and asked to quickly replace one, they tend to undo mentally the second letter in the sequence (Kahneman and Tversky 1982). People focus on the most recent event for sequences of more than just a couple of events (Segura, Fernandez-Berrocal, and Byrne 2002). They focus on the last event to occur in the sequence even when it is mentioned first in the description (Byrne et al. 2000). And they focus on the last event not only when the outcome is bad, but also when it is good. For good outcomes, they judge that the second player, for example, Jenny, will feel more relief than Lisa (Byrne et al. 2000). Why do people mentally alter the most recent event when they imagine a counterfactual alternative to reality?

Clues from Reasoning: The Case of "Only If" Conditionals

The tendency to alter the most recent event may reflect a more general property of thinking, namely, that people mentally represent possibilities in a way that preserves information about the temporal order of occurrence of events in the world. People may tend to imagine counterfactual alternatives that focus on the most recent event because their mental representations preserve information about the order of occurrence of events in the world and they allocate a special status to the first event in a sequence. A demonstration of the effect of temporal order in the possibilities that people think about occurs for "only if" conditionals—for example, "Alicia went swimming only if she slept well." People maintain the order of occurrence of events in the world in their mental representations even when the order of mention of the events in a description is the opposite to their order of occurrence.

"Only If" Conditionals and Inferences

People often produce counterfactual conditionals such as "if only the weather had been good we would have had a picnic." But *only* is a flexible word and its position in an assertion can change the meaning of the assertion. Compare for example, the factual conditional, "if Alicia went swimming then she slept well" to an "only if" conditional "Alicia went swimming only if she slept well." You may be surprised to find that "if A then B" and "A only if B" are usually logically equivalent (see table 7.1). A moment's reflection will verify the equivalence. For example, what possibility is ruled out by "Alicia went swimming only if she slept well"? Most people judge accurately that the assertion rules out the possibility that Alicia went swimming and she did not sleep well. This is the same possibility that is ruled out by the conditional, "if Alicia went swimming then she slept well" (Jeffrey 1981).

But the two assertions are not psychologically equivalent, (Keenan 1971; Evans 1977). When you know that, "Alicia went swimming only if she slept well," which event do you believe occurs first, Alicia went swimming, or she slept well? The "only if" conditional seems to work best when its second clause, "Alicia slept well," refers to a state of affairs that holds prior to the state referred to in its first clause, "Alicia went swimming" (Cheng and Holyoak 1985; Evans and Beck 1981; Marcus and Rips 1979; Thompson and Mann 1995). In fact, "only if" is often used to express a permission, for example, "you can go out to play only if you tidy your room" (Girotto, Mazzocco, and Cherubini 1992).

People make different inferences from "only if" and "if" conditionals. Suppose you know that "Alicia went swimming only if she slept well" and

Table 7.1
Possibilities that are true and false for "if" and "only if"

If Alicia went swimming then she slept well (if A then B)
True possibilities
  Alicia went swimming and slept well
  Alicia did not go swimming and did not sleep well
  Alicia did not go swimming and slept well
False possibilities
  Alicia went swimming and did not sleep well
Alicia went swimming only if she slept well (A only if B)
True possibilities
  Alicia went swimming and slept well
  Alicia did not go swimming and did not sleep well
  Alicia did not go swimming and slept well
False possibilities
  Alicia went swimming and did not sleep well
If Alicia slept well then she went swimming (if B then A)
True possibilities
  Alicia went swimming and slept well
  Alicia did not go swimming and did not sleep well
  Alicia went swimming and did not sleep well
False possibilities
  Alicia did not go swimming and slept well

then you find out that "Alicia did not sleep well." What would you conclude? Many people conclude readily that "Alicia did not go swimming." The modus tollens (not-B therefore not-A) inference, which is difficult to make from an "if" conditional, is made readily from the "only if" conditional. For the conditional, "if Alicia went swimming then she slept well," people make the modus ponens inference (Alicia went swimming therefore she slept well) far more readily than the modus tollens one (Alicia did not sleep well therefore she did not go swimming). But there is no such difference for "Alicia went swimming only if she slept well." People readily make both inferences (Evans and Beck 1981; Roberge 1978). Why are the inferences so easy from the "only if" conditional?

The answer is that "only if" requires people to think about more possibilities from the outset than "if" (Johnson-Laird and Byrne 1989). As we have seen in previous chapters, people reason by thinking about possibilities (see table 7.2). They usually think about true possibilities and not about false

Table 7.2
Summary of principles thus far

1. True possibilities: *People keep in mind true possibilities.*
2. Few possibilities: *People keep in mind few possibilities.*
3. Dual possibilities: *Some ideas require people to think about two possibilities.*
4. Counterfactual possibilities: *People think about possibilities that once may have been true possibilities but can be true no longer.*
5. Mutability of dual possibilities: *People readily imagine a counterfactual alternative to a possibility if it is mentally represented with a second possibility.*
6. Forbidden possibilities: *People think about the forbidden possibility as well as the permitted possibility when they understand an obligation.*
7. Temporal possibilities: *The possibilities people think about encode the temporal order of events in the world.*

I. Actions: *People think about two possibilities when they understand an action.*
II. Single possibilities: *People can switch from thinking about one possibility to thinking about two possibilities e.g., for inactions.*
III. Controllable events: *People think about two possibilities when they understand controllable events.*
IV. Causes: People think about a single possibility when they understand a strong causal relation (*cause and outcome*). They can readily access a second possibility for an enabling condition (*enabler and outcome, no enabler and no outcome*).
V. Semifactual alternatives: When people mentally represent a semifactual assertion they think about two possibilities, A and B, and not-A and B. When they mentally represent a weak causal relation they can readily access the same two possibilities.
VI. Anchored possibilities: People think of the first element in a possibility as immutable.

ones, and they tend to think initially about very few possibilities. However, some ideas require people to keep in mind two possibilities from the outset. They must also keep track of the status of the possibilities, for example, as an imagined possibility or as the facts. When people understand an obligation, they think about the permitted possibility and the forbidden possibility noted as "forbidden." The possibilities that people mentally represent affect the counterfactual alternatives they imagine. They can more readily imagine a counterfactual alternative to the facts when they have mentally represented the facts by thinking about two possibilities from the outset, than when they have thought about just a single possibility. The possibilities that people think about explain the counterfactual alternatives they imagine to actions, controllable events, and socially unacceptable events. They explain the focus of counterfactual thoughts on enabling causal relations and semifactual thoughts on weak causal relations. The

Table 7.3
Possibilities that people mentally represent initially for factual and counterfactual "if" and "only if"

	Factual	Counterfactual
If A then B	A and B	A and B (imagined)
		Not-A and not-B (facts)
A only if B	B and A	B and A (imagined)
	Not-B and not-A	Not-B and not-A (facts)

possibilities that people keep in mind also explain their reasoning about "only if."

People understand "Alicia went swimming only if she slept well" by thinking about the possibility, "Alicia went swimming and she slept well," and they also think about the possibility "Alicia did not go swimming and she did not sleep well" (Johnson-Laird and Byrne 1989). "Only if" prompts people to think of dual possibilities. As a result, they can readily make both the modus ponens (A therefore B) and the modus tollens (not-B therefore not-A) inferences. But there is more to the mental representation of "only if" then keeping in mind two possibilities. People think about the possibilities in a way that preserves a record of the temporal order of the events in the world (see table 7.3).

Possibilities Preserve Temporal Order
Temporal information is conveyed implicitly by many "only if" conditionals, such as "Alicia went swimming only if she slept well." The information about the temporal order of events is preserved in the possibilities that people think about. People think about the possibility, "Alicia sleeps well and she goes swimming" (B and A), and the possibility, "Alicia does not sleep well and she does not go swimming" (not-B and not-A).

Some evidence to support this suggestion comes from studies of inferences. In fact, there are few inference studies of "only if." Instead, most studies of "only if" have been based on "truth-table tasks" that require people to evaluate the truth of different situations, for example, "Alicia did not go swimming and she slept well" (Evans, Clibbens, and Rood 1995, 1996). Other studies have been based on Wason's selection task (Evans, Legrenzi, and Girotto 1999; see chapter 4 for a description of the task). Nonetheless, existing inference studies show that people make two inferences more often from "Alicia went swimming only if she slept well" compared to "if Alicia went swimming then she slept well." They make the affirmation of the consequent inference (Alicia slept well therefore she went swimming) and the modus tollens inference (Alicia did not sleep well therefore she did not go swimming) (Evans and Beck 1981). These inferences are in a "backward" direction, from B to A. Their relative ease suggests a preference for processing information from B to A for "A only if B." (The evidence that the forwards inferences, modus ponens (A therefore B) and denial of the antecedent (not-A therefore not-B), are made more often for "if" than for "only if" is less robust.) The order in which people think about information affects the ease with which they make certain inferences, as the cartoon in figure 7.1 illustrates.

Further evidence to support the idea that people keep in mind the two possibilities for "only if" in the order in which they are assumed to have occurred in the world, comes from priming studies (Santamaría and Espino 2002). When people read an "only if" conditional such as, "there were tulips only if there were daffodils" (A only if B), they are primed to read quickly the conjunction, "there were daffodils and there were tulips" (B and A), and also "there were no daffodils and there were no tulips" (not-B and not-A). They read "there were no daffodils and there were no tulips" reliably faster after they had read an "only if" conditional than an "if" conditional. The result supports the view that people think about two possibilities when they understand "only if." Moreover, people do not read "there were no tulips and there were no daffodils" (not-A and not-B) more quickly after the "only if" conditional than the "if" conditional (Santamaría and Espino 2002). The result supports the view that people keep in mind the possibilities in a way that encodes their implied order of occurrence in the world.

The principle that people preserve the temporal order of events in their mental representations is summarized as follows:

7. Principle of temporal possibilities: *The possibilities that people think about encode the temporal order of events in the world.* For example, people think about "A only if B" by keeping in mind two possibilities in the order of B and A, and not-B and not-A.

THE FAR SIDE® By GARY LARSON

"Well, lemme think. ... You've stumped me, son.
Most folks only wanna know how to go
the other way."

Figure 7.1

Counterfactual "Only If" Conditionals People understand a factual "only
if" conditional such as "Peg went for a walk only if she felt well" by
thinking about the possibility, "Peg felt well and she went for a walk,"
and the possibility, "Peg did not feel well and she did not go for a walk."
Consider the counterfactual "only if" conditional, "Peg would have gone
for a walk only if she had felt well." The counterfactual is understood by
keeping in mind the same two possibilities, the conjecture, and the presupposed facts. As a result, the theory predicts that people should make the
same inferences from factual and counterfactual "only if."

Suzanne Egan, Juan García-Madruga, and I have compared factual conditionals such as "Peg went for a walk only if she felt well" to their counterfactual analogues, such as "Peg would have gone for a walk only if she had felt well" (Byrne, García-Madruga, and Egan 2003). We also compared factual conditionals such as "if Peg went for a walk then she felt well" to counterfactual conditionals, such as "if Peg had gone for a walk then she would have felt well." In the experiment we gave forty participants factual and counterfactual conditionals. One group received factual conditionals based on "if" and "only if," and the other group received counterfactual conditionals based on "if" and "only if." As the theory predicts, participants did not make reliably more of the negative inferences from the counterfactual "only if" conditional compared to the factual "only if" conditional. They did not make more denial of the antecedent (not-A therefore not-B) inferences from the counterfactual than the factual conditional:

Counterfactual conditional, 68 percent; factual conditional, 79 percent

And they did not make more of the modus tollens (not-B therefore not-A) inferences:

Counterfactual conditional, 92 percent; factual conditional, 96 percent

There were no reliable differences for the affirmative inferences either. The results support the view that people consider two possibilities when they understand factual "only if" conditionals, just as they do for counterfactual conditionals. Counterfactual conditionals generally elicit more negative inferences than factual conditionals, but counterfactual and factual "only if" conditionals both elicit the negative inferences readily. These results have been replicated with factual and counterfactual "unless" (see García-Madruga et al. 2004).

What "Only If" Does Not Mean   The results from these inference and priming studies rule out a number of alternative views about how people understand "only if." The results rule out the idea that people understand an "only if" conditional such as "there were tulips only if there were daffodils" by keeping in mind a single possibility in the reverse order, "there were daffodils and there were tulips" (Evans 1993; Santamaría and Espino 2002). The single-possibility view cannot explain the priming data which show that people read the possibility "there were no daffodils and there were no tulips" more quickly after "only if" compared to "if." In fact, the single-possibility account cannot explain the inference data either: it cannot explain the greater frequency of modus tollens (not-B therefore not-A) inferences from "only if" compared to "if."

The results also rule out the suggestion that an "only if" assertion such as "Peg went for a walk only if she felt well" conveys a double negative, similar to "if Peg did not feel well then she did not go for a walk" (if not-B then not-A) (Braine 1978). The thrust of this suggestion is that the modus tollens inference (Peg did not feel well therefore she did not go for a walk) is easy from "Peg went for a walk only if she felt well" because it is in effect a modus ponens inference from "if Peg did not feel well then she did not go for a walk" (Peg did not feel well therefore she did not go for a walk) (Braine 1978). But this view must predict that the modus ponens inference (Peg went for a walk therefore she felt well) should be difficult from "Peg went for a walk only if she felt well" because it is in effect a modus tollens inference from "if Peg did not feel well then she did not go for a walk." And the inference is not difficult (Johnson-Laird and Byrne 1989).

The results also rule out a third suggestion that "only if" is interpreted as a biconditional. If it were, high rates of both the denial of the antecedent (not-A therefore not-B) and affirmation of the consequent (B therefore A) would be expected because on a biconditional interpretation these inferences are not contradicted. It is true that the affirmation of the consequent (B therefore A) inference is generally made more readily and more quickly from "only if" than from "if" (Evans 1977; Evans and Beck 1981; Johnson-Laird and Byrne 1989). But, the frequency of the denial of the antecedent (not-A therefore not-B) inference is unstable. Some studies show that it is made more often from "only if" (Johnson-Laird and Byrne 1989; García-Madruga et al. 2004). Others show it is made less often, for example when implicit negation is used (Evans and Beck 1981). Still others show it is the same from "only if" and "if" (Evans 1977), and so we can rule out the biconditional explanation.

Finally, the results rule out the suggestion that people simply omit the "only" and interpret "Peg went for a walk only if she felt well" as if it meant "Peg went for a walk, if she felt well" (A, if B), in other words, "if Peg felt well, she went for a walk" (if B, A). The truth conditions for "if Peg felt well, she went for a walk" are different from the truth conditions of "if Peg went for a walk, she felt well" (if A, B), as table 7.1 shows. For example, what situation do you think is false, given "if Peg felt well, she went for a walk" (if B, A)? Most people judge accurately that the conditional rules out the possibility that Peg felt well and she did not go for a walk (B and not-A). Suppose you know that Peg went for a walk. What would you infer? Few people would infer that Peg felt well. But given "Peg went for a walk only if she felt well, Peg went for a walk," most people readily infer that Peg felt well.

Conditionals, such as "Peg went for a walk only if she felt well" are understood by thinking about two possibilities, but the possibilities preserve information about the presupposed temporal order of the events, that Peg first felt well, and then she went for a walk. This "directional" aspect of the possibilities that people consider provides a clue to understanding why imagined counterfactual alternatives tend to focus on the most recent event.

The Rational Imagination: Why People Change Recent Events

People think about possibilities in the temporal order that the events occurred in the world. The temporal order affects what people can mentally alter most readily when they imagine counterfactual alternatives. Consider again a game of the following sort:

Imagine two individuals who take part in a television game show. Each is given a bag of marbles, and each one picks a marble from their own bag. If the two marbles they pick are of the same color (i.e., both blue marbles or both white marbles) each individual wins $1,000. However, if the two marbles are not the same color, neither individual wins anything. Steven goes first and picks a blue marble from his bag. Paul goes next and the marble that he picks is a white marble.

Most people complete the assertion "the players could have won if only one of them had picked a different-color marble, for example, if ..." by suggesting the players could have won if only Paul had picked a blue marble. The result provides a clue about the sorts of possibilities that people consider when they understand the scenario. They may understand it by keeping in mind the true possibility: "Steven picks blue and Paul picks white and they lose," and they note that this possibility corresponds to the facts. But they can also think about the counterfactual possibilities, of which there are several, as table 7.4 shows. The "temporal-order" effect is that people imagine a counterfactual alternative to the second event, and they say "if only Paul had picked blue ...". Their assertion indicates that they can most readily imagine the counterfactual alternative, "Steven

Table 7.4

Possibilities people think about when they understand the marbles scenario

Fully explicit set of possibilities

   Steven picks blue and Paul picks white and they lose (facts)

   Steven picks blue and Paul picks blue and they win (imagined)

   Steven picks white and Paul picks white and they win (imagined)

   Steven picks white and Paul picks blue and they lose (imagined)

Initial possibilities

   Steven picks blue and Paul picks white and they lose (facts)

   Steven picks blue and Paul picks blue and they win (imagined)

picks blue and Paul picks blue and they win." They imagine a counterfactual alternative by mentally altering the most recent event. Why do they do so?

The answer is that people mentally represent the facts and the ways in which the players can win by keeping in mind certain possibilities. There are three counterfactual possibilities for this game and people tend to think about just one of them, the possibility "Steven picks blue and Paul picks blue and they win." They do not think about the possibility "Steven picks white and Paul picks blue and they lose" because it is not an *effective* counterfactual alternative. It does not change the outcome: the players still lose (Byrne 1997). But why do people not think about the possibility, "Steven picks white and Paul picks white and they win"?

People think about possibilities that preserve the order in which the events are presumed to have occurred in the world. When people imagine a counterfactual alternative to the marble game, they hold constant the first player's selection, for example, "Steven picked blue," and they change the second player's selection, for example, "Paul picked white." The first player's selection is presupposed (Miller and Gunasegaram 1990). It provides the background against which later events are perceived (Sherman and McConnell 1996). The first player's choice sets the stage, and subsequent choices are interpreted in the light of this context (Byrne et al. 2000). The game is now "about" picking blue marbles once the first player has picked a blue one, because winning depends on the second player's selection fitting in with the first player's selection (see also Byrne, Culhane, and Tasso 1995). A corollary to the principle of temporal possibilities can be described in the following way:

Corollary 6 for thoughts about anchored possibilities: People encode the first part of a possibility as immutable.

The earlier event is presupposed because it provides the cornerstone of the possibility. An experimental test of this idea is described, after a brief sketch of a computer program that simulates it.

A Program to Simulate Temporal Anchoring

Suppose you wanted to create a robot that had enough artificial intelligence to be able to imagine counterfactual alternatives. Let's start with a computer program that behaves like a person who is given the marble story. The program should generate the same sorts of counterfactual alternatives as people do. It should focus on the most recent event. What information does the program need in order to carry out the task in the way that the theory proposes people do? The answer is, it needs to be able to keep a record of certain sorts of possibilities, and to make changes to those possibilities.

Clare Walsh and I have constructed a computer program to simulate this account of the temporal-order effect (Walsh and Byrne 2001). The program, which is written in LISP, takes as input a simple description of a game such as the marble one, for example "if the two marbles are of the same color (both blue or both white), each player wins $1,000." It produces as output a counterfactual conjecture about how the events could have turned out differently, for example, "if Paul had picked blue they would have won." The program makes a record of the facts described in the story, "Steven picks blue and Paul picks white and they lose." It also makes a record of the set of counterfactual possibilities suggested by the story, that is, the possibilities in which the players would have won (Walsh and Byrne 2004b). The possibilities in which the players would have won are as follows:

Steven picks blue and Paul picks blue and they win.
Steven picks white and Paul picks white and they win.

The program compares its record of the facts,

Steven picks blue and Paul picks white and they lose.

to the two possibilities in which the players would have won (see table 7.5). It generates a counterfactual alternative by changing aspects of its record of the facts to be like aspects of its record of the possibilities in which the players would have won.

Table 7.5
An algorithm that uses the facts and the winning possibilities to generate a counter-factual

---

Example 1 "If they both pick the same color marble (both blue or both white) they each win $1,000"
Facts
  Steven picks blue and Paul picks white and they lose
Winning possibilities
  Steven picks blue and Paul picks blue and they win
  Steven picks white and Paul picks white and they win
Algorithm
  Select the first element (Steven picks blue) from "facts."
  Search for match in "winning possibilities."
  A match is found: the first element in "facts" matches the first element in the first possibility in "winning possibilities."
  Select the first possibility in "winning possibilities" to use as a base for a counterfactual. Change the second element of "facts" to be like the second element of the selected "winning possibility."
  Output: Steven picks blue and Paul picks blue and they win
Counterfactual
  If only Paul had picked blue (second event changed)

Example 2 "If Lisa or Jenny but not both pick a white marble they each win $1,000"
Facts
  Lisa picks blue and Jenny picks blue and they lose
Winning possibilities
  Lisa picks blue and Jenny picks white and they win
  Lisa picks white and Jenny picks blue and they win
Initial representation of winning possibilities
                        Jenny picks white
  Lisa picks white
Algorithm
  Select the first element (Lisa picks blue) from "facts."
  Search for match in (the initial representation of) "winning possibilities."
  No match is found to the first element in any possibility in "winning possibilities."
  Negate the selected element from facts (Lisa picks blue) to be: "Lisa picks white."
  Search for a match in (the initial representation of) "winning possibilities."
  A match is found: the first element in "facts" matches the first element in the second possibility in (the initial representation of) "winning possibilities."
  Select the second possibility in (the initial representation of) "winning possibilities" to use as a base for a counterfactual. Change the first element of "facts" to be like the first element of the selected "winning possibility." Complete the initial representation of "winning possibility" to include "Jenny picks blue."
  Output: Lisa picks white and Jenny picks blue and they win
Counterfactual
  If only Lisa had picked white (first event changed)

The program relies on a simple algorithm. It selects the first player's play in its record of the facts—that is, Steven picks blue. It seeks a match for it in the possibilities in which the players could have won. In this case, it finds a match in the first possibility: "Steven picks blue and Paul picks blue and they win." Because it readily finds a match for the first player's play in its record of the winning possibilities, it changes the second player's play from its record of the facts (Paul picks white), to be like the second player's play in this winning possibility (Paul picks blue). It describes this counterfactual alternative with the conditional, "if Paul had picked blue, they would have won." The program illustrates the key principle: because Steven is the first player mentioned in the facts, his selection is the anchor and it is held constant. Accordingly the program alters the second player's selection to fit with the possibilities in which the players could have won (for further details see Walsh and Byrne 2001). A novel prediction of the program is examined, after some experimental evidence that people anchor possibilities in this way.

Anchored Possibilities and Dual Possibilities

Do the possibilities that people think about contain some immutable aspects as anchors? When people understand "Steven picks blue and Paul picks white," the first player's selection, "Steven picks blue" becomes anchored. An anchored idea is *immutable*. Just as fault lines in the mental representation of reality are mutable, so too anchors in the mental representation of reality are immutable. An anchored idea is akin to a single possibility idea in that people do not readily think of an alternative to it.

But just as a single-possibility idea can be transformed into a dual possibility one, so too an anchored idea can be transformed into a more mutable one. How is it possible for an anchored idea to be transformed into a more mutable one? The key lies in the mutability of dual possibilities. People can imagine a counterfactual alternative more readily to a possibility when they have mentally represented a second possibility, than when they have thought about a single possibility. For example, they can imagine a counterfactual alternative readily to an action, such as "Laura was in company A and she decided to switch to company B" because they have thought about two possibilities, the pre-action possibility, "Laura was in company A," and the postaction possibility, "Laura was in company B." They can create a counterfactual alternative by mentally changing the post-action possibility to be like the preaction possibility. The theory predicts that people should be able to imagine a counterfactual alternative even to an anchor such the first player's selection, when they have thought about two possibilities rather than a single possibility.

Suppose in the television game show with blue and white marbles described earlier, there is a technical hitch, as follows:

Steven goes first and picks a blue marble from his sack. At this point, the game-show host has to stop the game because of a technical difficulty. After a few minutes, the technical problem is solved and the game can be restarted. Steven goes first again, and this time the marble that he draws is a white one. Paul goes next and the marble that he draws is a blue one.

Suppose you were asked to think about "how the players could each have won $1,000 if only one of them had picked a different-color marble, for example, if ...". How would you complete this thought? In this "technical hitch" story, the first player's posthitch selection is different from his prehitch selection. The first event, Steven picks blue, is the anchor but the technical hitch provides an alternative to it, Steven picks white. The idea that Steven picks white is the new anchor, but its effects are undermined by the availability of a counterfactual alternative, the prehitch event. People think about two possibilities, the prehitch and posthitch plays. As a result they can readily imagine a counterfactual alternative in which they mentally change the first event. The prehitch play provides a ready made counterfactual. The theory predicts that participants should complete the sentence by saying, "if only Steven had picked blue."

We tested this prediction in an experiment in which we gave 75 participants technical hitch scenarios (Byrne et al. 2000). One group received the technical hitch scenario in which Steven's prehitch and posthitch selections were different. The second group received a control version of the story in which Steven's posthitch selection was the same as his prehitch selection, he picked white the first time, then there was a technical hitch, and he picked white again; Paul went next and he picked blue, and they lost (see table 7.5). The theory predicted that the effects of the anchor should be overridden when it is pitted against the effects of a ready-made counterfactual alternative in the technical hitch scenario (Byrne et al. 2000).

The results corroborated the prediction and showed that it is possible to shake loose an anchor, and render the first event mutable by making available a counterfactual alternative to it. Participants were asked, "Steven and Paul could each have won $1,000 if only one of them had picked a different marble, for instance if ...". They sometimes imagined a counterfactual alternative in which the technical hitch had not happened, but more often they imagined a counterfactual alternative to the first event or the second event. They imagined a counterfactual alternative to the first event just as often as the second event when the technical hitch provided a ready-made alternative to it:

Technical hitch: second player, 44 percent; first player, 42 percent

The typical temporal-order effect, of focusing on the most recent event, was eliminated. But the second group, who read the control scenario in which the technical hitch did not provide an alternative to the anchor, showed the typical temporal-order effect and imagined a counterfactual alternative to the second event reliably more often than to the first event:

Control technical hitch: second player, 59 percent; first player, 23 percent

The experiment shows that anchoring is overridden by the technical hitch scenario in which the first player's prehitch play is an alternative to the first player's posthitch play. The anchoring role of the first event and the dual possibilities made available by the technical hitch act as opposing determinants of the mutability of the events. Some participants' judgments are guided by the anchored event to focus on the second player and they exhibit a temporal-order effect, whereas others are guided by the available alternative to focus on the first player instead.

We also asked participants questions about emotions and social ascriptions, for example, "who would you predict would experience more guilt?" The technical hitch story eliminated the tendency to judge that the second person would experience more guilt:

Technical hitch: first person, 31 percent; second person, 44 percent

And in the control version of the technical hitch story, participants judgments of guilt exhibited the standard temporal-order effect:

Control technical hitch: first person, 10 percent; second person, 77 percent

(see Byrne et al. 2000 for details).

The results rule out the possibility that the temporal-order effect occurs simply because the recent event is fresh in working memory, or more available to a backward search through the entries. Miller and Gunase-garam (1990, 1117) briefly considered the possibility that "later events in a temporal sequence may be assigned more causal responsibility because they are more available in memory." If so, the effect should be observed in both versions of the story, since the second player's selection is most recent in either version. The results also rule out the possibility that it is the unusual nature of the technical hitch that eliminates the temporal-order effect. A technical hitch occurred in the control version also, and the partic-ipants given the control version showed the standard temporal order effect, so exceptionality is not the key.

Finally the results rule out the suggestion that people believe the second player has a greater causal role because they calculate the probability of a good outcome after each players' contribution (Spellman 1997). In the coin toss story, the probability of a good outcome is 50:50 before either play; it remains 50:50 after the first player's selection, but after the second player's selection, the probability of a good outcome changes, to either 1 or 0. On this account, people update their probability estimates after each play, and they consider the second play to have a greater causal role be-cause it determines the probability of the outcome more (Spellman 1997). But, the technical hitch manipulations do not alter the probabilities: The calculation remains the same for both versions of the story. On the proba-bility explanation, the temporal order effect should continue even when the alternative possibility is available for the first player's play.

The elimination of the temporal-order effect occurs because two oppos-ing tendencies weigh against each other: the anchor is weighed against the dual possibilities created by the prehitch alternative. In the technical hitch scenario, people keep track of the prehitch play and the posthitch play:

Steven picks blue (prehitch)
Steven picks white and Paul picks blue (posthitch)

When they imagine a counterfactual alternative, they rely on the informa-tion they have already mentally represented in these two possibilities. They imagine an alternative by mentally changing the current reality to be like the past, now counterfactual, possibility. In other experiments we have found that people sometimes think of two possibilities from the outset when they understand the first player's selection, when an alternative is available from memory, or even when one is available from the linguistic convention about the usual order of terms—for example, "heads or tails" rather than "tails or heads." The temporal order effect depends on the order of the occurrence of events in the world, not their order of mention. When people are told "Paul picked a blue marble, before him, Steven picked a white marble" they still imagine a counterfactual alternative by mentally altering the second event to occur in the world, even though it corresponds to the first event in the description (see Byrne et al. 2000 for details).

The Space of Counterfactual Possibilities

The algorithm described earlier implies that people imagine a counterfactual alternative by thinking about the facts and also some of the counterfactual possibilities—for instance, the possibilities in which the players win (Walsh and Byrne 2004b). People imagine a counterfactual alternative by mentally changing an aspect of the facts to fit with an aspect of one of the possibilities in which the players win. Clare Walsh and I have shown that the way that people mentally represent the winning possibilities has a dramatic effect on the counterfactual alternatives they imagine (Walsh and Byrne 2004b). The demonstration depends on the key principle that people think of few possibilities.

For example, suppose you know that there are only blue and white marbles in a bag. Consider the disjunction, "Lisa or Jenny but not both pick a blue marble." What do you think about when you understand it? It corresponds to two true possibilities. In one, Lisa picks a blue marble and Jenny picks a white one, and in the other Lisa picks a white marble and Jenny picks a blue one, as follows:

Lisa picks blue and Jenny picks white.
Lisa picks white and Jenny picks blue.

But people think about only some aspects of the true possibilities, the aspects mentioned in the assertion, and their thoughts on other aspects remain unformed (Johnson-Laird and Byrne 1991, 2002). When they are told that "Lisa or Jenny but not both pick a blue marble," they think about one possibility in which Lisa picks a blue marble, and they think about another separate possibility in which Jenny picks a blue marble. They do not think through the idea that in the possibility in which Lisa picks a blue marble, Jenny picks a white one. Instead they leave that information

unformed in their thoughts, which is captured as a blank space in the following diagram:

Lisa picks blue.

                    Jenny picks blue.

In the first possibility, "Lisa picks blue" is thought about fully. In this
possibility, Jenny does not pick blue, she picks white, but that information
remains unformed, a thought that can be developed at a later time if
needed (see Johnson-Laird and Byrne 2002). Their incomplete representation can be completed if necessary.

   Consider the same disjunction, but described somewhat differently: "Lisa
or Jenny but not both pick a *white* marble." What do you think about when
you understand it? It is consistent with the same full set of possibilities as
the "blue marbles" disjunction:

Lisa picks blue and Jenny picks white.
Lisa picks white and Jenny picks blue.

However, people think about the "white marbles" disjunction differently
because they represent just some information explicitly. They think about
one possibility in which Jenny picks white, and another separate possibility
in which Lisa picks white:

                    Jenny picks white.
Lisa picks white.

Consider now a game based on such a disjunction. The two assertions "if
Lisa or Jenny but not both pick a blue marble they each win $1,000" and
"if Lisa or Jenny but not both pick a *white* marble they each win $1,000"
mean the same thing, they are consistent with the same possibilities in
which the players can win. But they are mentally represented in different
ways, as table 7.6 shows. Because people mentally represent the assertions
in different ways, they imagine very different counterfactual alternatives to
them.

   Suppose you know that the rule for the new marble game is that if Lisa or
Jenny but not both pick a white marble they each win $1,000. Suppose you
are told that the outcome was that Lisa goes first and picks a blue marble
from her bag. Jenny goes next and the marble that she picks is a blue
marble. As a result, they lose. How do you think the game could have
turned out differently? You might say, "if only Lisa had picked a white

Table 7.6
Initial mental representations of the winning possibilities for the "blue" and "white"
disjunctions

Blue disjunction: "Lisa or Jenny but not both pick a <u>blue</u> marble"
Explicit winning possibilities
  Lisa picks blue and Jenny picks white
  Lisa picks white and Jenny picks blue
Initial (incomplete) possibilities
  Lisa picks blue

         Jenny picks blue
White disjunction: "Lisa or Jenny but not both pick a <u>white</u> marble"
Explicit winning possibilities
  Lisa picks blue and Jenny picks white
  Lisa picks white and Jenny picks blue
Initial (incomplete) possibilities
         Jenny picks white

Lisa picks white

---

marble ...". But this counterfactual assertion focuses on the first player not
the most recent one: it is the reverse of the standard temporal order effect.
Our computer program exhibits this reversal and it is informative to examine why.

We gave the program the facts:

Lisa picks blue and Jenny picks blue and they lose.

and we gave it the new game described in terms of *white* marbles "if Lisa or
Jenny but not both pick a white marble they each win $1,000." It con-
structs incomplete possibilities to represent the conditions under which
the players can win:

       Jenny picks white.
Lisa picks white.

The simple algorithm relies on selecting the first fact "Lisa picks blue"
(the anchor in the facts) and searching for a match to it in the winning
possibilities. But in this example, unlike in the earlier example, the program does not find a match (because the possibilities are represented in an
incomplete manner). Instead, it must turn to its next tactic (see example 2
in table 7.5).

When the program fails to find a match to the first fact, it looks for a match to the opposite of the fact (the opposite of "Lisa picks blue" in this binary game is "Lisa picks white"). It finds a match for "Lisa picks white" in the second possibility. It completes this selected possibility:

Lisa picks white and Jenny picks blue and they win.

It describes the counterfactual alternative and produces the output, "if only Lisa had picked white." The program produces the reverse of the temporal-order effect, when it is given the "white marbles" disjunction.

The program's performance illustrates an important point: the description of the conditions by which the players can win determines how accessible certain possibilities are. The theory predicts that when people are given the "white marbles" disjunction they should exhibit a reversal of the temporal-order effect, and say "if only Lisa picked white"; when they are given the "blue marbles" disjunction they should exhibit the standard temporal-order effect, and say "if only Jenny had picked white."

In one experiment we gave 148 participants a scenario about two individuals participating in a game of this sort (Walsh and Byrne 2004b). The experimental group were given a disjunction of the following sort "If one or the other but not both picks a *white* marble, each individual wins $1,000." In the scenario, Lisa goes first and selects a blue marble, Jenny goes second and the marble that she selects is also blue, and the outcome is that both players lose. The control group were given a simple conjunction to describe the winning conditions. All of the participants were asked to complete the sentence "Lisa and Jenny could each have won $1,000 if only one of them had picked a different marble, for instance, if ...". The results showed that the temporal-order effect was reversed. Reliably more participants focused on the first player's selection and said "if only Lisa had picked a white marble" than on the second player's selection:

White marbles: first player, 40 percent; second player, 24 percent

In a second experiment we gave 152 students the same scenario but this time the experimental group were given a disjunction of the following sort "If one or the other but not both picks a *blue* marble, each individual wins $1,000." Once again, in the story Lisa goes first and selects a blue marble, Jenny goes second and the marble that she selects is also blue, and the outcome is that both players lose. The blue disjunction produced the standard temporal-order effect. Reliably more participants focused on the second player and said "if only Jenny had selected a white marble" than on the first player:

Blue marbles: first player, 25 percent; second player, 38 percent

The two versions of the story differed only in a single word in the description of how the players could win, "blue" or "white." The facts were the same (both picked blue), and the possibilities in which the players could win were the same (the players would win in the possibility in which Lisa picks blue and Jenny white, or Lisa picks white and Jenny blue); all that differed was a single word in the description of the winning conditions. Yet the imagined counterfactual alternatives were dramatically different.

The experiments show that imagined counterfactual alternatives are sensitive to the way in which possibilities have been mentally represented. However, emotions may be more impermeable. In the experiments we asked participants to judge various emotional and social ascriptions—for example, who would experience more guilt. The participants judged that the second player would feel more guilt than the first player regardless of whether the description was about blue or white marbles. The dissociation between emotions and counterfactual thoughts suggests that emotional judgments may be affected most by the factual outcome and the conditions under which the players can win, rather than by the nature of the description. Nonetheless the experiments show that people mentally represent possibilities that preserve the temporal order of events in the world. They encode the first part of a possibility as immutable, and this anchor influences their imagination of counterfactual alternatives.

Summary

People imagine counterfactual alternatives that focus on the more recent event in an independent sequence of events. A clue from reasoning is that people preserve the temporal order of events in the possibilities they think about. A conditional, such as "Alicia went swimming only if she slept well" (A only if B) is understood by thinking about two possibilities, "Alicia slept well and she went swimming" (B and A) and "Alicia did not sleep well and she did not go swimming" (not-B and not-A). The possibilities preserve the presumed temporal order of the events in the world, Alicia slept well occurred first, and she went swimming second. As a result, inferences in the direction from B to A, such as the affirmation of the consequent (Alicia slept well therefore she went swimming) and modus tollens (Alicia did not sleep well therefore she did not go swimming) are made more readily from "only if" then from "if." People also keep in mind the same two possibilities when they understand a counterfactual "only if" conditional such as "Alicia would have gone swimming only if she had slept well."

This clue from reasoning sheds light on the phenomenon that people imagine counterfactual alternatives by mentally changing the most recent event. People understand a sequence of events such as "Steven picked a blue marble and Paul picked a white marble" by mentally representing the facts anchored by the earlier event, Steven picked a blue marble. The anchor is usually immutable but it can be overridden when people mentally represent an alternative possibility, for example, when there is a technical hitch and a player's prehitch selection is different from their posthitch selection. They can imagine a counterfactual alternative to the earlier event just as readily as the recent event when they have mentally represented an alternative to the earlier event. Sometimes they imagine a counterfactual alternative to an earlier event rather than a recent event because they have mentally represented the events in an incomplete way.

The idea of a "last chance" is a powerful one. When people try to understand why someone carried out an inexplicable act, such as a school massacre, they often focus on the events that occurred immediately prior to the crime. Their focus reflects the belief that the bad outcome was precipitated by the event that immediately preceded it, "the straw that broke the camel's back." It arises because people can readily imagine a counterfactual alternative in which the last event did not happen, and so the outcome was prevented.

People differ in the way they think about possibilities. One illustration of how they differ comes from the way in which they deal with contradictions. In Rex Stout's 1949 story *Instead of Evidence*, a man is killed when he smokes a cigar that has an explosive hidden in it. The police discover that several of the cigars in the man's cigar box have been skillfully rewrapped with explosive hidden inside them. Underneath all of the cigars there are several strands of long hair. Inspector Cramer suspects that the murderer is the man's wife, Martha. He believes that if Martha's hair is in the box then she is the murderer. He also believes that the hair in the box *is* Martha's hair. He concludes that Martha is the murderer. But the heroes of the novel, Nero Wolfe and Archie Goodwin do not believe that Martha is the murderer. She is their client. How can they resolve the contradiction between their beliefs and Inspector Cramer's conclusions?

The story provides a good illustration of how different individuals think about possibilities (Byrne and Walsh, forthcoming). Nero Wolfe and Archie Goodwin resolve the contradiction in two different ways. Archie Goodwin focuses on a single possibility, the claim that the hair in the cigar box is Martha's. He denies this possibility and tells Inspector Cramer that the hair in the cigar box is *not* Martha's. His denial is plausible in the pre-DNA analysis days of 1949. Nero Wolfe focuses instead on the possibilities expressed in the conditional hypothesis, if Martha's hair is in the box then she is the murderer. He argues that if Martha's hair is in box then she is *not* the murderer: "those hairs, far from being evidence that Martha killed her husband, are instead evidence that she did not kill her husband!" His view is that any murderer methodical enough to rewrap cigars with hidden explosives in them would not leave his or her hair in the cigar box. The hairs must have been deliberately planted there to frame Martha. There are many ways in which the two detectives differ, as fans of Stout's stories will appreciate, and one way is in the sorts of possibilities they think about. Unfortunately, in this rare case neither detective thought about the possibility that turns out to be true. Martha did kill her husband and the hairs in the box were hers. She had planted them there herself to throw everyone off her trail.

People imagine counterfactual alternatives by thinking about particular sorts of possibilities. This view has several implications and this chapter sketches two of them. The idea that the imagination depends on thinking about possibilities has implications for understanding the nature of differences between individuals in imaginative thoughts, and the first section considers these implications. The idea also has implications for the relation of counterfactual thoughts to other sorts of creative thoughts, and the second section considers the creative imagination.

Individual Differences in Imaginative Thoughts

Most people exhibit the sorts of regularities described in the earlier chapters, such as the tendency to imagine alternatives to actions or to controllable events or to forbidden events. But a minority of people do the opposite. People may create different counterfactual alternatives depending on their motivation, for example to console a victim or to allocate blame (Seeleu et al. 1995; McMullen and Markman 2000). They may imagine different alternatives depending on their goals, for example to improve their performance, or to feel better about their failure (Roese, Sanna, and Galinsky 2005). As chapter 1 outlined, their tendency to create counterfactual alternatives may be affected by characteristics of their personalities, such as high self-esteem, or by emotional disorders such as depression (Kasimatis and Wells 1995; Sanna, Turley-Ames, and Meier 1999; Roese and Olson 1993a). Differences between individuals in the imagination of counterfactual alternatives may also be affected by cognitive differences.

People may create different counterfactual alternatives because of differences in their ability to think about possibilities of various sorts. People differ in their cognitive abilities in many ways. For example, cognitive differences in spatial and linguistic abilities underlie many differences between individuals in reasoning (Sternberg 1985). Cognitive differences may be correlated with differences in making judgments and decisions of various sorts (Stanovich 1999).

Cognitive differences may exist in how people think about possibilities. For example, people may differ in their ability to think about true possibilities. They may differ in their ability to generate alternative true possibilities (Torrens, Thompson, and Cramer 1999). The ability to think about alternative possibilities develops as children get older (Barrouillet and Lecas 1998, 1999), perhaps because improvements in working memory facilitate the consideration of counterexamples (Oakhill and Johnson-Laird 1986). Adults also differ in their ability to keep in mind alternative true possibilities perhaps because of differences in working memory abilities (García-Madruga et al., forthcoming). For example, people differ in their tendency to interpret "if" as a biconditional, or as a conditional (Markovits 1984). The biconditional is consistent with two possibilities and the conditional is consistent with three possibilities, and the tendency to interpret "if" as one or the other may depend in part on the ease with which people can think about different possibilities.

People may also differ in their ability to think about counterfactual possibilities. The ability to think about counterfactual possibilities develops as children get older (Riggs et al. 1998; Leevers and Harris 1999). Adults also differ in their ability to think about counterfactual possibilities. Some people tend to focus on the facts when they understand a counterfactual conditional, whereas other people tend to think about the imagined alternative (Byrne and Tasso 1999). Imagine Mary got 50 percent on a test, and her teacher says "if you had studied harder you would have got 70 percent." The counterfactual conditional is consistent with at least two possibilities, the presupposed facts, Mary did not study hard and she did not get 70 percent (not-A and not-B), and the conjecture, Mary studied hard and she got 70 percent (A and B). Some people seem to focus on the facts, whereas others seem to focus on the imagined alternative.

Facts and Other Possibilities
Little is known about the circumstances that lead people to focus more on the facts or the imagined alternative. But one factor is the nature of the counterfactual itself. Some counterfactuals describe a worse world. For example, Mary may think, "I could have obtained only 20 percent." This thought may focus attention on the good aspects of the facts: they are

better than the imagined alternative (McMullen and Markman 2000). Other counterfactuals describe a better world. For example, Mary may think, "I could have obtained 70 percent." This thought focuses attention on the counterfactual possibility: it is better than the facts.

But there may also be differences in the way that different individuals think about the same counterfactual, even when it is about a neutral topic, such as "if there had been a circle on the blackboard then there would have been a triangle." Some individuals may tend to focus more on the facts and others on the imagined possibility. Alessandra Tasso and I have found that different individuals focus on the two possibilities differently (Byrne and Tasso 1999). What two shapes do you think would best fit the counterfactual description? In one experiment we gave people this task (Byrne and Tasso 1999). We allocated thirty-eight students to two groups, and we gave one group the counterfactual conditional and the other group a factual conditional, "if there was a circle on the blackboard then there was a triangle." People consider a single possibility when they understand the factual conditional and it contains the two shapes, a circle and a triangle. The theory predicts that they should judge that these two shapes best fit the factual conditional. And most people generated this possibility (78 percent). People consider two possibilities when they understand the counterfactual conditional, the imagined possibility of a circle and a triangle, and the presupposed facts of no circle and no triangle. The theory predicts that they will be torn between these two possibilities. And they were. Half of the participants said the two shapes that would best fit the counterfactual were the circle and the triangle, and the other half said the two shapes that would best fit the counterfactual were not a circle and not a triangle.

Consider again the factual conditional: "if there was a circle on the blackboard then there was a triangle." What two shapes do you think would definitely go against the description? We gave this task to the participants in the experiment. The theory predicts it should be a difficult one. People tend to keep in mind true possibilities. They do not think about the possibility that goes against the description, a circle and not a triangle (A and not-B). They may have to think about all of the possibilities that are consistent with the conditional before they can work out which possibilities are inconsistent with it. Some of the participants (44 percent) were able to work out that the shapes that went against the factual conditional were a circle and not a triangle. But some of them thought that the two shapes that went against the conditional were not a circle and not a triangle (44 percent). The negation of a conditional is difficult and some people may simply negate its components (Byrne and Handley 1994).

Now consider what two shapes you think would definitely go against the counterfactual, "if there had been a circle on the blackboard then there would have been a triangle"? The participants' answers revealed an interesting tendency. One-third of participants were able to generate the possibility that is inconsistent with the conditional, a circle and not a triangle. But more often, participants identified one of the two possibilities that the theory proposes they already had in mind. One-third of them believed the presupposed facts, not a circle and not a triangle, went against the counterfactual, and one-third of them believed the conjectured possibility, a circle and a triangle, went against the counterfactual. No one thought the possibility of a circle and a triangle went against the factual conditional. The experiment shows that people have different opinions about which possibility makes a counterfactual true, and which possibility makes it false.

Multiple Possibilities

Does everyone think about two possibilities when they understand the counterfactual conditional? Valerie Thompson and I have found that there may be even more fundamental differences in the way different individuals interpret counterfactual conditionals (Thompson and Byrne 2002). A minority of individuals seem to think about just a single possibility. In one experiment we categorized participants into different groups based on their understanding and reasoning from counterfactuals such as "if Mark had gone to Moose Jaw then Karl would have gone to Medicine Hat" (Byrne and Thompson 2000). We were able to discern four distinct categories (as table 8.1 shows).

1. Most of the participants kept in mind two possibilities when they thought about the counterfactual conditional. They thought about the conjecture, "Mark went to Moose Jaw and Karl went to Medicine Hat," and they also thought about the presupposed facts, "Mark did not go to Moose Jaw and Karl did not go to Medicine Hat." We established that they thought about these two possibilities by their answers to two tasks. First, when they judged what someone who uttered the assertion meant to imply, they judged the person meant to imply "Mark did not go to Moose Jaw" or "Karl did not go to Medicine Hat," or both. Second, when they

Table 8.1
Differences between individuals in understanding factual and counterfactual conditionals

	Possibilities thought about	Judgments made
Counterfactual: If A had been then B would have been		
1. Dual-possibility group:	*not-A and not-B*	Implies "not-A" or "not-B"
	A and B	"A and B" is consistent
2. Single-possibility group:	*not-A and not-B*	Implies "not-A" or "not-B"
		"A and B" is inconsistent
Factual: If A then B		
3. Dual-possibility group:	*A and B*	Implies "A" or "B" or nothing
	. . .	"not-A and not-B" consistent
4. Single-possibility group:	*A and B*	Implies "A" or "B" or nothing
		"not-A and not-B" inconsistent

judged whether different situations were consistent or inconsistent with the assertion, they judged the situation, "Mark went to Moose Jaw and Karl went to Medicine Hat" to be *consistent* with it. On these criteria, 77 percent of our participants (51 out of 66 observations) thought about two possibilities when they understood the assertion.

2. A minority of the participants focused on a single possibility, the facts, "Mark did not go to Moose Jaw and Karl did not go to Medicine Hat." First, when they were asked what someone who uttered the assertion meant to imply, they judged they meant to imply "Mark did not go to Moose Jaw" or "Karl did not go to Medicine Hat," or both, like the first group. But unlike the first group, when they judged whether different situations were consistent or inconsistent with the assertion, they judged the situation "Mark went to Moose Jaw and Karl went to Medicine Hat" to be *inconsistent* with it. On these criteria, 23 percent of our participants (15 of the 66 observations) kept in mind a single possibility when they understood the assertion.

After we categorized the participants in this way, we then examined their performance on an inference task. We found that the two groups reasoned differently. The group who thought about just the single possibility, "Mark did not go to Moose Jaw and Karl did not go to Medicine Hat," made fewer modus ponens (A therefore B) inferences compared to the group who thought about two possibilities (60 versus 84 percent). When they were told that "Mark went to Moose Jaw" they did not infer as readily, "therefore, he went to Medicine Hat." The group who thought about just the single possibility also made fewer affirmation of the consequent (B therefore A) inferences compared to the group who thought about two possibilities (40 versus 67 percent). The differences are small but they provide some validation for the classification. The single-possibility group do not think initially about the possibility, "Mark went to Moose Jaw and Karl went to Medicine Hat" and so they make fewer inferences that rely on this possibility.

In the experiment, the participants were given subjunctive and indicative conditionals. We examined differences between individuals not only in their counterfactual interpretations but also in their factual interpretations.

3. When participants were given the factual conditional, "if Mark went to Moose Jaw then Karl went to Medicine Hat" most of them kept in mind a single possibility "Mark went to Moose Jaw and Karl went to Medicine Hat." But their interpretation was not entirely conjunctive and they appreciated that there may be alternative possibilities consistent with the conditional. First, when they judged what someone who uttered the conditional meant to imply, they judged the person meant to imply "Mark went to Moose Jaw" or "Karl went to Medicine Hat," or that nothing was implied (which is the logically correct answer). Second, when they judged whether different situations were consistent or inconsistent with the conditional, they judged the situation "Mark did not go to Moose Jaw and Karl did not go to Medicine Hat," to be *consistent* with it. On these criteria, 78 percent of our participants (120 out of 153 observations) kept in mind a single possibility when they understood the conditional but their understanding was not entirely conjunctive and they allowed that there may be other possibilities consistent with it.

4. A minority of the participants focused on a single possibility, the facts, "Mark went to Moose Jaw and Karl went to Medicine Hat," and their interpretation seemed entirely conjunctive. First, when they were asked what someone who uttered the conditional meant to imply, they judged they meant to imply "Mark went to Moose Jaw" or "Karl went to Medicine Hat," or that nothing was implied, like the previous group. But unlike them, when they judged whether different situations were consistent or inconsistent with the conditional, they judged the situation "Mark did not

go to Moose Jaw and Karl did not go to Medicine Hat" to be *inconsistent* with it. On these criteria, 22 percent of our participants (33 of the 153 observations) thought about a single possibility when they understood the conditional, and their interpretation seems conjunctive.

Once again, after we categorized the participants in this way, we then examined their performance on an inference task. Again we found that the two groups reasoned differently. The group who thought about just the single possibility, "Mark went to Moose Jaw and Karl went to Medicine Hat," in a conjunctive interpretation made fewer denial of the antecedent (not-A therefore not-B) inferences compared to the group who thought about a single possibility but allowed that there may be alternatives (27 versus 45 percent). The group who thought about just the single possibility in a conjunctive way also made fewer modus tollens (not-B therefore not-A) inferences compared to the group who thought about a single possibility but allowed that there may be alternatives (21 versus 53 percent). The differences again provide some validation for the classification. The conjunctive single possibility group did not think about other possibilities.

The results indicate that there are differences between different individuals in how willing or able they are to consider more than one possibility. Most people think about two possibilities when they come to a counterfactual interpretation, but a minority of individuals, up to a quarter of the individuals we encountered, thought about a single possibility only, the presupposed facts. Differences between individuals in reasoning about counterfactual conditionals may reflect differences in the ability to imagine counterfactual alternatives to reality. These differences in the imagination of possibilities when people understand a counterfactual conditional may have consequences for the impact of counterfactual thoughts. An individual who interprets a counterfactual "if Bert had driven fast, he would have been injured," by thinking only of the facts "Bert was not driving fast and he was not injured" may not benefit from the preparatory effects of counterfactual alternatives (Bert should not drive fast in the future), or from their emotional amplification (Bert feels relieved at his lucky escape this time).

People differ in their ability to keep in mind more than one possibility. Perhaps more importantly, they differ in their ability to keep in mind a possibility that may be false (Bert was driving fast and he was injured), and which they may need to assume to be true, temporarily. Difficulties in thinking about false possibilities are pervasive in many sorts of thought. They may underlie differences in the way that people confirm or falsify hypotheses (Mynatt, Doherty, and Tweney 1978; Wason 1966). For example, chess masters are able to test their hypotheses about good play sequences by thinking about potential refutations. They attempt to falsify their plans more often than less accomplished experts (Cowley and Byrne 2004). Difficulties in thinking about false possibilities may underlie differences in susceptibility to reasoning illusions (Johnson-Laird and Savary 1999). They may underlie differences in resolving contradictions and revising beliefs (Elio and Pelletier 1997; Revlin, Cate, and Rouss 2001; Byrne and Walsh 2002). The ability to think about a false possibility, and perhaps even to assume temporarily that it is true, is essential for the appreciation of fiction, for example, in literature, theater, and film, and for the suspension of disbelief in general. Our results suggest that there may be fundamental cognitive differences between different individuals in this ability.

Heuristics and Strategies

Differences between individuals may reflect differences in cognitive capacity, but they may also reflect differences in the adoption of different strategies. For example, people develop strategies to help them to solve complex deductions. Different people develop different strategies and their strategies are evident in their inferences (Byrne and Handley 1997). People also develop shortcuts (Kahneman, Slovic, and Tversky 1982; Kahneman and Frederick 2002). For example, they may judge probability by relying on quick estimates of the similarity of an instance to a general category (Kahneman and Tversky 1982). Their "rules of thumb" may be a collection of useful heuristics that lead to the correct answer sometimes but not always (Kahneman and Tversky 1982; Evans 1989; Slovic et al. 2002).

One possibility is that heuristics have been shaped by evolution to adapt to the ecological landscape (Gigerenzer and Todd 1999). But the idea that people reason by thinking about possibilities suggests that they may develop shortcuts that reflect their *internal* cognitive landscape—that is, the sorts of mental representations they construct. People may develop "principled heuristics" that reflect the operation of an algorithm applied to an abbreviated representation. For example, people sometimes make an inference on the basis of just a single possibility that they have kept in mind. When people know "if Alicia went to the stables then she rode Starlight," and they hear that "Alicia rode Starlight," many infer "Alicia went to the stables." They have kept in mind a single possibility, "Alicia went to the stables and she rode Starlight." They do not think through the full set of possibilities to discover any counterexamples to this affirmation of the consequent (B therefore A) inference. But when they are asked to judge whether the following possibility is consistent with the conditional "Alicia did not go to the stables and she rode Starlight," people can often judge that it is (the pony may live in a nearby field). They can think through the full set of possibilities when they are prompted to do so by the consistency judgment. Some individuals may develop a strategy to make an inference based on the initial possibility that they have thought about. The strategy can lead to the correct answer for some inferences but at other times it will be wrong. The strategy is a principled heuristic in that the algorithm is applied to a shortcut version of the fuller representation. Principled heuristics may explain the observation that performance errors can be systematic and related across tasks (Stanovich 1999).

Creative Thoughts

The counterfactual imagination is implicated in many everyday mental activities (Roese and Olson 1995). The ability to create alternatives to reality may provide the basis for daydreams and fantasies. Counterfactual thoughts play a role in pretence, including children's pretend play (Harris 2000). As chapter 1 outlined, everyday imaginative thoughts can seem more mundane than other sorts of creative thoughts (Finke, Ward, and Smith 1992). Creative thoughts are relied on to write a poem, paint a picture, compose a piece of music, design an experiment, or invent a new product. These sorts of activities can seem very different from the imagination of a counterfactual alternative to reality. But counterfactual imaginative thoughts may share some similarities with other sorts of creative thoughts. In the next section three sorts of creative thought illustrate some of the similarities.

Inventing New Instances of a Category

Take a moment to imagine a new alien life form. You might like to sketch your new creature. It is a task that faces the creators of comic book heroes and science fiction novels and films. The results are diverse, from the giant plants in *The Day of the Triffids*, to the fluid metal of the robots in *Terminator 2*. How do people imagine a new creature? Participants in experiments have been asked to draw a front and side view of a creature from a planet somewhere else in the universe, and to provide information on its diet and habitat and nonvisible properties (Ward 1994). They have been asked to draw another member of the species, and members of a different species. Their drawings differed very widely. But they also exhibited some very informative regularities. For example, people tended to make sure that their alien creature had sensory organs, most commonly eyes, and functional appendages, most commonly legs.

These regularities across creative products are as important as the originality and novelty of the creatures (Finke, Ward, and Smith 1992). They suggest that when people imagine new creatures, they may access some sort of exemplar of the existing concept (Rosch 1976). They modify it to create a new instance (Ward et al. 2004). Inventions of new instances of a category appear to be structured by existing conceptual knowledge. For example, when participants were asked to draw a creature that had feathers, they tended to include correlated attributes such as a beak and wings, more than when they were asked to draw a creature with fur (Ward 1994). The imagined home environment of the creature influences the sort of creature people imagine (Ward et al. 2004), as fans of the cartoon Spongebob Squarepants (who lives in a pineapple under the sea) will appreciate. Indeed, the structured nature of creations of new instances emerges even in children by the age of 5 years (Cacciari, Levorato, and Cicogna 1997). It is also evident in highly creative instances, such as the creatures in *Star Wars* (Ward 1994).

The task of conceptual expansion faces designers whenever they produce a new coffee mug, a better car, or a fashionable "new look." How do people invent new instances? They may think about a category by keeping in mind some possibilities. They may think of possibilities corresponding to true instances of the category, and they may not think about possibilities that are false. For example, they may consider an instance of the category "bird" that possesses the characteristics of wings and feathers such as a sparrow, rather than an instance that does not possess these characteristics such as a penguin. They may think about just a few of the true possibilities, for example they may recall a specific instance of a sparrow, rather than all of the true possibilities. They may imagine an alternative creature by making a minimal change to their representation of the facts, that is, to the exemplar they have in mind.

There are fault lines in categories and concepts just as there are in events and episodes. The fault lines may correspond to those aspects of reality for which people can readily think of dual possibilities. People can readily think of alternative possibilities for the size, shape, and color of creatures. For example, known birds come in many different sizes and so people can readily think of more than a single possibility. They can alter mentally these aspects of the category more readily than others. People may think of just a single possibility to mentally represent other aspects, such as the presence of the sensory organ of eyes. (People may think of several possibilities to represent the size and shape of eyes, but they are unlikely to represent their presence and as an alternative, their absence.) These aspects of reality seem immutable because people do not mentally represent them from the outset by thinking about two possibilities. Are there any known birds without eyes? The way in which people imagine alternative instances of a category shares similarities with the way they imagine alternatives to events and episodes. Imaginative thoughts about alternatives to a category follow the same principles, concerning the representation of true possibilities and few possibilities and the mutability of multiple possibilities, as imaginative thoughts about alternatives to an event.

Concept Combination

How do people come up with new ideas? One way is to expand an existing concept by thinking of new instances of a category. Another way is to combine several existing concepts to form a new one. Suppose you read the noun-noun combination "robin snake." What do you think it means? People can understand and produce new combinations that they have never heard before (Wisniewski and Gentner 1991; Costello and Keane 2000). New concept combinations enter into everyday language use regularly. New knowledge may emerge from the interaction of existing ideas.

How do people combine two concepts? Suppose you hear for the first time the combination "corn oil." What do you think it means? You may decide it is oil made from corn. Now imagine you hear for the first time, "baby oil." What does it mean? You are unlikely to decide it is oil made from babies. It is more likely you will conclude it is oil to rub on babies' skin. Now, what is "lamp oil"? It is unlikely you will say it is oil made from lamps, or oil to rub on lamps. Instead you might say it is oil to fuel lamps (Wisniewski 1996). People combine two ideas to create a new one in different ways. Most combinations go beyond a simple conjunction of the individual concepts. For example, "red apple" may be a conjunction of "red things," and "apples," but "fake gun" is not a member of the category "gun." Even when an instance is a member of the combined category and each individual category, it may not be a good instance of each one. For example, a "guppy" may be a good example of a "pet fish" but it is not a good example of either a "pet" or a "fish" (Hampton 1991).

When people combine two concepts they often transfer aspects of the first concept to change something about the second concept. What did you decide a "robin snake" was? You might think it is a snake with a red breast. Sometimes when people combine two concepts, they map the properties of the first concept onto the second. Alternatively, you might decide that a robin snake is a snake that eats robins. Sometimes when people combine two concepts, they create a relation between them that is not based on property mapping (Murphy 1988). There can be many different sorts of relations between two concepts, for example a mountain stream is a stream *in* a mountain, an electric shock is a shock *caused* by electricity and a honey bee is a bee that *makes* honey (Gagne and Shoben 1997). People may map the diagnostic aspects of a concept, for example, what is a "cactus fish"? You might consider that it is a fish that has prickly spines. Prickly spines are diagnostic of cactii, there are few other plants that have them (Costello and Keane 2001). Diagnostic aspects of a concept may be those aspects that are least mutable.

People may combine concepts by identifying the most *immutable* aspect of the first concept and the most *mutable* aspect of the second concept. Imaginative thoughts about combinations of concepts may also follow the same principles as imaginative thoughts about alternatives to an event. People may think about what snakes eat or the shapes and colors of fish by thinking about several possibilities from the outset. The perceived fault lines of the concept correspond to the aspects for which people can readily think of several possibilities. Because they mentally represent some aspects of a concept, for example, what snakes eat, by more than a single possibility from the outset they can alter those aspects readily. People may think about the prickly spines of a cactus or the color of a robin's breast by thinking about just a single possibility from the outset. They may not be able to think readily of alternative possibilities for this aspect of the concept, that is, a cactus that does not have prickly spikes, or a robin that does not have a red breast. Such aspects of a concept seem immutable. The way in which people create new ideas shares similarities with the way they imagine counterfactual alternatives.

Insight

In the sciences and arts, individuals sometimes report experiencing a moment of "insight" in which a new idea "pops" into mind (Eysenck and Keane 2000). There are also regularities in what people think about when they experience creative insights (Sternberg and Davidson 1995). Consider Duncker's candle problem: In a room there is a table pressed against a wall. On the table are a candle, a box of tacks, and a packet of matches. Your task is to attach the candle to the wall above the table in such a way that the wax from the lighted candle will not drip onto the table or the floor. How would you solve this problem? Most participants do not solve it (Weisberg and Suls 1973). The solution is that you should use the box containing the tacks as a candleholder. Use some of the tacks to attach it to the wall, light the candle and melt some of the wax into the box, and secure the candle in the box. The difficulty is that people tend to think about the box as a container for the tacks only, and not as a platform for the candle. This "functional fixity" hinders their creative problem solving.

Suppose now you are asked to describe how to throw a Ping-Pong ball so that it will go a short distance, come to a dead stop, and then reverse itself. You are not allowed to bounce the ball against any object or attach anything to it (Ansburg and Dominowski 2000). What solution would you suggest? Most people suggest throwing the ball so that it curves back to them (but this solution violates the constraint that the ball comes to a dead stop). Others suggest throwing the ball against a wall or to another person (but this solution violates the constraint not to bounce the ball against any object). Few people reach the correct solution, to throw the ball up into the air.

Why are these problems hard to solve? Problems that require "insight" have puzzled psychologists for many decades (Mayer 1995; Novick and Sherman 2003). People may think about problems such as the candle-box problem or the Ping-Pong one by thinking about just a few of the true possibilities. The possibilities that they think about are limited by their previous experience with similar situations (Keane 1997; Keane, Ledgeway, and Duff 1994). For example, they may mentally represent some aspects of the facts by thinking about a single possibility. They do not change the usual function of the thumbtack box as a container and they do not change the usual horizontal trajectory of a Ping-Pong ball in play. People often add mistaken assumptions to their mental representation when they try to solve such problems (Ohlsson 1992; Ormerod, MacGregor, and Chronicle 2002). They can solve them when they are primed to think about alternatives (Galinsky and Moskovitz 2000).

People may add the usual horizontal trajectory of a Ping-Pong ball in play to their mental representation of the problem. They may think about the trajectory of the ball by keeping in mind just this single possibility, and they may not entertain alternatives to it. But they may not add the horizontal trajectory assumption to their mental representation of other sorts of ball in play. For example, other balls travel in both vertical and horizontal trajectories when in play. This account predicts that in a basketball version of the problem, the trajectory of the ball should become a fault line in the mental representation of reality—that is, an aspect of the facts for which people can think of dual possibilities. Aisling Murray and I tested this idea (Murray and Byrne 2004). In one experiment we gave thirty-eight participants problems such as the Ping-Pong one. We gave one group of participants the Ping-Pong version and another group a basketball version. The problems differed in just one word: *Ping-Pong ball* or *basketball*. Only 29 percent of participants solved the Ping-Pong version but 53 percent solved the basketball version. The description of the ball as a Ping-Pong ball or as a basketball cues different knowledge from memory about the ball, such as its usual trajectory in play, and its weight. People are more readily able to think about several possibilities for the trajectory of a basketball. Moments of insight may be moments of mutability, when a previously immutable aspect of the mental representation of reality is transformed into a fault line.

There are many sorts of creative thoughts. Some of them share some commonalities with the counterfactual imagination, as illustrated by the three sorts outlined here, category expansion, concept combination, and insight. The brief sketch of each sort illustrates how the principles that underlie the counterfactual imagination may also underlie other sorts of creative thoughts. Of course, there are also differences between counterfactual thoughts and these other sorts of creative thoughts. Counterfactual thoughts may be common and spontaneous and they may occur as part of mundane daily mental life. Other sorts of creative thoughts may be more exotic and rare and they may occur in the service of deliberate goals (Sternberg and Davidson 1995). Nonetheless, they may share at least some cognitive processes in common.

Summary

There are many implications of the theory that people create counterfactual alternatives by thinking about possibilities guided by a small set of principles. One implication is that differences between individuals in their imaginative thoughts may depend on differences in the sorts of possibilities that they focus on, and differences in whether or not they think readily about a single possibility or dual possibilities. Another implication is that the counterfactual imagination may share some commonalities with other sorts of creative cognition. For example, similar sorts of processes may underlie the invention of new instances of a category, the creation of new ideas by combining concepts, and the role of insight in solving problems.

9 The Idea of a Rational Imagination

... a priest of the eternal imagination transmuting the daily bread of experience into the radiant body of ever living life.

—James Joyce, *A Portrait of the Artist as a Young Man*

The human imagination is one of the last frontiers of the mind. People create counterfactual alternatives to reality often in their daily mental lives. Imaginative thoughts about what might have been are so commonplace that they may be taken for granted. What would life be like without the ability to think "if only ..."? The answer is that it would be very different from normal life. People who could not create counterfactual alternatives to reality would be stuck with the facts. They could not conjecture how things might have turned out differently, or the same, and so they would experience neither a sense of inevitability about events, nor a sense that something else "almost" happened (Byrne 1997; Roese and Olson 1995). They might find it hard to mull over their mistakes in a constructive way to avoid similar ones in the future. They might be limited in their ability to create novel ideas or products. They may even lack the capacity to console others or to placate them or to provide excuses based on what might have been. They may have impoverished experiences of hope or relief, and feel little regret or guilt or remorse. Their tendency to attribute blame or to establish fault and responsibility might be curtailed. In fact, some people do appear to lose the capacity to create counterfactual alternatives. Brain injury to the frontal cortex can impair the ability to imagine counterfactual possibilities (Knight and Grabowecky 1995; see also Damasio 1994). A mental life occupied solely by facts would lack the rich variety of cognitive, emotional, and social experiences that most people take for granted.

The counterfactual imagination is a central part of human mental life. The aim of this book has been to explain how the mind creates counterfactual alternatives to reality. This final chapter summarizes the key argument of the book: the counterfactual imagination is rational. It outlines the principles that underlie the rational imagination and their application to the core phenomena of counterfactual thought. It finishes with a discussion of the extent to which the counterfactual imagination is genuinely rational.

Reality and Other Possibilities

Is it crucial to establish whether the counterfactual imagination is rational or irrational? One of the reasons people create alternatives to reality may be to learn from mistakes and prepare for the future (Roese 1994). Imaginative thoughts about how events in the past could have turned out differently may help people try to make sure that similar events in the future do turn out differently. Emotional experiences such as regret may help people to make better decisions (Ritov and Baron 1995). A counterfactual alternative may provide a plan for how to prevent mistakes (Markman et al. 1993; Mandel and Lehman 1996). Another reason people create alternatives to reality may be to help them work out causal relations (Roese and Olson 1997). Thoughts about what might have happened "if only ..." or "even if ..." may help people make sense of their personal histories. What are the consequences of a rational counterfactual imagination, or an irrational counterfactual imagination? If the counterfactual imagination is an irrational process, its usefulness and reliability are in doubt.

The claim that the counterfactual imagination is rational depends on three steps. The first step is that humans are capable of rational thought. People can make rational inferences, as illustrated by evidence about their deductions. But people also make mistakes. Does the existence of error undermine the idea of rational thought? Perhaps, not. People may be rational in principle—that is, they have the mental machinery to make rational inferences. But they may err in practice—that is, their performance is constrained by various factors such as working-memory limitations, as well as their knowledge, beliefs, and interest in different topics (Johnson-Laird and Byrne 1991). Just as people may have a competence in their native language, so too can they have a competence in reasoning. Their competence rests on the ability to imagine alternatives, including counterexamples to conclusions. Just as they may be unable to articulate the grammar that underlies their utterances or be conscious of its operation, so too can they be unaware of the rational competence that underlies their inferences. And just as they may make ungrammatical utterances at times, so too can they make irrational inferences. The idea that human reasoning is rational is crucial to the idea that the counterfactual imagination is rational. If reasoning itself is not rational, it is implausible that imaginative thought is rational.

The second step toward the conclusion that the counterfactual imagination is rational depends on the idea that people make inferences by thinking about possibilities. There are several alternative theories of reasoning, such as that it depends on inference rules that detect the underlying logical form of an argument, or that it depends on inference rules that encapsulate knowledge, for instance about social interaction (Braine and O'Brien 1998; Rips 1994; Fiddick, Cosmides, and Tooby 2000; Holyoak and Cheng 1995). But only one theory places imagination at the heart of reasoning and that is the view that people make inferences by imagining alternative possibilities (Johnson-Laird and Byrne 2002). There is extensive experimental support for this theory of reasoning (for a review see Johnson-Laird 2001). For example, many experiments have corroborated the proposal that people think about true possibilities, not false possibilities. Their tendency to think about what is true and not about what is false extends far beyond deductive inference. It characterizes their thoughts about how to test hypotheses (Cowley and Byrne 2004; Poletiek 1996). It figures in their judgments about probability and risk (Girotto and Gonzalez 2001; Johnson-Laird et al. 1999; McCloy, Byrne, and Johnson-Laird 2004). It can lead to illusory inferences (Johnson-Laird and Savary 1999). It may underlie belief persistence and stereotype maintenance (Baron 2000). Many experiments have also corroborated the proposal that people think of only a few of the true possibilities. Indeed, they tend to keep in mind a single possibility. When they try to make an inference that requires them to think about more than one possibility, they make more mistakes and they take longer (Johnson-Laird and Byrne 1991). The idea that human reasoning depends on the imagination of possibilities is crucial to the idea that the counterfactual imagination is rational.

The third step toward the conclusion that the imagination is rational is that counterfactual thoughts rely on thinking about possibilities, just as

Table 9.1
Summary of principles

1. True possibilities: *People keep in mind true possibilities.*
2. Few possibilities: *People keep in mind few possibilities.*
3. Dual possibilities: *Some ideas require people to think about two possibilities.*
4. Counterfactual possibilities: *People think about possibilities that once may have been true possibilities but can be true no longer.*
5. Mutability of dual possibilities: *People readily imagine a counterfactual alternative to a possibility if it is mentally represented with a second possibility.*
6. Forbidden possibilities: *People think about the forbidden possibility as well as the permitted possibility when they understand an obligation.*
7. Temporal possibilities: *The possibilities people think about encode the temporal order of events in the world.*

rational thoughts do. This book has been about the set of principles that guide the possibilities that people think about when they create counterfactual alternatives to reality. The next section provides a summary of the principles and how they apply to counterfactual thoughts. Then I will discuss the conclusion that the counterfactual imagination is rational.

Possibilities and Principles

The key insight from the study of human reasoning is that people think about possibilities. The sorts of possibilities they think about are guided by a small set of principles (see table 9.1). The first principle is that people think about true possibilities. Suppose you hear that a friend of yours has been in a car accident. You do not know whether he has been injured. But you do know that he has a tendency to drive fast. You might conjecture, "if James was driving fast, he was injured" (if A then B). The conditional is consistent with several possibilities—for example, the possibility, "James was driving fast and he was injured" (A and B). People do not think about the false possibility, "James was driving fast and he was not injured" (A and not-B) (Johnson-Laird and Byrne 2002).

The second principle is that initially people think about just a few of the true possibilities. There are several possibilities that are consistent with the conditional—for example, "James was driving fast and he was injured" (A and B), "James was not driving fast and he was not injured" (not-A and not-B), and "James was not driving fast and he was injured" (not-A and B). Most people think about the first possibility. Their interpretation is not entirely conjunctive: they know that there are alternative possibilities that are also compatible with the conditional, but these possibilities remain unformed in their minds at the outset (Johnson-Laird and Byrne 1991).

The key principles of most interest for the creation of alternative realities concern dual possibilities. The third principle is that some ideas are dual-possibility ideas: they require people to keep in mind two possibilities. Suppose you know that in fact your friend James was not driving fast and he was not injured, and you say "if James had been driving fast he would have been injured." People understand a counterfactual conditional by thinking about two possibilities from the outset (at least when it is about known situations). They think about the conjecture, "James was driving fast and he was injured" (A and B), but they also think about the presupposed facts, "James was not driving fast and he was not injured" (not-A and not-B).

The fourth principle is that when people think about dual possibilities, they sometimes think about counterfactual possibilities—that is, possibilities that once could have been true possibilities but they could be true no longer. Counterfactuals are intriguing in part because they often require people to envisage a possibility they know or presuppose to be false. People may assume temporarily that the possibility is true. Generally people think about things that are true, but imaginative thoughts often focus on things that are not true. People keep track of the status of the possibilities they have thought about. They note that the possibility "James was driving fast and he was injured" is "imagined", and the possibility "James was not driving fast and he was not injured" corresponds to the presupposed "facts."

In the counterfactual conditional about your friend James, the facts are that he was not driving fast and he was not injured. The counterfactual alters one aspect of the facts, "if he had been driving fast ...", and this change leads to a different outcome, "he would have been injured." When people create an alternative to reality, they can mentally change some aspects of their representation of the facts more easily than others. A key principle is that an idea that is mentally represented from the outset by thinking about two possibilities is more easily changed than one that is mentally represented from the outset by thinking about a single possibility. Suppose you live in a remote area with no public transportation to the city and so you drive to work. When there is heavy traffic you may wish that you were not stuck in it, and you may wish that you did not have to go to work. But suppose instead you live in a suburban area with a good light-rail service to the city. When you choose to drive to work and there is heavy traffic you may more easily create a counterfactual alternative—for example, "if only I had taken the train ...". The availability of a second possibility makes the counterfactual alternative particularly easy to create. The fifth principle is that people can readily imagine how the facts might have turned out differently if they have mentally represented the facts with a second possibility from the outset.

The sixth principle is that people think about forbidden possibilities when they understand an obligation. Suppose you know the regulation, "if staff members earn any outside income, they must declare it to the university's finance office." Most people understand the regulation by thinking about the permitted possibility, staff members who earn outside income and declare it to the finance office (A and B). And they also think about the forbidden possibility, staff members who earn outside income and do not declare it to the finance office (A and not-B). They note this possibility as "forbidden."

The seventh principle is that the possibilities people keep in mind reflect the temporal order of events in the world. For example, people think about the conditional "Alicia goes to her karate class only if she gets home early" (A only if B) by thinking about two possibilities, and they think about the events in the order in which they are assumed to occur in the world, "Alicia gets home early and she goes to her karate class" (B and A), and "Alicia does not get home early and she does not go to her karate class" (not-B and not-A). These seven principles can explain the key phenomena of the counterfactual imagination.

The Counterfactual Imagination
When people create a counterfactual alternative to reality, they zoom in on fault lines in their conceptions of reality (Kahneman and Miller 1986). People show extraordinary similarities in their imagination of alternatives to reality, in Western cultures and in other similar cultures. Each of the chapters in the book outlined a commonly perceived fault line of reality and detected a clue from the study of reasoning to help understand the phenomenon. It sketched an explanation of each phenomenon based on the core principles (see table 9.2).

Table 9.2
Summary of corollaries

I. Actions: *People think about two possibilities when they understand an action.*

II. Single possibilities: *People can switch from thinking about one possibility to thinking about two possibilities e.g. for inactions.*

III. Controllable events: *People think about two possibilities when they understand controllable events.*

IV. Causes: People think about a single possibility when they understand a strong causal relation (*cause and outcome*). They can readily access a second possibility for an enabling condition (*enabler and outcome, no enabler and no outcome*).

V. Semifactual alternatives: When people mentally represent a semifactual assertion they think about two possibilities, A and B, and not-A and B. When they mentally represent a weak causal relation they can readily access the same two possibilities.

VI. Anchored possibilities: People think of the first element in the possibility as immutable.

Actions People tend to imagine alternatives to their actions, rather than to their inactions. Suppose two mothers decide whether to vaccinate their children against a new disease. Patricia decides to vaccinate her child and he becomes seriously ill from an allergic reaction to the vaccine. Brigid decides not to vaccinate her child and he becomes seriously ill from contracting the new illness. Who do you think will regret her decision more? Most participants in experiments judge that Patricia will regret her decision to vaccinate her child, more than Brigid will regret her decision not to vaccinate her child (Kahneman and Tversky 1982; Ritov and Baron 1990). The action effect arises because certain ideas are dual-possibility ideas—that is, they require people to think about two possibilities.

People make different inferences when they think about two possibilities than when they think about a single possibility. For example, people can readily make inferences from the counterfactual "if James had been driving fast he would have been injured" because they think about two possibilities, the conjecture "James drove fast and he was injured," and the presupposed facts "James did not drive fast and he was not injured." They make more inferences from the counterfactual than from a factual conditional, "if James drove fast he was injured," because they initially think about just a single possibility for the factual conditional, "James drove fast and he was injured." For example, when they are told that James was not injured, they can more readily make the inference that he was not driving fast from the counterfactual than from the factual conditional (Byrne and Tasso 1999).

Likewise, an action, such as the decision to vaccinate a child, is a dual-possibility idea—that is, people tend to think about it by keeping in mind two possibilities from the outset. When people understand the action, "Patricia vaccinated her child," they envisage two possibilities, one corresponding to the preaction possibility, Patricia did not vaccinate her child, and one to the postaction possibility, Patricia vaccinated her child. When they understand an inaction, "Brigid did not vaccinate her child," they envisage a single possibility, Brigid did not vaccinate her child (Byrne and McEleney 2000). People imagine an alternative to an action because they can mentally "rewind" the postaction possibility to be like the preaction one, and say, "if only Patricia had not vaccinated her child ...".

An inaction is usually a single-possibility idea—that is, people tend to think about it by keeping in mind just a single possibility from the outset. But people can think about two possibilities from the outset for an inaction in some situations, such as when its consequences over time are considered, or when there are good reasons to act. Suppose Sam and Jim think about whether or not to move to a new college, and Jim decides to transfer and Sam decides to stay. Most people judge that *in the long run* Sam will regret his inaction more than Jim will regret his action (Gilovich and Medvec 1995a). The imagined alternative to the inaction "if only Sam had transferred ..." leads to consequences that are unknown—he might have been happy had he moved or he might have been unhappy—and at least some of the imagined consequences are better than the actual outcome. In contrast, the imagined alternative to the action "if only Jim had stayed ..." leads to known consequences—he was unhappy in his first college—and the imagined consequence is not better than the actual outcome. People say "if only ..." about Sam's inaction because there is an imbalance in the consequences from the inaction and the action, which becomes apparent when the long-term perspective prompts people to consider the consequences. People think about a single possibility when they understand an inaction in some circumstances, but they can think about more possibilities for it, for example, when they take a long-term perspective.

Obligations People sometimes think about what should *not* have been when they imagine alternatives to reality. An important clue about why they do so comes from reasoning. People understand the obligation "if staff members earn outside income then they must declare it to the university's finance office" by keeping in mind the permitted possibility, "staff members earn outside income and they declare it," as well as the forbidden possibility, "staff members earn outside income and they do not declare it," which is noted as forbidden. They can make some inferences more readily about an obligation than about a neutral topic, because they have thought about what is forbidden (Quelhas and Byrne 2003). For example, when people know that staff members did not declare any income, they can infer that they did not earn any.

People can readily create a counterfactual alternative to a forbidden possibility. Suppose you know about a colleague who earns outside income but decides not to declare it. Your colleague is caught and he has to pay a large tax bill. When you imagine an alternative, you can mentally change the forbidden possibility to be like the permitted one, and say "if only he had declared his income ...". The permitted possibility provides a ready-made alternative. People change a forbidden possibility to be like the permitted possibility, but not vice versa. For example, they imagine counterfactual alternatives to controllable events more than to uncontrollable events (Girotto, Legrenzi, and Rizzo 1991; Markman et al. 1993). But they imagine alternatives to socially unacceptable controllable events even more than to socially acceptable ones (McCloy and Byrne 2000). Suppose another colleague declares her extra income and she has to pay a large tax bill. When you imagine an alternative, you are unlikely to mentally change the permitted possibility to be like the forbidden one, and say "if only she had not declared her income ...". Instead you may find other aspects to mentally change—for example, "if only taxes were not so high ..." (Walsh and Byrne 2004). Obligations can seem immutable because people do not change the permitted possibility to be like the forbidden one.

Causes   A curious aspect of the counterfactual imagination is its relation to causal thoughts. People imagine counterfactual alternatives to an event, even when they know it was not the cause of the outcome. People wish the baggage handlers had detected the hijackers' weapons, even though they do not consider the baggage handlers to have caused the September 11 attack. Causal thoughts influence counterfactual thoughts. For example, a causal belief, such as the belief that nuclear deterrence works, can influence judgments about the plausibility of a counterfactual conjecture, such as "if Kennedy had listened to his hawkish advisers then the Cuban missile crisis would have become nuclear" (Tetlock and Lebow 2001). Counterfactual thoughts also influence causal thoughts. A taxi driver refused a couple a lift and they were killed when a bridge they drove over collapsed; the taxi driver managed to drive over the bridge just before it collapsed. People can readily create a counterfactual alternative, "if only the taxi driver had given the couple a lift ...", and they judge that the taxi driver had a causal role in the couple's deaths (Wells and Gavanski 1989; Roese and Olson 1993b). But counterfactual thoughts often focus on antecedents that did not cause the outcome. For example, even though people say "if only ..." about the taxi driver, they identify the collapsing bridge as the cause of the outcome (Mandel and Lehman 1996; N'gbala and Branscombe 1995).

The clue from reasoning is that there are different sorts of causal relations. People can distinguish strong causal relations and enabling relations (Goldvarg and Johnson-Laird 2001). A strong cause—for instance, "the drunk driver overtook James and caused the crash"—is consistent with two possibilities, "the drunk driver overtook James and the crash occurred," and "the drunk driver did not overtake James and the crash did not occur." But most people understand the strong causal relation by keeping in mind just a single possibility from the outset, "the drunk driver overtook James and the crash occurred." The drunk driver's overtaking is the only cause they think about for the crash. In contrast, an enabling relation—for example, "James driving home by that route made it possible for the crash to happen"—is consistent with several possibilities, "James drove home by that route and the crash occurred," "James did not drive home by that route and the crash did not occur," and "James drove home by that route and the crash did not occur," perhaps because there was no drunk driver. People can think readily about the first two possibilities when they understand the enabling relation.

Enabling conditions affect the inferences people make. For instance, when they know James drove home by that route, and they are aware of other conditions, such as the need for there to have been a drunk driver on that route, they do not infer that the crash occurred (Byrne, Espino, and Santamaría 1999). This clue from reasoning helps to explain the relation between counterfactual and causal thoughts. Counterfactual thoughts focus on enablers, as in "if only James had not driven by that route the crash would not have occurred." Enablers are dual-possibility ideas—that is, people can think about two possibilities when they understand them, and the second possibility provides a ready-made counterfactual. In contrast, the mental representation of a strong causal relation is different from the mental representation of a counterfactual conditional. People think about a single possibility when they understand a strong cause, whereas they think about two possibilities when they understand a counterfactual conditional. Indeed, they spontaneously generate twice as many causal thoughts as counterfactual thoughts (McEleney and Byrne 2000).

Semifactual Thoughts When people imagine how an outcome could have turned out the same—for example, "even if there had been good weather, the crash would still have occurred"—they judge that the weather was not a strong cause of the crash (Branscombe et al. 1996; McCloy and Byrne 2002). Why do semifactual "even if ..." alternatives reduce the judgment of the causal role of an event? The clue from reasoning is that people understand a semifactual by keeping in mind two possibilities. They think about the conjecture, "there was good weather and the crash occurred," and the presupposed facts, "there was bad weather and the crash occurred." Most people make different inferences from "even if ..." semifactuals compared to factual conditionals (Moreno-Ríos, García-Madruga, and Byrne 2004). For example, when they know that there was bad weather, they do not infer there was no crash. Instead they often infer that there *was* a crash. This clue helps to explain why the imagination of an "even if ..." alternative can affect causal judgments. When people imagine an "even if ..." alternative, they think about the possibility that the cause did not happen and the outcome did. The possibilities they keep in mind correspond to a weak causal relation. A weak causal relation, such as "bad weather caused the crash" (when the drunk driver is also a known cause), is consistent with three possibilities, "bad weather and the crash," "no bad weather and no crash," and "no bad weather and the crash." Most people think about the possibility "there was bad weather and the crash occurred," but they can also think readily about a second possibility, "there was no bad weather and the crash occurred."

Temporal Order People imagine counterfactual alternatives to the more recent event in a sequence of events—for example, the last runner in a relay race, or the penalty shoot-out in a soccer match (Miller and Guna-segaram 1990). A clue from reasoning is that people encode the temporal order of events in the world. People think about the conditional "Mary works hard only if she is well paid" by thinking about the two possibilities, "Mary is well paid and she works hard," and "Mary is not well paid and she does not work hard." Most people can readily make inferences from B to A from the "only if ..." conditional—for instance, when they know that Mary was not well paid, they can make the inference that she did not work hard (García-Madruga et al. 2004). This clue from reasoning sheds light on the phenomenon that people imagine counterfactual alternatives to the most recent event. The possibilities that people consider when they understand a sequence of events, such as Lisa tossed heads and Jenny tossed tails, preserve the temporal order of events. The possibilities are anchored by the earlier event, Lisa tossed heads, and the anchor is immutable (Byrne et al. 2000; Walsh and Byrne 2004).

The exploration of the counterfactual imagination in this book has been guided by the set of principles that govern the possibilities that people envisage. There are of course other phenomena of the counterfactual imagination, and the ones explored here by no means constitute an exhaustive list. And sometimes different people create different alternatives. For example, some people understand a counterfactual conditional "if Mark had changed jobs he would have moved" by thinking about just a single possibility, the presupposed facts, "Mark did not change jobs and he did not move." The phenomena considered illustrate how *most* people create counterfactual alternatives. The phenomena illustrate the way the counterfactual imagination may be explained by the set of principles that guide the possibilities people think about.

The Rationality of the Counterfactual Imagination

My claim is that the counterfactual imagination is rational. The three steps to this conclusion are that humans are capable of rational thought, the principles that underlie rational thought guide the sorts of possibilities that people think about, and these principles underlie the counterfactual imagination. Is it possible to accept these three steps, and yet reject the conclusion? Perhaps. The answer depends on what it means for the counterfactual imagination to be rational.

A strong version of the claim is that the counterfactual imagination is rational in that the cognitive processes that underpin it are capable of producing the best counterfactual thoughts (and I will return to the notion of "best" shortly). A weaker version of the claim is that the counterfactual imagination shares the same principles as rational thought. On the strong view, if you accept each of the three steps, then you are committed to the conclusion that the counterfactual imagination is rational. Reasoning can be considered rational because people have an underlying competence—that is, they have the cognitive machinery capable of producing valid inferences, even though their competence is sometimes limited by performance factors such as working-memory constraints. So too, counterfactual thoughts may be rational if people have the underlying competence to produce the best counterfactual thoughts, even though their competence may sometimes be limited by performance factors.

Of course, there are many examples of irrational outputs from the counterfactual imagination (Miller, Turnbull, and McFarland 1990; Ritov and Baron 1992). For example, when people can readily imagine a woman who was attacked doing something differently, say, walking home by a different route, or not accepting a lift, they tend to blame the victim for her fate (Branscombe et al. 1997). Their judgments of fault and responsibility and causality are swayed by how readily they can imagine an alternative. So too are their judgments of regret and guilt (Roese and Olson 1995). And how readily they can imagine an alternative sometimes depends merely on the way the information about the facts was presented to them (Walsh and Byrne 2004). But just as the existence of ungrammatical utterances or invalid deductions does not indict human competence in language or reasoning, neither does the existence of irrational judgments indict human competence in counterfactual imaginative thought.

The argument about whether the counterfactual imagination is rational or irrational may hinge on what it means for a counterfactual thought to be the "best" one. There is no normative standard against which to judge whether an imaginative thought is best. In contrast, it is possible to judge whether an inference is valid. The inference can be compared to a normative theory that specifies what counts as a rational inference. Of course, there is considerable debate about which normative theory provides the best standard of comparison for rational thought (Manktelow and Over 1993). It may be set by traditional logical analyses (Jeffrey 1981) or by an analysis of the environment (Oaksford and Chater 1999; but see Oberauer, Wilhelm, and Dias 1999). The appropriate normative model may be provided within the limitations of specific domains (Cheng and Holyoak 1985), or evolutionary ecology (Gigerenzer and Todd 1999; Cosmides and Tooby 1992), or personal goals (Evans and Over 1996). A deductive conclusion may be viewed as irrational when it is compared to one of these standards—for example, the propositional calculus—but as rational when it is compared to another standard, such as an environmental one (Oaksford and Chater 1999). There are disagreements about which normative model is the appropriate one to which inferences should be compared. Nonetheless there is considerable consensus that it should be possible to judge whether an inference is rational or irrational.

Could it be possible to judge whether a counterfactual thought is the best one? There are several options. One option is that a normative theory of imaginative thought is impossible. Another option is that counterfactual thoughts could be judged by how imaginative their output is. But it is difficult to make such a judgment even about deliberately creative thoughts. History is full of examples of creative products that were not recognized as creative initially because of the prevailing social and cultural standards, such as Vincent Van Gogh's paintings or James Joyce's novels. Conversely, poor ideas or products may be judged to be creative because they fit the current trend (Sternberg and Davidson 1995). The imaginative nature of the output may not be a guide to the imaginative nature of the process that led to it. For example, an individual may create an original and novel idea but unbeknownst to them, it is already familiar to the wider community (Johnson-Laird 1993; Boden 1990).

Another option is that counterfactual thoughts could be judged to be good by whether or not they serve their purpose well. For example, a counterfactual thought could be judged to be good if it helps people to learn from mistakes and provides a "roadmap for the future" (Roese, Sanna, and Galinsky 2005). The usefulness of a counterfactual may depend on the accuracy of the causal inferences it suggests (Roese and Olson 1997). But of course counterfactual thoughts can be unhelpful. People may imagine what might have been different even when such thoughts are not useful for preparing for the future. Counterfactual thoughts often focus on controllable events, even when they are not the cause. This tendency can become dysfunctional when someone dwells on their own role, as in "if only I had swerved out of the way ...", even when they know the cause of the accident lies elsewhere—for instance, a drunk driver crossing into oncoming traffic (Davis et al. 1995). When people imagine how a traumatic attack could have been avoided, their imagination of a better possibility is often not helpful given that the facts of the traumatic attack cannot be reversed and the likelihood of another one is low (Branscombe et al. 2003). Alternatively, a counterfactual thought could be judged to be good if it helps people feel better. But counterfactual thoughts that just consider how things could have been worse may be a panacea, and lull people into a false complacency.

A final option is that a counterfactual thought could be judged to be the best one by how plausible it is. For example, historical "if only ..." conjectures can be considered illuminating or merely whimsical (Tetlock and Parker 2005). The difference may depend on whether people made *minimal* changes to their representation of reality to create the counterfactual alternative (Lewis 1973; Stalnaker 1968, 1999; Pollock 1986). The remarkable regularities people exhibit have been considered to reflect the limitations of the imagination. The perceived fault lines in the mental representation of reality have sometimes been viewed as constraints on the imagination. Instead, they may be the very hallmark of its rationality. The minimal changes that characterize the counterfactual imagination may not reflect a limitation, they may be its strength. People do not tend to imagine "miracle-world" alternatives. The regularities they exhibit in their counterfactual alternatives may reflect a rational exploitation of fault lines that occur in their representation of reality.

People do not appear to create counterfactual alternatives to every possible factor and then select one that fits their current goal. Instead their understanding of the factual reality leads them to represent it in certain ways. Their representation of the facts makes dual possibilities available for some factors. People think about two possibilities from the outset when they understand certain ideas, such as choices, actions, controllable events, forbidden actions, and so on. Dual-possibility ideas correspond to the fault lines in the representation of reality. Flights of fancy may be reined in by the principles that guide the possibilities people think about.

People create counterfactual alternatives by making minimal changes to their mental representation of the facts because the facts must be recoverable from the imagined possibility (Byrne 1997). They are recoverable when people create a counterfactual alternative to facts that they have mentally represented from the outset by thinking about two possibilities. For example, people mentally represent the action "Patricia vaccinated her child" by thinking about two possibilities from the outset, the preaction possibility, "Patricia did not vaccinate her child," and the postaction possibility, "Patricia vaccinated her child." They can create a counterfactual alternative based on a minimal change by replacing one of the possibilities, "Patricia vaccinated her child," with the other possibility that they have envisaged from the outset, "Patricia did not vaccinate her child." People may tend to understand a counterfactual alternative in the context of the facts from which it was created. They can appreciate the import of the counterfactual by the comparison between the counterfactual's conjecture and the presupposed facts. Minimal changes may ground imaginative thoughts in the bedrock of rationality.

Creating Different Counterfactuals

Can people be helped to create counterfactual alternatives that are more imaginative than the ones they tend to create? The endeavor may be an interesting one to bridge the gap between imaginative thoughts that are counterfactual and other sorts of creative thoughts. For example, people tend to invent a new instance of a category, such as an alien from another planet, by relying heavily on their knowledge of the existing category. Their inventions may be limited by their inability to consider alternatives to some aspects of the facts, such as the presence of sensory organs. But people may be helped to design more exotic instances when they are given a general framework, for example to design a new handheld container for hot liquids, rather than a specific one, such as to design a new coffee mug (Ward, Patterson, and Sifonis 2004; Ward, Smith, and Vaid 1997). Likewise, it may be possible to change the sorts of counterfactual alternatives that people create. People may create counterfactual alternatives that focus on less common aspects of their mental representation of reality when they are prompted to represent the facts more fully. They can be encouraged to represent the facts by thinking not only about the single possibility that comes to mind from the outset, but also by thinking about other possibilities.

Are some people poorer at creating counterfactual alternatives than others? The existence of differences between people in the ways they think about counterfactual conditionals suggests that some people might be poorer than others. Some people understand "if he had worn his seatbelt he would not have been injured" by keeping in mind just a single possibility, corresponding to the facts, "he did not wear his seatbelt and he was injured." Is their tendency to do so an irrational one? It might be. They may not benefit as much from the preparatory influence of counterfactual thoughts as someone who has also kept in mind the imagined possibility, "he wore his seatbelt and he was not injured." People who think about both possibilities may be more readily able to formulate a plan for the future based on the counterfactual alternative. Likewise, some people tend to think about how things might have been better, whereas others tend to think about how things might have been worse (Kasimatis and Wells 1995). The opportunity to identify causal relations and learn from past mistakes may be reduced for people who tend to think only about how things might have been worse. Three- and four-year-old children can be helped to answer a counterfactual question about a story, such as "if Bobby the Bunny had gone to the field when it was empty would he have been able to play with the other bunnies?", when they are told to "make a picture in your mind" (Meehan and Byrne 2004). The instruction to form a mental image of the current reality described in the story (the field was full of bunnies) or the past, now counterfactual, possibility (the field was empty) may help them to focus on the relevant possibilities.

Can adults be encouraged to create counterfactual thoughts that are better than the ones they create? Some events may be so traumatic for an individual that they cannot help but create the same counterfactual alternative repeatedly. When thoughts about "if only ..." alternatives become dysfunctional, is it possible to help people change the focus of their imagined alternatives? When someone dwells on their own controllable actions—for example, "if only I had swerved out of the way ..." even when they know their actions did not cause the accident—it may be possible to switch their attention to the cause. For example, when an individual's attention is drawn to the first cause in a causal sequence, it may help to divert attention from other causes (Wells, Taylor, and Turtle 1987). Victims may not blame themselves as much if they are encouraged to think about how their actions prevented the attack from being worse (Branscombe et al. 2003). Semifactual thoughts about how an outcome could have turned out the same "even if ..." an antecedent had been different reduce judgments that the antecedent played a causal role (McCloy and Byrne 2002).

Counterfactual thoughts can amplify emotions, and the emotions people experience may be affected by the sorts of counterfactual alternatives they create. For example, when people imagine how an individual who betrayed a friend's trust might think and feel about the situation, they judge the individual to feel shame when they say "if only ..." about the individual's personality, as in "if only she wasn't such an unreliable person ...". But they judge the individual to feel guilt when they say "if only ..." about the individual's actions, as in "if only she hadn't done that ..." (Niedenthal, Tangney, and Gavanski 1994). Likewise, when thoughts are directed away from what could have or should have been done in the past, to what might be done in the future, individuals may experience less self-blame and regret (Boninger, Gleicher, and Strathman 1994).

People may sometimes regret their failures to act because they forget the concerns and worries that led them to decide not to act (Savitsky, Medvec, and Gilovich 1997). When they recall the reason for their decision not to act, it may alleviate their counterfactual thoughts about their failure to act. Reasons can shift the focus of counterfactual thoughts a little (Walsh and Byrne 2004). Dysfunctional counterfactual thoughts may be considered irrational. It may be possible to help people overcome them. People may have an underlying competence to create the best counterfactual alternatives to reality—alternatives that result in plausible and useful counterfactual possibilities, and that are based on changes that are minimal and that allow the facts to be recovered from the counterfactual. When people create counterfactual alternatives, they may be rational in principle, but they may err in practice.

Summary

This book has sketched seven principles derived from the study of reasoning that explain imaginative thoughts. People think about possibilities, and the sorts of possibilities they think about are true possibilities. They do not tend to think about false possibilities. They also tend to think about just a few of the true possibilities. People can think about dual possibilities: some ideas require them to keep in mind more than one possibility. When they think about counterfactual possibilities, they can think about a possibility that is false, and they may even suppose it to be true. They keep track of whether the possibilities they think about are real or imagined. Dual possibilities are more mutable than single possibilities: people can more readily create a counterfactual alternative to a possibility when they have mentally represented it from the outset with a second possibility. People understand obligations by thinking about the forbidden possibility as well as the permitted possibility. They can imagine how a situation should have been different by mentally changing a forbidden possibility to be more like the permitted possibility. The possibilities people envisage encode temporal information about the order of events in the world. The seven principles are not intended as an exhaustive set; nonetheless this fragment provides the beginnings of an explanation of the counterfactual imagination. The principles help to explain some of the remarkable regularities in the counterfactual alternatives that people create. For example, they explain why people create counterfactual alternatives to actions, to controllable events, to forbidden events, and to recent events. They explain why counterfactual thoughts focus on enabling causal relations and semifactual thoughts focus on weak causal relations.

My claim is that the counterfactual imagination is rational. The claim rests on three steps: human reasoning is rational, human reasoning depends on the imagination of possibilities, and the set of principles that guide the possibilities people think about when they reason also guide their imaginative thoughts. Reality can seem to shimmer with glimpses of counterfactual alternatives. Is the creation of counterfactual alternatives a uniquely human capacity? Perhaps. But there is as yet little evidence to indicate whether animals reflect on their past mistakes and create counterfactual alternatives about what might have been. There is abundant evidence that people do so. The human mind can take the facts of the present or the past and transform them into a new creation, an imaginative alternative to reality. Human mental life is made undeniably richer by the existence of the counterfactual imagination.

References

Adams, E. W. 1975. *The Logic of Conditionals*. Dordrecht: Reidel.

Ansburg, P. I., and Dominowski, R. L. 2000. Promoting insightful problem-solving. *Journal of Creative Behaviour*, 34(1), 30–60.

Anscombe, G. E. M. 1963. *Intention*. 2nd ed. Oxford: Blackwell.

Athanasiadou, A., and Dirven, R., eds. 1997. *On Conditionals Again*. Amsterdam: John Benjamins.

Au, T. K. 1983. Chinese and English counterfactuals: The Sapir-Whorf hypothesis revisited. *Cognition*, 15, 155–187.

Avni-Babad, D. 2003. Mental undoings of actions and inactions in the absence of counterfactuals. *British Journal of Psychology*, 94, 213–222.

Ayers, M. R. 1965. Counterfactuals and subjunctive conditionals. *Mind*, 347–364.

Barker, S. 1991. Even, still and counterfactuals. *Linguistics and Philosophy*, 14, 1–38.

Baron, J. 2000. *Thinking and Deciding*. 3rd ed. Cambridge: Cambridge University Press.

Barrouillet, P., and Lecas, J.-F. 1998. How can mental models theory account for content effects in conditional reasoning: A developmental perspective. *Cognition*, 67, 209–253.

Barrouillet, P., and Lecas, J.-F. 1999. Mental models in conditional reasoning and working memory. *Thinking and Reasoning*, 5, 289–302.

Barwise, J. 1986. Conditionals and conditional information. In E. C. Traugott, A. ter Meulen, J. S., Reilly, and C. Ferguson, *On Conditionals*. Cambridge: Cambridge University Press.

Beckett, S. 1977. *Collected Poems in English and French*. London: John Calder.

Bennett, J. 1982. Even if. *Linguistics and Philosophy*, 5, 403–418.

Boden, M. 1990. *The Creative Mind*. London: Weidenfeld & Nicolson.

Bohner, G., Bless, N., Schwarz, N., and Strack, F. 1988. What triggers causal attributions? The impact of valence and subjective probability. *European Journal of Social Psychology*, 18, 335–345.

Bonatti, L. 1994. Propositional reasoning by model? *Psychological Review*, 101, 725–733.

Boninger, D. S., Gleicher, F., and Strathman, A. 1994. Counterfactual thinking: From what might have been to what may be. *Journal of Personality and Social Psychology*, 67, 297–307.

Bonnefon, J. F., and Hilton, D. J. 2002. The suppression of modus ponens as a case of pragmatic preconditional reasoning. *Thinking and Reasoning*, 8, 21–40.

Bonnefon, J. F., and Hilton, D. J. 2004. Consequential conditionals: Invited and suppressed inferences from valued outcomes. *Journal of Experimental Psychology: Learning, Memory, and Cognition*, 30, 28–37.

Bouts, P., Spears, R., and Van Der Pligt, J. 1992. Counterfactual processing and the correspondence between events and outcomes: Normality vs. value. *European Journal of Social Psychology*, 22, 387–396.

Braine, M. D. S. 1978. On the relation between the natural logic of reasoning and standard logic. *Psychological Review*, 85, 1–21.

Braine, M. D. S., and O'Brien, D. P. 1991. A theory of IF: A lexical entry, reasoning program, and pragmatic principles. *Psychological Review*, 98, 182–203.

Braine, M. D. S., and O'Brien, D. 1998. *Mental Logic*. Mahwah, NJ: Erlbaum.

Branscombe, N. R., N'gbala, A., Kobrynowicz, D., and Wann, D. L. 1997. Self and group protection concerns influence attributions but they are not determinants of counterfactual mutation focus. *British Journal of Social Psychology*, 36, 387–404.

Branscombe, N. R., Owen, S., Garstka, T. A., and Coleman, J. 1996. Rape and accident counterfactuals: Who might have done otherwise and would it have changed the outcome? *Journal of Applied Social Psychology*, 26, 1042–1067.

Branscombe, N. R., Wohl, M. J. A., Owen, S., Allison, J. A., and N'gbala, A. 2003. Counterfactual thinking, blame assignment, and well-being in rape victims. *Basic and Applied Social Psychology*, 25, 265–273.

Brem, S., and Rips, L. J. 2000. Evidence and explanation in informal argument. *Cognitive Science*, 24, 573–604.

Bucciarelli, M., and Johnson-Laird, P. N. Forthcoming. Foundations of deontic meaning and reasoning. *Cognitive Psychology*.

Burke, E. 1770. Thoughts on the cause of the present discontents. In H. Froude 1909. *The Works of the Right Honourable Edmund Burke*. Oxford: Oxford University Press. (Attributed quotation).

Byrne, R. M. J. 1989a. Everyday reasoning with conditional sequences. *Quarterly Journal of Experimental Psychology*, 41A, 141–166.

Byrne, R. M. J. 1989b. Suppressing valid inferences with conditionals. *Cognition*, 31, 61–83.

Byrne, R. M. J. 1996. Towards a model theory of imaginary thinking. In J. Oakhill and A. Garnham, eds., *Mental Models in Cognitive Science: Essays in Honour of Phil Johnson-Laird*, 155–174. Hove, UK: Erlbaum, Taylor and Francis.

Byrne, R. M. J. 1997. Cognitive processes in counterfactual thinking about what might have been. In D. Medin, ed., *The Psychology of Learning and Motivation: Advances in Research and Theory*, vol. 37, pp. 105–154. San Diego, CA: Academic Press.

Byrne, R. M. J. 2002. Mental models and counterfactual thinking. *Trends in Cognitive Sciences*, 6, 405–445.

Byrne, R. M. J. Forthcoming. Whether, although, and other conditional connectives. In W. Schaeken, A. Vandierendonck, W. Schroyens, and G. d'Ydewalle, eds., *The Mental Models Theory of Reasoning: Extensions and Refinements*. Mahwah, NJ: Erlbaum.

Byrne, R. M. J., Culhane, R., and Tasso, A. 1995. The temporality effect in thinking about what might have been. In J. D. Moore and J. F. Lehman, eds., *Proceedings of the 17th Annual Conference of the Cognitive Science Society*, 385–390. Hillsdale, NJ: Erlbaum.

Byrne, R. M. J., and Egan, S. 2004. Counterfactual and pre-factual conditionals: Reasoning about future and past possibilities. *Canadian Journal of Psychology*, 58, 82–89.

Byrne, R. M. J., Espino, O., and Santamaría, C. 1999. Counterexamples and the suppression of inferences. *Journal of Memory and Language*, 40, 347–373.

Byrne, R. M. J., Egan, S., and García-Madruga, J. 2003. Counterfactual "only if" reasoning. In R. Alterman and D. Kirsh, eds., *Proceedings of the 25th Annual Conference of the Cognitive Science Society*. Hillsdale, NJ: Erlbaum.

Byrne, R. M. J., and Handley, S. J. 1992. Reasoning strategies. *Irish Journal of Psychology*, 13, 111–124.

Byrne, R. M. J., and Handley, S. J. 1997. Reasoning strategies for suppositional deductions. *Cognition*, 62, 1–49.

Byrne, R. M. J., Handley, S. J., and Johnson-Laird, P. N. 1995. Reasoning with suppositions. *Quarterly Journal of Experimental Psychology*, 48A, 915–944.

Byrne, R. M. J., and Johnson-Laird, P. N. 1989. Spatial reasoning. *Journal of Memory and Language*, 28, 564–575.

Byrne, R. M. J., and Johnson-Laird, P. N. 1992. The spontaneous use of propositional connectives. *Quarterly Journal of Experimental Psychology*, 45A, 89–110.

Byrne, R. M. J., and McEleney, A. 1997. Cognitive processes in regret for actions and inactions. In M. Shafto and P. Langley, eds., *Proceedings of the 19th Annual Conference of the Cognitive Science Society*, 73–78. Hillsdale, NJ: Erlbaum.

Byrne, R. M. J., and McEleney, A. 2000. Counterfactual thinking about actions and failures to act. *Journal of Experimental Psychology: Learning, Memory, and Cognition*, 26, 1318–1331.

Byrne, R. M. J., Segura, S., Culhane, R., Tasso, A., and Berrocal, P. 2000. The temporality effect in counterfactual thinking about what might have been. *Memory and Cognition*, 28, 264–281.

Byrne, R. M. J., and Tasso, A. 1994. Counterfactual reasoning: Inferences from hypothetical conditionals. In A. Ram and K. Eiselt, eds., *Proceedings of the 16th Annual Conference of the Cognitive Science Society*, 124–129. Hillsdale, NJ: Erlbaum.

Byrne, R. M. J., and Tasso, A. 1999. Deductive reasoning with factual, possible, and counterfactual conditionals. *Memory and Cognition*, 27, 726–740.

Byrne, R. M. J., and Thompson, V. 2000. Individual differences in counterfactual reasoning. Paper presented at the International Conference on Thinking, Durham, UK.

Byrne, R. M. J., and Walsh, C. 2002. Contradictions and counterfactuals: Generating belief revisions in conditional inference. In W. D. Gray and C. D. Schunn, eds., *Proceedings of the 24th Annual Conference of the Cognitive Science Society*, 160–165. Mahwah, NJ: Erlbaum.

Byrne, R. M. J., and Walsh, C. Forthcoming. Resolving contradictions. In P. N. Johnson-Laird and V. Girotto, eds., *The Shape of Reason: Essays in Honour of Paolo Legrenzi*. Hove: Psychology Press.

Cacciari, C., Levorato, M. C., and Cicogna, P. 1997. Imagination at work: Conceptual and linguistic creativity in children. In T. B. Ward, S. M. Smith, and J. Vaid, eds., *Creative Thought*, 145–178. Washington, DC: American Psychological Association.

Carpenter, P. A. 1973. Extracting information from counterfactual clauses. *Journal of Verbal Learning and Verbal Behavior*, 12, 512–520.

Catellani, P., and Milesi, P. 2001. Counterfactuals and roles: Mock victims' and perpetrators' accounts of judicial cases. *European Journal of Social Psychology*, 31, 247–264.

Chan, D., and Chua, F. 1994. Suppression of valid inferences: Syntactic views, mental models, and relative salience. *Cognition*, 53, 217–238.

Cheng, P. W., and Holyoak, K. J. 1985. Pragmatic reasoning schemas. *Cognitive Psychology*, 17, 391–416.

Cheng, P. W., and Holyoak, K. J. 1989. On the natural selection of reasoning theories. *Cognition*, 33, 285–313.

Cheng, P. W., Holyoak, K. J., Nisbett, R. E., and Oliver, L. M. 1986. Pragmatic versus syntactic approaches to training deductive reasoning. *Cognitive Psychology*, 18, 293–328.

Cheng, P. W. 1997. From covariation to causation: A causal power theory. *Psychological Review*, 104, 367–405.

Cheng, P. W., and Novick, L. R. 1991. Causes versus enabling conditions. *Cognition*, 40, 83–120.

Chisholm, R. M. 1946. The contrary-to-fact conditional. *Mind*, 55, 289–307.

Cohen, L. J. 1981. Can human irrationality be experimentally demonstrated? *Behavioral and Brain Sciences*, 4, 317–370.

Connolly, T., Ordóñez, L. D., and Coughlan, R. 1997. Regret and responsibility in the evaluation of decision outcomes. *Organizational Behavior and Human Decision Processes*, 70, 73–85.

Connolly, T., and Zeelenberg, M. 2002. Regret in decision making. *Current Directions in Psychological Science*, 11, 212–216.

Cosmides, L. 1989. The logic of social exchange. *Cognition*, 31, 187–276.

Cosmides, L., and Tooby, J. 1992. Cognitive adaptations for social exchange. In J. Barkow, L. Cosmides, and J. Tooby, eds., *The Adapted Mind*. New York: Oxford University Press.

Costello, F. J., and Keane, M. T. 2000. Efficient creativity: Constraint guided conceptual combination. *Cognitive Science*, 24, 299–349.

Costello, F. J., and Keane, M. T. 2001. Testing two theories of conceptual combination: Alignment versus diagnosticity in the comprehension and production of combined concepts. *Journal of Experimental Psychology: Learning, Memory, and Cognition*, 27, 255–271.

Costello, T., and McCarthy, J. 1999. Useful counterfactuals. *Linkoping Electronic Articles in Computer and Information Science*, 3, 1–28.

Cowley, M., and Byrne, R. M. J. 2004. Chess masters' hypothesis testing. In K. D. Forbus, D. Gentner, and T. Rogers, eds., *Proceedings of the Twenty-Sixth Annual Conference of the Cognitive Science Society*, 250–255. Mahwah, NJ: Erlbaum.

Cowley, R., ed. 2001. *What If? Military Historians Imagine What Might Have Been*. London: Pan Macmillan.

Craik, K. 1943. *The Nature of Explanation*. Cambridge: Cambridge University Press.

Crawford, M. T., McConnell, A. R., Lewis, A. C., and Sherman, S. J. 2002. Reactance, compliance, and anticipated regret. *Journal of Experimental Social Psychology*, 38, 56–63.

Cummins, D. D. 1995. Naive theories and causal deduction. *Memory and Cognition*, 23, 5, 646–658.

Cummins, D. D., Lubart, T., Alksnis, O., and Rist, R. 1991. Conditional reasoning and causation. *Memory and Cognition*, 19, 274–282.

Damasio, A. 1994. *Descartes' Error: Emotion, Reason, and the Human Brain*. Avon Books.

Davidson, D. 1963. Actions, reasons, and causes. *Journal of Philosophy*, 60, 685–700.

Davis, C. G., Lehman, D. R., Silver, R. C., Wortman, C. M., and Ellard, J. H. 1996. Self-blame following a traumatic event: The role of perceived avoidability. *Personality and Social Psychology Bulletin*, 22, 557–567.

Davis, C. G., Lehman, D. R., Wortman, C. M., Silver, R. C., and Thompson, S. C. 1995. The undoing of traumatic life events. *Personality and Social Psychology Bulletin*, 21, 109–124.

De Neys, W., Schaeken, W., and d'Ydewalle, G. 2003. Inference suppression and semantic memory retrieval: Every counterexample counts. *Memory and Cognition*, 31, 581–595.

Dick, P. K. 1968. *Do Androids Dream of Electric Sheep?* New York: Del Rey Ballantine Books.

Dieussaert, K., Schaeken, W., Schroyens, W., and d'Ydewalle, G. 2000. Strategies during complex conditional inferences. *Thinking and Reasoning*, 6, 125–160.

Dudman, V. H. 1988. Indicative and subjunctive. *Analysis*, 48, 113–122.

Dunbar, K. 1997. How scientists think: On-line creativity and conceptual change in science. In T. B. Ward, S. M. Smith, and J. Vaid, eds., *Creative Thought*, 461–494. Washington, DC: American Psychological Association.

Dunning, D., and Parpal, M. 1989. Mental addition versus subtraction in counterfactual reasoning: On assessing the impact of personal actions and life events. *Journal of Personality and Social Psychology*, 57, 5–15.

Einhorn, H. J., and Hogarth, R. M. 1986. Judging probable cause. *Psychological Bulletin*, 99, 3–19.

Elio, R. 1997. What to believe when inferences are contradicted: The impact of knowledge type and inference rule. In M. Shafto and P. Langley, eds., *Proceedings of the 19th Annual Conference of the Cognitive Science Society*, 211–216. Hillsdale, NJ: Erlbaum.

Elio, R., and Pelletier, F. J. 1997. Belief change as propositional update. *Cognitive Science*, 21, 419–460.

Evans, J. St. B. T. 1977. Linguistic factors in reasoning. *Quarterly Journal of Experimental Psychology*, 29, 297–306.

Evans, J. St. B. T., and Beck, M. A. 1981. Directionality and temporal factors in conditional reasoning. *Current Psychological Research*, 1, 111–120.

Evans, J. St. B. T., Clibbens, J., and Rood, B. 1995. Bias in conditional inference: Implications for mental models and mental logic. *Quarterly Journal of Experimental Psychology*, 48, 644–670.

Evans, J. St. B. T., Clibbens, J., and Rood, B. 1996. The role of explicit and implicit negation in conditional reasoning. *Journal of Memory and Language*, 35, 392–409.

Evans, J. St. B. T., Legrenzi, P., and Girotto, V. 1999. The influence of linguistic form on reasoning: The case of matching bias. *Quarterly Journal of Experimental Psychology*, 52, 185–216.

Evans, J. St. B. T. 1989. *Bias in Reasoning*. Hove, UK: Erlbaum.

Evans, J. St. B. T. 1993. The mental model theory of conditional reasoning: Critical appraisal and revision, *Cognition*, 48, 1–20.

Evans, J. St. B. T., Newstead, S., and Byrne, R. M. J. 1993. *Human Reasoning: The Psychology of Deduction*. Hove, UK: Erlbaum.

Evans, J. St. B. T., and Over, D. E. 1996. *Rationality and Reasoning*. Hove, UK: Psychology Press.

Eysenck, M., and Keane, M. T. 2000. *Cognitive Psychology: A student's Handbook*. Hove, UK: Psychology Press.

Fairley, N., Manktelow, K. I., and Over, D. E. 1999. Necessity, sufficiency and perspective effects in causal conditional reasoning. *Quarterly Journal of Experimental Psychology*, 52A, 771–790.

Feeney, A., Gardiner, D. R., and McEvoy, R. J. 2001. Short term regret for actions versus failures to act and self esteem. Unpublished manuscript, Department of Psychology, University of Durham.

Feeney, A., and Handley, S. J. 2001a. Anchored cost/benefit comparisons underlie the scenario based action effect in judgements of regret. Unpublished manuscript, Department of Psychology, University of Durham.

Feeney, A., and Handley, S. J. 2001b. Decisions about organ donation: Evidence for an inaction effect in judgements of regret. Unpublished manuscript, Department of Psychology, University of Durham.

Feldman, J., Miyamoto, J., and Loftus, E. F. 1999. Are actions regretted more than inactions? *Organisational Behaviour and Human Decision Processes*, 78, 232–255.

Fiddick, L., Cosmides, L., and Tooby, J. 2000. No interpretation without representation: The role of domain-specific representations and inferences in the Wason selection task. *Cognition*, 77, 1–79.

Fillenbaum, S. 1974. Information amplified: Memory for counterfactual conditionals. *Journal of Experimental Psychology*, 102, 44–49.

Fillenbaum, S. 1993. Deductive reasoning: What are taken to be the premises and how are they interpreted? *Behavioral and Brain Sciences*, 16, 348–349.

Finke, R. A., Ward, T., and Smith. 1992. *Creative Cognition: Theory, Research, and Applications*. Cambridge, MA: MIT Press.

Fischhoff, B. 1977. Hindsight ≠ foresight: The effect of outcome knowledge on judgement under uncertainty. *Journal of Experimental Psychology: Human Perception and Performance*, 1, 288–299.

Ford, R. 1986. *The Sportswriter*. London: Harville Press.

Gagne, C. L., and Shoben, E. 1997. Influence of thematic relations on the comprehension of modifier-noun combinations. *Journal of Experimental Psychology: Learning, Memory, and Cognition*, 23, 71–87.

Galinsky, A. D., and Moskowitz, G. B. 2000. Counterfactuals as behavioural primes: Priming the simulation of heuristics and consideration of alternatives. *Journal of Experimental Social Psychology*, 36, 384–409.

Galotti, K. M. 2002. *Making Decisions That Matter*. Hillsdale, NJ: Erlbaum.

García-Madruga, J., Byrne, R. M. J., Egan, S., Moreno-Ríos, S., Quelhas, C., and Juhos, C. 2004. Counterfactual "only if" and "unless." Unpublished manuscript, Department of Psychology, UNED Madrid, Spain.

García-Madruga, J. A., Gutiérrez, F., Carriedo, N., Luzón, J. M., and Vila, J. O. Forthcoming. Working memory and propositional reasoning: Searching for new working memory tests. In V. Girotto and P. N. Johnson-Laird, eds., *Essays in Honour of Paolo Legrenzi*. Hove: Psychology Press.

Gavanski, I., and Wells, G. L. 1989. Counterfactual processing of normal and exceptional events. *Journal of Experimental Social Psychology*, 25, 314–325.

Geis, M. L., and Zwicky, A. M. 1971. On invited inferences. *Linguistic Inquiry*, 11, 561–566.

George, C. 1999. Evaluation of the plausibility of a conclusion derivable from several arguments with uncertain premises. *Thinking and Reasoning*, 5, 245–281.

Gigerenzer, G., and Hug, K. 1992. Domain specific reasoning: Social contracts, cheating, and perspective change. *Cognition*, 43, 127–171.

Gigerenzer, G., and Selten, R., eds. 2001. *Bounded rationality: The adaptive toolbox*. Cambridge, MA: MIT Press.

Gigerenzer, G., and Todd, P. M. 1999. *Simple Heuristics That Make Us Smart*. Oxford: Oxford University Press.

Gilovich, T., and Medvec, V. H. 1994. The temporal pattern to the experience of regret. *Journal of Personality and Social Psychology*, 67, 357–365.

Gilovich, T., and Medvec, V. H. 1995a. The experience of regret: What, when, and why. *Psychological Review*, 102, 379–395.

Gilovich, T., and Medvec, V. H. 1995b. Some counterfactual determinants of satisfaction and regret. In N. J. Roese and J. M. Olson, eds., *What Might Have Been: The Social Psychology of Counterfactual Thinking*, 259–282. Mahwah, NJ: Erlbaum.

Gilovich, T., Medvec, V. H., and Chen, S. 1995. Commission, omission, and dissonance reduction: Coping with regret in the "Monty Hall" problem. *Personality and Social Psychology Bulletin*, 21, 182–190.

Gilovich, T., Medvec, V., and Kahneman, D. 1998. Varieties of regret. *Psychological Review*, 102, 379–395.

Gilovich, T., Wang, R. F., Regan, D., and Nishina, S. 2003. Regrets of action and inaction across cultures. *Journal of Cross Cultural Psychology*, 34, 61–71.

Ginsberg, M. L. 1986. Counterfactuals. *Artificial Intelligence*, 30, 35–79.

Girotto, V., Blaye, A., and Farioli, F. 1989. A reason to reason: Pragmatic basis of children's search for counterexamples. *European Bulletin of Cognitive Psychology*, 9, 297–321.

Girotto, V., Gilly, M., Blaye, A., and Light, P. 1989. Children's performance in the selection task: Plausibility and familiarity. *British Journal of Psychology*, 80, 79–95.

Girotto, V., and Gonzalez, M. 2001. Solving probabilistic and statistical problems: A matter of information structure and question form. *Cognition*, 78, 247–276.

Girotto, V., Kemmelmeier, M., Sperber, D., and van der Henst, J.-B. 2001. Inept reasoners or pragmatic virtuosos? Relevance and the deontic selection task. *Cognition*, 81, B69–B76.

Girotto, V., Legrenzi, P., and Rizzo, A. 1991. Event controllability in counterfactual thinking. *Acta Psychologia*, 78, 111–133.

Girotto, V., Light, P. H., and Colbourn, C. J. 1988. Pragmatic schemas and conditional reasoning in children. *Quarterly Journal of Experimental Psychology*, 40A, 469–482.

Girotto, V., Mazzocco, A., and Cherubini, P. 1992. Judgements of deontic relevance in reasoning: A reply to Jackson and Griggs. *Quarterly Journal of Experimental Psychology*, 45A, 547–574.

Gleicher, F., Kost, K. A., Baker, S. M., Strathman, A. J., Richman, S. A., and Sherman, S. J. 1990. The role of counterfactual thinking in judgments of affect. *Personality and Social Psychology Bulletin*, 16, 284–295.

Goldman, A. 1970. *A Theory of Human Action*. Englewood Cliffs, NJ: Prentice-Hall.

Goldvarg, E., and Johnson-Laird, P. N. 2001. Naive causality: A mental model theory of causal meaning and reasoning. *Cognitive Science*, 25(4), 565–610.

Goodman, N. 1973. *Fact, Fiction and Forecast*. 3rd ed. Cambridge, MA: Harvard University Press.

Green, D. W. 2001. Understanding mircoworlds. *Quarterly Journal of Experimental Psychology*, 54A, 879–902.

Green, D. W., and Larking, R. 1995. The locus of facilitation in the abstract selection task. *Thinking and Reasoning*, 1, 183–199.

Green, D. W., McClelland, A., Mucki, L., and Simmons, C. 1999. Arguments and deontic decisions. *Acta Psychologica*, 101, 27–47.

Greene, S. B. 1992. Multiple explanations for multiply quantified sentences: Are multiple models necessary? *Psychological Review*, 99, 184–187.

Grice, H. P. 1975. Logic and conversation. In P. Cole and J. L. Morgan, eds., *Syntax and Semantics, Vol. 3: Speech Acts*. New York: Seminar Press.

Griggs, R. A., and Cox, J. R. 1983. The effects of problem content and negation on Wason's selection task. *Quarterly Journal of Experimental Psychology*, 35A, 519–533.

Hampton, P. 1991. The combination of prototype concepts. In P. Schwanenflugel, ed., *The Psychology of Word Meanings*. Hillsdale, NJ: Erlbaum.

Harris, P. 2000. *The Work of the Imagination*. London: Blackwell.

Harris, P., German, T., and Mills, P. 1996. Children's use of counterfactual thinking in causal reasoning. *Cognition*, 61, 233–259.

Hart, H. L., and Honore, A. M. 1959. *Causation and the Law*. Oxford: Clarendon Press.

Heaney, S. 1995. *Crediting Poetry*. http://www.nobel.se/literature/laureates/1995/heaney-lecture.html.

Hilton, D. J. 1990. Conversational processes and causal explanations. *Psychological Bulletin*, 107, 65–81.

Hilton, D. J., and Slugowski, B. R. 1986. Knowledge-based causal attribution: The abnormal conditions focus model. *Psychological Review*, 93, 75–88.

Hiraishi, K., and Hasegawa, T. 2001. Sharing rule and detection of free riders in cooperative groups. *Thinking and Reasoning*, 7, 255–294.

Hofstadter, D. R. 1985. *Metamagical Themas: Questing for the Essence of Mind and Pattern*. London: Penguin.

Holyoak, K. J., and Cheng, P. W. 1995. Pragmatic reasoning with a point of view. *Thinking and Reasoning*, 1, 289–313.

Hume, D. [1739] 2000. *A Treatise of Human Nature*. Reprint edition edited by D. F. Norton and M. J. Norton. Oxford: Oxford University Press.

Isard, S. D. 1974. What would you have done if.... *Journal of Theoretical Linguistics*, 1, 233–255.

Jackson, F. 1987. *Conditionals*. Oxford: Blackwell.

Jackson, S. L., and Griggs, R. A. 1990. The elusive pragmatic reasoning schemas effect. *Quarterly Journal of Experimental Psychology*, 42A, 353–373.

Jeffrey, R. 1981. *Formal Logic: Its Scope and Limits* 2nd ed. New York: McGraw-Hill.

Johnson, J. T. 1986. The knowledge of what might have been: Affective and attributional consequences of near outcomes. *Personality and Social Psychology Bulletin*, 12, 51–62.

Johnson-Laird, P. N. 1982. Ninth Bartlett memorial lecture: Thinking as a skill. *Quarterly Journal of Experimental Psychology*, 34A, 1–29.

Johnson-Laird, P. N. 1983. *Mental Models*. Cambridge: Cambridge University Press.

Johnson-Laird, P. N. 1986. Conditionals and mental models. In E. C. Traugott, A. ter Meulen, J. S. Reilly, and C. A. Ferguson, eds., *On Conditionals*. Cambridge: Cambridge University Press.

Johnson-Laird, P. N. 1993. *The Computer and the Mind*. 2nd ed. London: Fontana.

Johnson-Laird, P. N. 2001. Mental models and deduction. *Trends in Cognitive Sciences*, 5, 434–442.

Johnson-Laird, P. N., and Bara, B. 1984. Syllogistic inference. *Cognition*, 16, 1–61.

Johnson-Laird, P. N., and Byrne, R. M. J. 1989. *Only* reasoning. *Journal of Memory and Language*, 28, 313–330.

Johnson-Laird, P. N., and Byrne, R. M. J. 1990. Meta-logical problems: Knights, knaves, and Rips. *Cognition*, 36, 69–84.

Johnson-Laird, P. N., and Byrne, R. M. J. 1991. *Deduction*. Hillsdale, NJ: Erlbaum.

Johnson-Laird, P. N., and Byrne, R. M. J. 1992. Modal reasoning, models, and Manktelow and Over. *Cognition*, 43, 173–182.

Johnson-Laird, P. N., and Byrne, R. M. J. 1993a. Models and deductive rationality. In K. I. Manktelow and D. E. Over, eds., *Rationality: Psychological and Philosophical Perspectives*, 177–210. London: Routledge.

Johnson-Laird, P. N., and Byrne, R. M. J. 1993b. Précis of *Deduction*. *Behavioral and Brain Sciences*, 16, 323–333.

Johnson-Laird, P. N., and Byrne, R. M. J. 1995. A model point of view. *Thinking and Reasoning*, 1, 339–350.

Johnson-Laird, P. N., and Byrne, R. M. J. 2002. Conditionals: A theory of meaning, pragmatics, and inference. *Psychological Review*, 109, 646–678.

Johnson-Laird, P. N., Byrne, R. M. J., and Schaeken, W. 1992. Propositional reasoning by model. *Psychological Review*, 99, 418–439.

Johnson-Laird, P. N., Byrne, R. M. J., and Schaeken, W. 1994. Why models rather than rules give a better account of propositional reasoning: A reply to Bonatti, and to O'Brien, Braine, and Yang. *Psychological Review*, 101, 734–739.

Johnson-Laird, P. N., Byrne, R. M. J., and Tabossi, P. 1989. Reasoning by model: The case of multiple quantification. *Psychological Review*, 96, 658–673.

Johnson-Laird, P. N., Byrne, R. M. J., and Tabossi, P. 1992. In defense of reasoning: A reply to Greene. *Psychological Review*, 99, 188–190.

Johnson-Laird, P. N., Legrenzi, P., Girotto, V., Sonino-Legrenzi, M., and Caverni, J.-P. 1999. Naive probability: A mental model theory of extensional reasoning. *Psychological Review*, 106, 62–88.

Johnson-Laird, P. N., Legrenzi, P., and Legrenzi, M. S. 1972. Reasoning and a sense of reality. *British Journal of Psychology*, 63, 395–400.

Johnson-Laird, P. N., and Savary, F. 1999. Illusory inferences: A novel class of erroneous deductions. *Cognition*, 71, 191–229.

Joyce, J. [1915] 1992. *A Portrait of the Artist as a Young Man*. New York: Random House.

Kahneman, D. 1995. Varieties of counterfactual thinking. In N. J. Roese and J. M. Olson, eds., *What Might Have Been: The Social Psychology of Counterfactual Thinking*, 375–396. Mahwah, NJ: Erlbaum.

Kahneman, D., and Frederick, S. 2002. Representativeness revisited: Attribute substitution in intuitive judgment. In T. Gilovich, D. Griffin, and D. Kahneman, eds., *Heu-*

ristics and Biases: The Psychology of Intuitive Judgment, 49–81. Cambridge: Cambridge University Press.

Kahneman, D., and Miller, D. 1986. Norm theory: Comparing reality to its alternatives. Psychological Review, 93, 136–153.

Kahneman, D., and Tversky, A. 1982. The simulation heuristic. In D. P. Kahneman, P. Slovic, and A. Tversky, eds., Judgment under Uncertainty: Heuristics and Biases, 201–208. New York: Cambridge University Press.

Kahneman, D., Slovic, P., and Tversky, A., eds. 1982. Judgment under Uncertainty: Heuristics and Biases. New York: Cambridge University Press.

Kahneman, D., and Varey, C. A. 1990. Propensities and counterfactuals: The loser that almost won. Journal of Personality and Social Psychology, 59, 1101–1110.

Kasimatis, M., and Wells, G. L. 1995. Individual differences in counterfactual thinking. In N. J. Roese and J. M. Olson, eds., What Might Have Been: The Social Psychology of Counterfactual Thinking, 81–101. Mahwah, NJ: Erlbaum.

Kavanagh, P. 1972. Collected Poems. London: Martin Brian & O'Keefe Ltd.

Keane, M. T. 1997. What makes an analogy difficult? The effects of order and causal structure in analogical mapping. Journal of Experimental Psychology: Learning, Memory, and Cognition, 123, 946–967.

Keane, M. T., Ledgeway, T., and Duff, S. 1994. Constraints on analogical mapping: A comparison of three models. Cognitive Science, 18, 287–334.

Keenan, E. 1971. Quantifier structures in English. Foundations of language, 7, 255–284.

Kelley, H. H. 1972. Attribution in social interaction. In E. E. Jones, D. E. Kanouse, H. H. Kelley, R. E. Nisbett, S. Valins, and B. Weiner, eds., Attribution: Perceiving the Causes of Behavior, 1–26. Morristown, NJ: General Learning Press.

King, M. L. 1968. "I've Been to the Mountaintop," speech delivered in Memphis, Tennessee, April 3. See http://www.americanrhetoric.com/speeches/mlkivebeentothemountaintop.htm.

Klauer, K. C., Jacobsen, T., and Migulla, G. 1995. Counterfactual processing: Test of an hierarchical correspondence model. European Journal of Social Psychology, 25, 577–595.

Knight, R. T., and Grabowecky, M. 1995. Escape from linear time: Prefrontal cortext and conscious experience. In M. S. Gazzaniga, ed., The Cognitive Neurosciences, 1357–1371. Cambridge, MA: MIT Press.

Konig, E. 1986. Conditionals, concessive-conditionals, and concessives: Areas of contrast, overlap and neutralisation. In E. C. Traugott, A. ter Meulen, J. S. Reilly, and C. Ferguson, eds., On Conditionals. Cambridge: Cambridge University Press.

Kuhn, D. 1991. *The Skills of Argument*. Cambridge: Cambridge University Press.

Kvart, I. 1986. *A Theory of Counterfactuals*. Indianapolis, IN: Hackett.

Landman, J. 1987. Regret and elation following action and inaction: Affective responses to positive versus negative outcomes. *Personality and Social Psychology Bulletin*, 13, 524–536.

Landman, J. 1993. *Regret: The Persistence of the Possible*. New York: Oxford University Press.

Landman, J., and Manis, J. D. 1992. What might have been: Counterfactual thought concerning personal decisions. *British Journal of Psychology*, 83, 473–477.

Lebow, R. N. 2000. What's so different about a counterfactual? *World Politics*, 52, 550–585.

Leevers, H. J., and Harris, P. L. 1999. Persisting effects of instruction on young children's syllogistic reasoning with incongruent and abstract premises. *Thinking and Reasoning*, 5, 145–174.

Legrenzi, P., Johnson-Laird, P. N., and Girotto, V. 1993. Focusing in reasoning and decision-making. *Cognition*, 49, 37–66.

Legrenzi, P., Politzer, G., and Girotto, V. 1996. Contract proposals: A sketch of a grammar. *Theory and Psychology*, 6, 247–265.

Lewis, D. 1973. *Counterfactuals*. Oxford: Blackwell.

Liberman, N., and Klar, Y. 1996. Hypothesis testing in Wason's selection task: Social exchange, cheating detection, or task understanding. *Cognition*, 58, 127–156.

Light, P. H., Girotto, V., and Legrenzi, P. 1990. Children's reasoning on conditional promises and permissions. *Cognitive Development*, 5, 369–383.

Lipe, M. G. 1991. Counterfactual reasoning as a framework for attribution theories. *Psychological Bulletin*, 108, 3–18.

Love, R. E., and Kessler, C. M. 1995. Focusing in Wason's selection task: Content and instruction effects. *Thinking and Reasoning*, 1, 153–182.

Mackie, J. L. 1974. *The Cement of the Universe: A Study of Causation*. London: Oxford University Press.

Macrae, C. N. 1992. A tale of two curries: Counterfactual thinking and accident-related judgments. *Personality and Social Psychology Bulletin*, 18(1), 84–87.

Mandel, D. R. 2003a. Counterfactuals, emotions, and context. *Cognition and Emotion*, 17, 139–159.

Mandel, D. R. 2003b. Effect of counterfactual and factual thinking on causal judgments. *Thinking and Reasoning*, 9, 245–265.

Mandel, D. R., and Lehman, D. R. 1996. Counterfactual thinking and ascriptions of cause and preventability. *Journal of Personality and Social Psychology*, 70, 450–463.

Mandel, D. R., and Lehman, D. R. 1998. Integration of contingency information in judgements of cause, covariation and probability. *Journal of Experimental Psychology: General*, 127, 269–285.

Manktelow, K. I. 1999. *Reasoning and Thinking*. Hove, UK: Psychology Press.

Manktelow, K. I., and Fairley, N. 2000. Superordinate principles in reasoning with causal and deontic conditionals. *Thinking and Reasoning*, 6(1), 41–66.

Manktelow, K. I., and Over, D. E. 1990. Deontic thought and the selection task. In K. J. Gilhooly, M. T. G. Keane, R. H. Logie, and G. Erdos, eds., *Lines of Thinking: Reflections on the Psychology of Thought*, vol. 1. Chichester: Wiley.

Manktelow, K. I., and Over, D. E. 1991. Social roles and utilities in reasoning with deontic conditionals. *Cognition*, 39, 85–105.

Manktelow, K. I., and Over, D. E., eds. 1993. *Rationality: Psychological and Philosophical Perspectives*. London: Routledge.

Marcus, S., and Rips, L. J. 1979. Conditional reasoning. *Journal of Verbal Learning and Verbal Behaviour*, 18, 199–223.

Markman, K. D., Gavanski, I., Sherman, S. J., and McMullen, M. N. 1993. The mental simulation of better and worse possible worlds. *Journal of Experimental Social Psychology*, 29, 87–109.

Markman, K. D., Gavanski, I., Sherman, S. J., and McMullen, M. N. 1995. The impact of perceived control on the imagination of better and worse possible worlds. *Personality and Social Psychology Bulletin*, 21, 588–595.

Markman, K. D., and Tetlock, P. E. 2000a. Accountability and close-call counterfactuals: The loser who nearly won and the winner who nearly lost. *Personality and Social Psychology Bulletin*, 26, 1213–1224.

Markman, K. D., and Tetlock, P. E. 2000b. I couldn't have known: Accountability, foreseeability, and counterfactual denials of responsibility. *British Journal of Social Psychology*, 39, 313–325.

Markovits, H. 1984. Awareness of the "possible" as a mediator of formal thinking in conditional reasoning problems. *British Journal of Psychology*, 75, 367–376.

Markovits, H., and Potvin, F. 2001. Suppression of valid inferences and knowledge structures. *Memory and Cognition*, 29, 736–744.

Mayer, R. E. 1995. The search for insight: Grappling with Gestalt psychology's unanswered questions. In R. J. Sternberg and J. E. Davidson, eds., *The Nature of Insight*, 3–32. Cambridge, MA: MIT Press.

McCloy, R., and Byrne, R. M. J. 1999. Thinking about what might have been: If only, even if, causality and emotions. In N. Hahn and S. C. Stoness, eds., *Proceedings of the 21st Annual Conference of the Cognitive Science Society*. Hillsdale, NJ: Erlbaum.

McCloy, R., and Byrne, R. M. J. 2000. Counterfactual thinking about controllable events. *Memory and Cognition*, 28, 1071–1078.

McCloy, R., and Byrne, R. M. J. 2002. Semifactual "even if" thinking. *Thinking and Reasoning*, 8, 41–67.

McCloy, R., Byrne, R. M. J., and Johnson-Laird, P. N. 2004. Cumulative risk judgements. Unpublished manuscript, Department of Psychology, Reading University, UK.

McEleney, A., and Byrne, R. M. J. 1999. Consequences of counterfactual reasoning and causal reasoning. In S. Bagnara, ed., *ECCS '99*, 199–205. Siena, Italy: University of Siena.

McEleney, A., and Byrne, R. M. J. 2000. Counterfactual thinking and causal explanation. In J. A. García-Madruga, N. Carriedo, and M. J. González-Labra, eds., *Mental Models in Reasoning*, 301–314. Madrid: UNED.

McGill, A. L., and Klein, J. G. 1993. Contrastive and counterfactual thinking in causal judgment. *Journal of Personality and Social Psychology*, 64, 897–905.

McMullen, M. N., and Markman, K. D. 2000. Downward counterfactuals and motivation: The wake-up call and the pangloss effect. *Personality and Social Psychology Bulletin*, 26, 575–584.

McMullen, M. N., and Markman, K. D. 2002. Affective impact of close counterfactuals: Implications of possible futures for possible pasts. *Journal of Experimental Social Psychology*, 38, 64–70.

Meehan, J., and Byrne, R. M. J. 2004. The role of imagery in counterfactual thinking in children. Unpublished manuscript, Department of Psychology, Trinity College, Dublin University, Ireland.

Mele, A. R. 1992. *Springs of Action: Understanding Intentional Behavior*. New York: Oxford University Press.

Mill, J. S. [1872] 1956. *A System of Logic, Ratiocinative and Inductive*. 8th ed. London: Longmans, Green, & Reader.

Miller, D. T., and Gunasegaram, S. 1990. Temporal order and the perceived mutability of events: Implications for blame assignment. *Journal of Personality and Social Psychology*, 59, 1111–1118.

Miller, D. T., and McFarland, C. 1986. Counterfactual thinking and victim compensation: A test of norm theory. *Personality and Social Psychology Bulletin*, 12, 513–519.

Miller, D. T., and Turnbull, W. 1990. The counterfactual fallacy: Confusing what might have been with what ought to have been. *Social Justice Research*, 4, 1–19.

Miller, D. T., Turnbull, W., and McFarland, C. 1990. Counterfactual thinking and social perception: Thinking about what might have been. In P. Zanna, ed., *Advances in Experimental Social Psychology*, vol. 22, pp. 305–331. San Diego, CA: Academic Press.

Miller, G., and Johnson-Laird, P. N. 1976. *Language and Perception*. Cambridge: Cambridge University Press.

Mitchell, P., and Riggs, K. J., eds. 2000. *Children's Reasoning and the Mind*. Hove, UK: Psychology Press.

Miyamoto, J. M., and Dibble, E. 1986. Counterfactual conditionals and the conjunction fallacy. *Proceedings of the 8th Annual Conference of the Cognitive Science Society*. Hillsdale, NJ: Erlbaum.

Moreno-Ríos, S., García-Madruga, J. A., and Byrne, R. M. J. 2004. The effects of linguistic mood on if: Semifactual and counterfactual conditionals. Unpublished manuscript, Department of Psychology, Granada University, Spain.

Morris, M. N., and Moore, P. C. 2000. The lessons we (don't) learn: Counterfactual thinking and organizational accountability after a close call. *Administrative Science Quarterly*, 45, 737–765.

Morris, M., Sim, D., and Girotto, B. 1998. Distinguishing sources of cooperation in the one round prisoner's dilemma. *Journal of Experimental Social Psychology*, 34, 494–512.

Murphy, G. L. 1988. Comprehending complex concepts. *Cognitive Science*, 12, 529–562.

Murray, M. A., and Byrne, R. M. J. 2004. Single step and multiple step insight problems. Unpublished manuscript, Department of Psychology, Dublin University, Trinity College, Ireland.

Mynatt, C. R., Doherty, M. E., and Tweney, R. D. 1978. Consequences of confirmation and disconfirmation in a simulated research environment. *Quarterly Journal of Experimental Psychology*, 30, 395–406.

Nario, M. R., and Branscombe, N. R. 1995. Comparison processes in hindsight and causal attribution. *Personality and Social Psychology Bulletin*, 21, 1244–1255.

Nario-Redmond, M. R., and Branscombe, N. R. 1996. It could have been better or it might have been worse: Implications for blame assignment in rape cases. *Basic and Applied Social Psychology*, 18, 347–366.

Newstead, S. E. 1990. Conversion in syllogistic reasoning. In K. Gilhooly, M. T. Keane, R. Logie, and G. Erdos, eds., *Lines of Thought: Reflections on the Psychology of Thinking*. London: Wiley.

Newstead, S. E., Ellis, M. C., Evans, J. St. B. T., and Dennis, I. 1997. Conditional reasoning with realistic material. *Thinking and Reasoning*, 3, 1–80.

Niedenthal, P. M., Tangney, J. P., and Gavanski, I. 1994. "If only I weren't" versus "If only I hadn't": Distinguishing shame from guilt in counterfactual thinking. *Journal of Personality and Social Psychology*, 67, 585–595.

N'gbala, A., and Branscombe, N. R. 1995. Mental simulation and causal attribution: When simulating an event does not affect fault assignment. *Journal of Experimental Social Psychology*, 31, 139–162.

N'gbala, A., and Branscombe, N. R. 1997. When does action elicit more regret than inaction and is counterfactual mutation the mediator of this effect? *Journal of Experimental Social Psychology*, 33, 324–343.

Novick, L., and Sherman, S. J. 2003. On the nature of insight solutions: Evidence from skill differences in anagram solution. *Quarterly Journal of Experimental Psychology*, 56A, 351–382.

Oakhill, J., and Johnson-Laird, P. N. 1985. Rationality, memory, and the search for counterexamples. *Cognition*, 20, 79–84.

Oaksford, M., and Chater, N. 1995. Theories of reasoning and the computational explanation of everyday inference. *Thinking and Reasoning*, 1, 121–152.

Oberauer, K., Wilhelm, O., and Diaz, R. R. 1999. Bayesian rationality for the Wason selection task? A test of optimal data selection theory. *Thinking and Reasoning*, 5, 115–144.

O'Brien, D. P. 1993. Mental logic and human irrationality: We can put a man on the moon so why can't we solve those logical-reasoning problems? In K. I. Manktelow and D. E. Over, eds., *Rationality*, 110–135. London: Routledge.

O'Brien, D., Braine, M. D. S., and Yang, Y. 1994. Propositional reasoning by mental models? Simple to refute in principle and practice. *Psychological Review*, 101, 711–724.

Ohlsson, S. 1992. Information-processing explanations of insight and related phenomena. In M. T. Keane and K. J. Gilhooly, eds., *Advances in the Psychology of Thinking*. London: Harvester-Wheatsheaf.

Ordóñez, L. D., and Connolly, T. 2000. Regret and responsibility: A reply to Zeelenberg et al. 1998. *Organisational Behaviour and Human Decision Processes*, 81, 132–142.

Ormerod, T. C., MacGregor, J. N., and Chronicle, E. P. 2002. Dynamics and constraints in insight problem-solving. *Journal of Experimental Psychology: Learning, Memory, and Cognition*, 28(4), 791–799.

Perner, J. 2000. In P. Mitchell and K. J. Riggs, eds., *Children's Reasoning and the Mind*, 367–402. Hove, UK: Psychology Press.

Poletiek, F. H. 1996. Paradoxes of falsification. *Quarterly Journal of Experimental Psychology*, 49, 447–462.

Politzer, G., and Nguyen-Xuan, A. 1992. Reasoning about conditional promises and warnings: Darwinian algorithms, mental models, relevance judgements or pragmatic schemas? *Quarterly Journal of Experimental Psychology*, 44, 401–412.

Pollock, J. L. 1986. *Subjunctive Reasoning*. Dordrecht, The Netherlands: Reidel.

Quelhas, A. C., and Byrne, R. M. J. 2000. Counterfactual conditionals: Reasoning latencies. In J. A. García-Madruga, N. Carriedo, and M. J. González-Labra, eds., *Mental Models in Reasoning*, 315–326. Madrid: UNED.

Quelhas, A. C., and Byrne, R. M. J. 2003. Reasoning with deontic and counterfactual conditionals. *Thinking and Reasoning*, 9, 43–66.

Quine, W. V. 1972. *Methods of Logic*. 3rd ed. New York: Holt, Rinehart & Winston.

Ramsey, S. P. 1931. *The Foundations of Mathematics and Other Logical Essays*. London: Kegan Paul.

Revlin, R., Cate, C. L., and Rouss, T. S. 2001. Reasoning counterfactually: Combining and rending. *Memory and Cognition*, 29, 1196–1208.

Riggs, K. J., and Peterson, D. M. 2000. Counterfactual thinking in preschool children: Mental state and causal inferences. In P. Mitchell and K. J. Riggs, eds., *Children's Reasoning and the Mind*. Hove, UK: Psychology Press.

Riggs, K. J., Peterson, D. M., Mitchell, P., and Robinson, E. 1998. Are errors in false belief tasks symptomatic of a broader difficulty with counterfactuality? *Cognitive Development*, 13, 73–90.

Rips, L. J. 1983. Cognitive processes in deductive reasoning. *Psychological Review*, 90, 38–71.

Rips, L. J. 1989. The psychology of knights and knaves. *Cognition*, 31, 85–116.

Rips, L. J. 1994. *The Psychology of Proof*. Cambridge, MA: MIT Press.

Rips, L. J. 2003. Circular reasoning. *Cognitive Science*, 26, 767–796.

Rips, L. J., and Marcus, S. L. 1977. Suppositions and the analysis of conditional sentences. In M. A. Just and P. A. Carpenter, eds., *Cognitive Processes in Comprehension*. Hillsdale, NJ: Erlbaum.

Ritov, I., and Baron, J. 1990. Reluctance to vaccinate: Omission bias and ambiguity. *Journal of Behavioral Decision Making*, 3, 263–277.

Ritov, I., and Baron, J. 1992. Status-quo and omission biases. *Journal of Risk and Uncertainties*, 5, 49–61.

Ritov, I., and Baron, J. 1995. Outcome knowledge, regret and omission bias. *Organisational Behaviour and Human Decision Processes*, 64, 119–127.

Ritov, I., and Baron, J. 1999. Protected values and omission bias. *Organisational Behaviour and Human Decision Processes*, 79, 79–94.

Roberge, J. J. 1978. Linguistic and psychometric factors in propositional reasoning. *Quarterly Journal of Experimental Psychology*, 30, 705–716.

Roese, N. J. 1994. The functional basis of counterfactual thinking. *Journal of Personality and Social Psychology*, 66, 805–818.

Roese, N. J. 1997. Counterfactual thinking. *Psychological Bulletin*, 121, 133–148.

Roese, N. J., Hur, T., and Pennington, G. L. 1999. Counterfactual thinking and regulatory focus: Implications for action versus inaction and sufficiency versus necessity. *Journal of Personality and Social Psychology*, 77(6), 1109–1120.

Roese, N. J., and Olson, J. M. 1993a. Self-esteem and counterfactual thinking. *Journal of Personality and Social Psychology*, 65, 199–206.

Roese, N. J., and Olson, J. M. 1993b. The structure of counterfactual thought. *Personality and Social Psychology Bulletin*, 19, 312–319.

Roese, N. J., and Olson, J. M. 1996. Counterfactuals, causal attributions, and the hindsight bias: A conceptual integration. *Journal of Experimental Social Psychology*, 32, 197–227.

Roese, N. J., and Olson, J. M. 1997. Counterfactual thinking: The intersection of affect and function. In M. P. Zanna, ed., *Advances in Experimental Social Psychology*, vol. 29, pp. 1–59. San Diego, CA: Academic Press.

Roese, N. J., and Olson, J. M., eds. 1995. *What Might Have Been: The Social Psychology of Counterfactual Thinking*. Mahwah, NJ: Erlbaum.

Roese, N. J., Sanna, L. J., and Galinsky, A. D. 2005. The mechanics of imagination: Automaticity and counterfactual thinking. In R. Hassin, J. Uleman, and J. A. Bargh, eds., *The New Unconscious*, 138–170. New York: Oxford University Press.

Rosch, E. 1976. Basic objects in natural categories. *Cognitive Psychology*, 8, 382–439.

Rumain, B., Connell, J., and Braine, M. D. S. 1983. Conversational comprehension processes are responsible for reasoning fallacies in children as well as adults. *Developmental Psychology*, 19, 471–481.

Sanna, L. J., and Meier, S. 2000. Looking for clouds in a silver lining: Self-esteem, mental simulations and temporal confidence changes. *Journal of Research in Personality*, 34, 236–251.

Sanna, L. J., Parks, C. D., Meier, S., Chang, E. C., Kassin, B. R., Lechter, J. L., Turley-Ames, K. J., and Miyake, T. M. 2003. A game of inches: Spontaneous use of counterfactuals by broadcasters during major league baseball playoffs. *Journal of Applied Social Psychology*, 33, 455–475.

Sanna, L. J., Schwarz, N., and Stocker, S. L. 2002. When debiasing backfires: Accessible content and accessibility experiences in debiasing hindsight. *Journal of Experimental Psychology: Learning, Memory, and Cognition*, 28, 497–502.

Sanna, L. J., and Turley, K. J. 1996. Antecedents to spontaneous counterfactual thinking: Effects of expectancy violation and outcome valence. *Personality and Social Psychology Bulletin*, 22(9), 909–919.

Sanna, L. J., and Turley-Ames, K. J. 2000. Counterfactual intensity. *European Journal of Social Psychology*, 30, 273–296.

Sanna, L. J., Turley-Ames, K. J., and Meier, S. 1999. Mood, self-esteem, and simulated alternatives: Thought provoking affective influences on counterfactual direction. *Journal of Personality and Social Psychology*, 76, 543–558.

Santamaría, C., and Espino, O. 2002. Conditionals and directionality: On the meaning of if versus only if. *Quarterly Journal of Experimental Psychology*, 55A, 41–57.

Santamaría, C., Espino, O., and Byrne, R. M. J. 2004. Counterfactual conditionals as primes. Unpublished manuscript, Department of Psychology, La Laguna University, Spain.

Santamaría, C., García-Madruga, J. A., and Johnson-Laird, P. N. 1998. Reasoning from double conditionals: The effects of logical structure and believability. *Thinking and Reasoning*, 4, 97–122.

Savitsky, K., Medvec, V. H., and Gilovich, T. 1997. Remembering and regretting: The Zeigarnik effect and the cognitive availability of regrets for action and inaction. *Personality and Social Psychology Bulletin*, 23, 248–257.

Schaeken, W., Johnson-Laird, P. N., and d'Ydewalle, G. 1996. Mental models and temporal reasoning. *Cognition*, 60, 205–234.

Schaeken, W., Schroyens, W., and Dieussaert, K. 2001. Conditional assertions, tense, and explicit negatives. *European Journal of Cognitive Psychology*, 13(4), 433–450.

Schroyens, W., Schaeken, W., and d'Ydewalle, G. 2001. A meta-analytic review of conditional reasoning by model and/or rule. Technical report, Leuven University.

Schustack, M. W. 1988. Thinking about causality. In R. J. Sternberg and E. E. Smith, eds., *The Psychology of Thinking*, 99–115. Cambridge: Cambridge University Press.

Schustack, M. W., and Sternberg, R. J. 1981. Evaluation of evidence in causal inference. *Journal of Experimental Psychology: General*, 110, 101–120.

Seeleu, E. P., Seeleu, S. M., Wells, G. L., and Windschitl, P. D. 1995. Counterfactual constraints. In N. J. Roese and J. M. Olson, eds., *What Might Have Been: The Social Psychology of Counterfactual Thinking*. Mahwah, NJ: Erlbaum.

Segura, S., Fernandez-Berrocal, P., and Byrne, R. M. J. 2002. Temporal and causal order effects in thinking about what might have been. *Quarterly Journal of Experimental Psychology*, 55, 1295–1305.

Shafir, E., and Tversky, A. 1992. Thinking through uncertainty: Nonconsequential reasoning and choice. *Cognitive Psychology*, 24, 449–474.

Sherman, S. J., and McConnell, A. R. 1995. Dysfunctional implications of counterfactual thinking: When alternatives to reality fail us. In N. J. Roese and J. M. Olson, eds., *What Might Have Been: The Social Psychology of Counterfactual Thinking*. Mahwah, NJ: Erlbaum.

Sherman, S. J., and McConnell, A. R. 1996. Counterfactual thinking in reasoning. *Applied Cognitive Psychology*, 10, 113–124.

Silverstein, S. 1996. *Falling up*. New York: HarperCollins.

Sloman, S. A., and Lagnado, D. A. 2003. Counterfactual undoing in deterministic causal reasoning. In R. Alterman and D. Kirsch, eds., *Proceedings of the 25th Annual Conference of the Cognitive Science Society*. Hillsdale, NJ: Erlbaum.

Slovic, P., Finucane, M., Peters, E., and MacGregor, D. G. 2002. The affect heuristic. In T., Gilovich, D. Griffin, and D. Kahneman, eds., *Heuristics and Biases: The Psychology of Intuitive Judgment*. New York: Cambridge University Press.

Sobel, D. M. Forthcoming. Exploring the coherence of young children's explanatory abilities: Evidence from generating counterfactuals. *British Journal of Developmental Psychology*.

Spellman, B. A. 1997. Crediting causality. *Journal of Experimental Psychology, General*, 126(4), 323–348.

Spellman, B. A., and Mandel, D. R. 1999. When possibility informs reality: Counterfactual thinking as a cue to causality. *Current Directions in Psychological Science*, 8, 120–123.

Sperber, D., Cara, F., and Girotto, V. 1995. Relevance theory explains the selection task. *Cognition*, 52, 3–39.

Sperber, D., and Girotto, V. 2002. Use of misuse of the selection task? Rejoinder to Fiddick, Cosmides and Tooby. *Cognition*, 85, 277–290.

Sperber, D., and Girotto, V. 2003. Does the selection task detect cheater detection? In J. Fitness and K. Sterelny, eds., *New Directions in Evolutionary Psychology*. Macquarie Monographs in Cognitive Science. Hove, UK: Psychology Press.

Sperber, D., and Wilson, D. 1986. *Relevance*. Oxford: Blackwell.

Stalnaker, R. C. 1968. A theory of conditionals. In N. Rescher, ed., *Studies in Logical Theory*. Oxford: Blackwell.

Stalnaker, R. C. 1999. *Context and Content*. Oxford: Oxford University Press.

Stanovich, K. E. 1999. *Who Is Rational?* Mahwah, NJ: Erlbaum.

Staudenmayer, H. 1975. Understanding conditional reasoning with meaningful propositions. In R. J. Falmagne, ed., *Reasoning: Representation and Process*. New York: Wiley.

Sternberg, R. J. 1985. *Beyond IQ: A Triarchic Theory of Human Intelligence*. New York: Cambridge University Press.

Sternberg, R. J. 1997. *Thinking Styles*. Cambridge: Cambridge University Press.

Sternberg, R. J., and Davidson, J. E. 1995. *The Nature of Insight*. Cambridge, MA: MIT Press.

Sternberg, R. J., and Gastel, J. 1989. If dancers ate their shoes: Inductive reasoning with factual and counterfactual premises. *Memory and Cognition*, 17, 1–10.

Stevenson, R. J., and Over, D. E. 1995. Deduction from uncertain premises. *Quarterly Journal of Experimental Psychology*, 48A, 613–643.

Stevenson, R. J., and Over, D. E. 2001. Reasoning from uncertain premises: Effects of expertise and conversational context. *Quarterly Journal of Experimental Psychology*, 7, 313–392.

Stout, R. 1949. *Instead of Evidence*. London: Viking Press.

Tanner, C., and Medin, D. 2004. Protected values: No omission bias and no framing effects. Unpublished manuscript, Department of Psychology, Northwestern University.

Tetlock, P. E., and Parker, G. 2005. Counterfactual thought experiments: Why we cannot live without them and how we can learn to live with them. In P. E. Tetlock, R. N. Lebow, and G. Parker, eds., *Unmaking the West: Counterfactuals, Contingency, and Causation*, 3–35. Ann Arbor: University of Michigan Press.

Tetlock, P. E., and Lebow, R. N. 2001. Poking counterfactual holes in covering laws: Cognitive styles and historical reasoning. *American Political Science Review*, 95, 829–843.

Thomas, N. J. T. 1999. Are theories of imagery theories of imagination? An active perception approach to conscious mental content. *Cognitive Science*, 23, 207–245.

Thompson, V. A. 1994. Interpretational factors in conditional reasoning. *Memory and Cognition*, 22, 742–758.

Thompson, V. A., and Byrne, R. M. J. 2002. Reasoning about things that didn't happen. *Journal of Experimental Psychology: Learning, Memory, and Cognition*, 28, 1154–1170.

Thompson, V. A., and Mann, J. M. 1995. Perceived necessity explains the dissociation between logic and meaning: The case of "only if." *Journal of Experimental Psychology: Learning, Memory, and Cognition*, 21, 1–14.

Tiegen, K. H., Evensen, P. C., Samoilow, D. K., and Vatine, K. B. 1999. Good luck and bad luck: How to tell the difference. *European Journal of Social Psychology*, 29, 981–1010.

Torrens, D., Thompson, V. A., and Cramer, K. M. 1999. Individual differences and the belief-bias effect: Mental models, logical necessity and abstract reasoning. *Thinking and Reasoning*, 5, 1–28.

Traugott, E. C., ter Meulen, A., Reilly, J. S., and Ferguson, C. A., eds. 1986. *On Conditionals*. Cambridge: Cambridge University Press.

Tversky, A., and Kahneman, D. 1982. Judgment under uncertainty: Heuristics and biases. In D. Kahneman, P. Slovic, and A. Tversky, eds., *Judgment under Uncertainty: Heuristics and Biases*, 201–208. New York: Cambridge University Press.

Tykocinski, O. E., and Pittman, T. S. 1998. The consequences of doing nothing: Inaction inertia as avoidance of anticipated counterfactual regret. *Journal of Personality and Social Psychology*, 75, 607–616.

Vadeboncoeur, I., and Markovits, H. 1999. The effect of instructions and information retrieval on accepting the premises in a conditional reasoning task. *Thinking and Reasoning*, 5, 97–113.

Von Wright, G. H. 1983. *Practical Reason*. Oxford: Blackwell.

Walsh, C. R., and Byrne, R. M. J. 2001. A computational model of counterfactual thinking: The temporal order effect. In J. D. Moore and K. Stenning, eds., *Proceedings of the 23rd Annual Conference of the Cognitive Science Society*, 1078–1083. Mahwah, NJ: Erlbaum.

Walsh, C., and Byrne, R. M. J. 2004a. Counterfactual thinking about reasons for acting. Unpublished manuscript, Department of Psychology, University of Plymouth.

Walsh, C. R., and Byrne, R. M. J. 2004b. Counterfactual thinking: The temporal order effect. *Memory and Cognition*, 32, 369–378.

Ward, T. B. 1994. Structured imagination. *Cognitive Psychology*, 27, 1–40.

Ward, T. B., Patterson, M. J., and Sifonis, C. 2004. The role of specificity and abstraction in creative idea generation. *Creativity Research Journal*, 16, 1–9.

Ward, T. B., Smith, S. M., and Vaid, J., eds. 1997. *Creative Thought*. Washington, DC: American Psychological Association.

Wason, P. 1966. Reasoning. In B. Foss, ed., *New Horizons in Psychology*. Harmondsworth, UK: Penguin.

Weiner, B. 1985. "Spontaneous" causal thinking. *Psychological Bulletin*, 97(1), 74–84.

Weisberg, R. W., and Suls, J. 1973. An information processing model of Duncker's candle problem. *Cognitive Psychology*, 4, 255–276.

Wells, G. L., and Gavanski, I. 1989. Mental simulation of causality. *Journal of Personality and Social Psychology*, 56, 161–169.

Wells, G. L., Taylor, B. R., and Turtle, J. W. 1987. The undoing of scenarios. *Journal of Personality and Social Psychology*, 53, 421–430.

Wisniewski, E. J. 1996. Construal and similarity in conceptual combination. *Journal of Memory and Language*, 35, 434–453.

Wisniewski, E. J., and Gentner, D. 1991. On the combinatorial semantics of noun pairs: Minor and major adjustments to meaning. In G. B. Simpson, ed., *Understanding Word and Sentence*. Amsterdam: Elsevier Science.

Wittgenstein, L. 1922. *Tractatus Logico-Philosophicus*. London: Routledge and Kegan Paul.

White, P. A. 2002. Causal judgement from contingency information: Judging interactions between two causal candidates. *Quarterly Journal of Experimental Psychology* 55A, 819–838.

Yarlett, D., and Ramscar, M. 2002. Uncertainty in causal and counterfactual inference. In W. D. Gray and C. D. Schunn, eds., *Proceedings of the 24th Annual Conference of the Cognitive Science Society*. Mahwah, NJ: Erlbaum.

Zeelenberg, M., van der Bos, K., van Dijk, E., and Pieters, R. 2002. The inaction effect in the psychology of regret. *Journal of Personality and Social Psychology*, 82, 314–327.

Zeelenberg, M., van der Pligt, J., and Manstead, A. S. R. 1998. Undoing regret on Dutch television. *Personality and Social Psychology Bulletin* 24, 1113–1119.

Zhang, J., Bonnefon, J.-F., and Deng, C. 2004. Regret and reasons to act or not to act. Unpublished manuscript, Sociology Institute, Shanghai Academy of Social Science.

Index